Japanese Architecture
as a Collaborative Process

Architects throughout the world hold Japan's best architecture in high regard, considering the country's buildings among the world's most carefully crafted and innovative. While many books, magazines and exhibitions have focussed on the results of architectural practice in Japan, this book is the first to explain the reasons for Japan's remarkable structures. Architectural design does not occur in isolation; Japan's architects are able to collaborate with a wide variety of people including both professional consultants and constructors.

Dana Buntrock discusses architecture as a part of the construction community, moving from historical precedents that predate the emergence of the architectural profession in Japan through to contemporary practices. Because Japanese architects are able to collaborate in making decisions, Buntrock includes detailed discussion of the role of contractors, fabricators and suppliers, using accessible non-technical language. She also explains the context for design, addressing educational differences, the importance of Japan's national government in supporting construction, and Japan's legal flexibility. Case studies interspersed throughout the text discuss how these opportunities are explored in architectural practices and highlight important work by some of Japan's leading architects, including Fumihiko Maki, Toyo Ito, Hajime Yatsuka and Kazuyo Sejima. Notable projects range from the ground-breaking Shonandai Culture Center to the newly acclaimed Sendai Mediatheque.

Buntrock has had a unique opportunity to observe architecture and construction practices by a number of highly regarded firms. The diversity of architects' approaches to practice suggests that Japan's construction community is extraordinarily flexible. Readers will find this book offers them both insights into the nature of architectural practice in their own communities and surprising alternatives.

London and New York

Japanese Architecture as a Collaborative Process
Opportunities in a flexible construction culture

Dana Buntrock

First published 2001 by Spon Press
11 New Fetter Lane, London EC4P 4EE

Simultaneously published in the USA and Canada by Spon Press
29 West 35th Street, New York, NY 10001

Spon Press is an imprint of the Taylor & Francis Group

© 2002 Dana Buntrock

The right of Dana Buntrock to be identified as the
Author of this Work has been asserted by her in accordance
with the Copyright, Designs and Patents Act 1988

Typeset in Joanna and Helvetica Neue by Wearset Ltd,
Boldon, Tyne & Wear
Printed and bound in Malta by Gutenberg Press Ltd

All rights reserved. No part of this book may be reprinted or
reproduced or utilized in any form or by any electronic, mechanical,
or other means, now known or hereafter invented, including
photocopying and recording, or in any information storage or
retrieval system, without permission in writing from the publishers.

The publisher makes no representation, express or implied, with
regard to the accuracy of the information contained in this book
and cannot accept any legal responsibility or liability for any errors
or omissions that may be made.

British Library Cataloguing in Publication Data
A catalogue record for this book is available from the British Library

Library of Congress Cataloging in Publication Data

Buntrock, Dana, 1958–
    Japanese architecture as a collaborative process:
  opportunities in a flexible construction culture / Dana Buntrock.
    p.cm.
Includes bibliographical references and index.
    1. Architectural practice–Japan. 2. Architecture,
  Japanese–20th century. 3. Construction industry–Japan.
  4. Interprofessional relations–Japan. I. Title.

NA1555 .B86 2001
720'.952–dc21

                                      2001020518

ISBN 0–419–25140–5

For all my teachers

"The lyfe so short, the craft so long to lerne . . ." Geoffrey Chaucer

Contents

ix	List of plates
xi	Foreword
xviii	Preface
xx	Acknowledgements
1	Introduction
6	**Historical precedents**
6	Craft in early modern Japan (1590–1868)
7	Drawing the line: The carpenter as architect
9	The problem of style
13	A challenge to traditional trades
16	Design in the nineteenth century
19	The emergence of architectural practice
23	**Education and the professions**
23	The university
25	The office
31	Transferring knowledge from the university
33	**Architectural practice today**
34	Four models of design development
39	Leading architects as "lead users"
41	A cluster of innovations
47	**The roots of collaborative practice**
48	Design teams
51	Linkages between professionals
54	Team players
58	Building cooperative teams
60	Trade-outs
62	Working in the midst of construction
72	**Contractors: Collaborators and competitors**
78	Consultants and constructors in alliance
81	Sejima's shopping bag
84	Innovating through team effort
91	**Selecting subcontractors**
93	The benefits of oligopoly
100	**Two paths to customization**
100	Architects and craft
102	The architect and crafter in alliance: Shonandai Bunka Center
105	The architect and industry
108	Implications in architecture
112	Lead users in collaborative design

117	Being flexible within clear boundaries	152	Contracts in Japan's architectural community
119	Genuine drawbacks of collaborative methods		
120	Working with customization	154	Political economists' justification for "incomplete contracts"
123	Ancient equipment		
		157	Tort: Covering the costs of liability and negligence
128	**Avant-garde architecture in the public realm**		
131	Political support	159	The judicial system
132	Government support	162	Discouraging litigation
134	Pressure to perform	164	Sendai Mediatheque in crisis
135	The role of public commissions		
140	Cronyism and "descending from heaven"	**169**	**Conclusion**
142	Riken Yamamoto and Saitama University	171	Increasingly innovative
		173	Learning from Japan
148	**Legal issues**		
148	Contracts	**177**	**Index**
151	Contracts in Japan's legal and social community		

List of plates

1.1	Fumihiko Maki's Tokyo Metropolitan Gymnasium	2
1.2	Toyo Ito's Yokohama Care Center	3
2.1	Shugakuin Villa	8
2.2	Katsura Imperial Villa	9
2.3	Toshogu roofscape	10
2.4	Interior of Katsura's Shōiken Pavilion	11
2.5	Toshogu ornament	12
2.6	Todaiji	15
2.7	Detail of steel strapping at Todaiji	15
2.8	Yamagata University	17
2.9	Saiseikan	18
3.1	An intern at work	24
3.2	On a *kengakkai*	26
4.1	Shizuoka Granship site office	37
4.2	A large site office	37
4.3	Toyo Ito's Sendai Mediatheque	42
4.4	Sendai Mediatheque structural tube	43
4.5	Floor section at fabricators	43
4.6	Architectural staff and subcontractors	44
4.6a	"Rockwall" in place	44
5.1	Jun Aoki's "Snow Village Future Foundation"	52
5.2	Promotional diagram	52
5.3	Shigeru Ban's Miyake Design Studio Gallery	52
5.4	Ota Rest House by Toyo Ito and Mutsuro Sasaki, exterior view	56
5.5	Ota Rest House interior	56
5.6	Kasai Rinkai Park by Yoshio Taniguchi	57
5.7	A relatively large weekly meeting	61
5.8	Mock-up of a concrete wall	65
5.9	Wall for Arata Isozaki's Shizuoka Granship	65
5.10	Mock-ups of duct and part of the structural system for Sendai Mediatheque	67
5.11	Test welding a mock-up	68
5.12	Ito's office tries out a proposed lighting grille on a mock-up	69
6.1	Office building in Tokyo, designed and built by Takenaka Komuten	75
6.2	Kazuyo Sejima at the Media Academy	82
6.3	Media Academy interior	82
6.4	Small mock-ups of fastener and finish joint alternatives	83
6.5	Dai'ichi Kōbō's Kumamoto Dome	85

6.6	View of ring at grade	86
6.7	Interior, Kumamoto Dome, before lift-up	87
6.8	Interior, Kumamoto Dome, after lift-up	87
7.1	Man hand-sanding precast concrete	94
7.2	Design team struggles with a problem	97
8.1	Shonandai Culture Center by Itsuko Hasegawa	103
8.2	Shonandai Culture Center tile "river" designed with Shuji Yamada	103
8.3	Concrete finish showing Akira Kusumi's input	103
8.4	Fujisawa Gymnasium, by Fumihiko Maki	110
8.5	Inspecting structural connectors for a publicly funded project	111
8.6	Photograph documenting an inspection	111
8.7	Hajime Yatsuka's Nagaoka "Earth Man and Sky" Folly	115
8.8	Ceramic wall designed to draw heat from prevailing winds	115
8.9	Fumihiko Maki's Church of Christ, exterior view	121
8.10	Interior of sanctuary	122
8.11	Models of light fixtures	123
8.12	Terunobu Fujimori's Tanpopo House, interior	124
8.13	Fujimori marking wood for cutting	126
9.1	Yoshio Taniguchi's Gallery of Horyuji Treasures in Tokyo, exterior	136
9.2	Yoshio Taniguchi's Gallery of Horyuji Treasures in Tokyo, interior	136
9.3	Saitama University, designed by Riken Yamamoto	143
9.4	Exterior wall, showing punched aluminum	145
9.5	Architectural staff with a mock-up of the same material	145
9.6	Interior at Saitama University	145
10.1	Two-story tube section, Mediatheque	165
10.2	Various approaches to fire resistance	165
10.3	Tube finished with "Taika-Arock"	165
10.4	Mediatheque nearing completion	165

Foreword

Making Architecture in Japan

Fumihiko Maki

The Tokyo of my childhood in the 1930s was still a city of abundant greenery and detached, mostly wooden, houses. At times, new construction would begin in the neighborhood. In those days, workmen did not mind the intrusion of curious children. We watched as carpenters sawed and planed wood. Using hammer and chisel, they shaped mortises. The sounds of men at work echoed pleasantly in the otherwise quiet residential district. The air was filled with the fragrance of fresh wood shavings. The carpenters wielded their tools with steady hands and, from time to time, examined intently their own handiwork. I remember these things quite vividly even now.

My first encounter with craftsmen thus took place at a time when I had as yet no idea I would become an architect.

More than sixty years have passed since then. I still live in the same district, but the houses today are mostly prefabricated or built of reinforced concrete. Few are built by carpenters. Now, the construction company seals off a site with a temporary enclosure once work is to begin, and the occasional noise of construction provides those outside with little hint of what is transpiring within. Eventually, the enclosure is removed, and the roughly completed building is unveiled. In the past, we were able to observe not only the work of carpenters but *performances* put on by craftsmen such as glassworkers and textile dyers. Today we have few such opportunities. Nevertheless, human beings must still confront materials or other human beings at certain points in the production process, even though wood and *shoji* have been replaced by metal and glass, and individual activity has given way to group activity. Those confrontations are where architectural culture in Dana Buntrock's sense, that is, as an expression of building construction, is made manifest. That culture lives on. If, for example, the installation of a complex element on a building site proves difficult, people of different trades will meet to discuss the problem with the architect. The tradesmen on such occasions have the same intent faces as the carpenters of my childhood. If a small metal piece needs to be affixed just so to the structure, the work is done with hands as steady as those of the craftsmen I watched long ago.

Today, less and less use is made of individual craftsmanship in the building production process. In what ways, then, does the spirit of craftsmanship live on in contemporary construction? I believe it lives on in the pride people take in the work they do and the things they create, no matter how small. Today, nearly a decade after the bursting of the Bubble, unit construction cost has fallen from two-thirds to one-half of what it was at its peak as a result of fierce price competition among construction companies. Yet the quality of building has not fallen to the same extent. Indeed there is little perceptible change in quality. Construction companies have managed to do this in part by trimming profits, which were indeed extremely high in the Bubble era, but they would seem to have only so much leeway. Western societies that have markedly more transparent price structures find it difficult to understand this phenomenon. Quality control is being maintained in Japan in many cases through the sacrifice of subcontractors and sub-subcontractors. The situation may be bleak, but people are refusing to use that as an excuse for lower quality. I find it inspiring to see these people continue to work with such dedication. People in Japan still take pride in their work, whatever the pay. That is, they feel a need, not only to achieve explicitly stated objectives, but to meet unspoken expectations. After receiving my undergraduate degree nearly half a century ago, I was briefly a member of Kenzo Tange's research group at Tokyo University. Tange, who was then professor, never gave explicit orders. We did our best, acting, as often as not, on what we understood to be his unspoken messages to us.

This mentality has been characteristic of, not only the master–disciple relationship but, as Buntrock points out, relationships in the fields of construction and design in *keiretsu* organizations. Takenaka Corporation, one of the biggest construction companies in Japan, has a proud tradition of high quality. Until recently, Takenaka had a special system of inspection for particularly important buildings. The inspection, which took place just before the completion of construction, was carried out by a number of people nearing retirement who had long experience at Takenaka in managing site offices. If the quality of the inspected building was not up to their expectations, the inspectors themselves undertook improvements on their own initiative. For the Takenaka personnel working at the site, the inspection was a major event that could impact their future careers. This was a system based on pride that was possible only in institutions practicing lifetime employment.

I believe the culture of building construction has always had two aspects: aesthetics and engineering. Devising appropriate ways to express the beauty and richness of materials has been a major aesthetic concern in Japanese architecture throughout history. It is a major concern in, for example, the work of Yoshio Taniguchi. The beauty that is sought is more a matter of *sensibility* than of intellectually understood concepts such as symmetry and the golden section. Many contemporary Japanese architects are extraordinarily insistent that builders achieve certain surface effects in concrete. A sensibility honed by a long history of love for, and preoccupation with, the texture of wood probably accounts for that insistence. Demand that building elements be "thinner and more transparent" is yet another way in which a special sensitivity to materials is expressed. It is also an impetus to devise means to achieve that condition. Japanese architecture has always been characterized by the confluence and simultaneous expression of beauty and technology.

The modernization of Japan that began around 1850 was in fact a Westernization. However, Japan was never subjugated by a colonial power. Japan thus differed from other Asian countries in that it could be highly selective in its process of Westernization. It looked to France for art and cuisine, Germany for medicine and technology and England for shipbuilding and shipping. In fields such as law and literature, where choosing from alternative models was difficult, Japan adopted separate, parallel fields of specialty, e.g., English literature and French literature.

Architectural education in Japan was first established in what later became Tokyo University. The department of architecture then closely resembled that of a German technical university and belonged to the faculty of engineering. Josiah Conder, the first professor on the faculty, was English. It is interesting to note that Kingo Tatsuno, one of the first four students Conder taught, and the first student sent overseas for further education, went on Conder's recommendation to not only an architectural firm but also to Thomas Cubitt, a leading builder in England at the time.

Even today, only a minority of those who graduate from engineering-oriented departments of architecture go to work for so-called atelier architects (that is, architects whose offices more closely resemble artists' ateliers than the offices of conventional professionals). In the early 1950s when I received my undergraduate degree, the overwhelming majority of graduates found employment with large construction companies. The rest became administrative officials in government or remained in graduate school to do research. After several years, practically all graduates, now as in the past, take an examination in order to qualify as a licensed architect. Those who pass are eligible to become a member of the prefectural Architects & Building Engineers Association. This association collectively represents the largest professional organization in the field. The Japan Institute of Architects, made up of individuals belonging to architectural design offices, has 5,300 members, but the Architects & Building Engineers Association has a total membership nearly twice as large. On the other hand, the Architectural Institute of Japan, which was established to promote research, study and the exchange of information in various fields of architecture including engineering and history, has 37,000 members, not all of whom are licensed architects. AIJ members, who include architects, scholars, engineers and people in different niches in various corporations, actively communicate with one another through sectional meetings and the annual general meeting. The AIJ Prizes, which are awarded each year at the general meeting, are considered the most prestigious of the many architectural prizes in Japan. As these two institutional examples make clear, cross-fertilization between different fields has played a large part in promoting both the pursuit of technology and the pursuit of beauty in the architecture of modern Japan.

The artistic autonomy of architecture became a much-debated subject upon the arrival of Postmodernism in the Japanese architectural world around 1970. Yet even Arata Isozaki, the leading advocate of the idea of the autonomy of architecture, has pursued technological themes in many works during his career.

Japan has a relatively weak tradition of locally based professional practice, no doubt accounted for by the fact that two-thirds of all architectural offices are concentrated in Tokyo. Architects of different generations and backgrounds are engaged instead in attempts to create thematic works of architecture. By participating in various competitions and proposals and using the few opportunities for actual work available to them to develop fresh ideas, young architects in particular must try to draw the interest of the media. This is true not only in Japan but in most large European cities. The pursuit of experimental ideas has been the architect's *raison d'être*. That experimental approach has had an effect on the building industry. For example, manufacturers of glass have expanded their lines to include doors and window frames, roofs and even the main supporting structure. They have begun to take part in all stages of a project, from initial design to construction. Such developments are leading to the emergence of new trades that cross the boundaries of established trades. People in these new trades are as yet few in number, but architects on the cutting edge are finding that collaborating with them can yield innovative designs.

Diverse systems of cooperation have thus been available to architects, engineers, fabricators and construction companies in Japan in the last several decades. Here I would like to describe in greater detail different ways in which architects and construction companies have collaborated, using as examples three masters of twentieth-century Japanese architecture: Togo Murano (1891–1985), Kunio Maekawa (1905–86) and Kenzo Tange (1913–).

Murano, who was active to the end of his life, visited a construction site the day before he died at the age of ninety-four. After graduating from a university, Murano apprenticed with an Osaka office and subsequently opened his own office in the same city. His work, which was mostly for the private sector, was not orthodox Modernist in style, having instead an Expressionist aspect. The architect, who was also accomplished in the *sukiya* style, remained creative even in old age. He designed not only architecture but furniture, lighting fixtures and ornament. Especially remarkable is the fact that Murano completed half of his life's work after the age of seventy. Close ties tend to develop between architect, builder and client in the Osaka area. The local culture has traditionally been conducive to their working together on a building project. Murano had at his disposal a full complement of collaborators for both design and construction work. The large construction company that was involved in many of Murano's works set aside for him a team of experienced designers and a site manager. Murano's office (Murano & Mori, Associated Architects) did not produce many design drawings prior to construction. The site manager familiar with Murano's work and a veteran estimator would calculate what the total cost of the building would be, based on past experience. Once construction work began, an architect from Murano's office and "Murano's" team of designers from the construction company would collaborate in producing detailed drawings. Numerous full-scale construction drawings and mock-ups of building elements would be prepared. Murano continued to make changes until he was satisfied and was not overly concerned about the increases in cost the changes entailed. The construction company, having already factored in Murano in their calculations, voiced few objections. For the company, the important thing was to carry out the work in an atmosphere of cooperation. In a small country such as Japan, an architect and a construction company often find themselves working together on many different projects. For a construction company, establishing trust is often a greater priority than making a little immediate profit. Murano continued into his nineties to channel much of his creative energy as an architect into on-site design. Naturally on a large project, some parts of the design task interested him more than others. Murano took a rational approach and left the design of those parts with which he was less concerned to the construction company. He was an architect who adopted in the latter half of the twentieth century the role of a medieval *meister*. Yet his favorite reading matter on the commuter train he took to his office in Osaka is said to have been *Das Kapital*.

Kenzo Tange was Murano's junior by more than twenty years, but their careers overlapped from the 1950s to the late 1970s. Tange, a figure in the mainstream of the Japanese architectural world, was on the faculty of Tokyo University when he designed his best-known works but also had a design office called Urtec outside the university. During those years, Tange designed each work around a different theme – e.g., the use of a new structural system to create a large space – as did his contemporaries Eero Saarinen and Paul Rudolph in the United States. Many of Tange's works demanded such a high standard of construction and involved the application of such new structural systems that new construction methods had to be developed for them. Unlike works by Murano, Tange's works required the participation of construction companies to solve technological problems of construction. To improve coordination on the site, a construction company would typically send several talented members of its design department to Urtec at an early stage in the design process and form a collaborative team with Tange's architects. That team would eventually move to the site office once construction began. The architect's word was law, in Tange's case as it was in the case of Murano. There were no qualms about making many changes during construction work.

Kunio Maekawa graduated from Tokyo University ten years before Tange in 1928, which happens to have been the year of my birth. Maekawa departed for Europe on the night of the day he graduated. Once in the Soviet Union, he took the Siberian Railway. Eventually he made his way to the atelier of Le Corbusier, where he stayed for approximately two years. In later years, Maekawa worked earnestly to improve the social standing of architects and to establish standards of professionalism. He served as the first president of the Japan Institute of Architects. Maekawa probably had the deepest understanding of European history and culture, including music and literature, of any Japanese architect of his generation.

Tange and Murano saw *aesthetic performance* as their ultimate objective in architecture. Maekawa, although naturally interested in aesthetic performance, was equally concerned with *building performance*. Ideally, of course, architectural design is a synthesis of the two, but that is difficult to achieve because aesthetic performance and building performance are by no means compatible. Building performance is a matter of the functionality and, above all, the durability of a building. Maekawa was an architect who dealt seriously with not only aesthetic problems but pragmatic problems that confront contemporary architecture, such as weathering and deterioration. In the case of any important building he designed, Maekawa is said to have assembled every year on the anniversary of the building's completion the builder, the engineers and the architect from his office who had been in charge of the project. Together they would inspect the building and afterwards discuss technical problems, including any deterioration that they had discovered.

In the 1950s and early 1960s, Maekawa tended to use exposed concrete as a building finish, as did his teacher Le Corbusier. However, he soon began to recognize that air pollution caused by increased industrialization and urbanization was damaging the surface of exposed concrete. The pre-set brick tiles that he later developed in collaboration with a manufacturer were among the most durable exterior finish materials developed in post-war Japan. Maekawa stopped using exposed concrete as an all-purpose material. Maekawa wrote:

> The great French author Zola once said that the fictional construct called the novel would not hold up even for a moment without "truth in the details." Ruskin pointed out that the white cloud in the sky that reminds us of a lamb is in fact nothing more than a cluster of water drops floating in the air. Truth in architecture seems to me to be something like the drops of water that create the illusion of a white lamb. . . . Architecture too is a grand work of fiction based on "truth in the details."[1]

I think of Maekawa as an architect who continued to bear the cross of Modernism throughout his life.

My generation was influenced by these outstanding architects. We listened to them speak about their design methods and philosophies and saw what they created. Today, each architect continues to search for an ideal way of coordinating design and construction. Buntrock offers an honest, detailed account of circumstances today. What then are the problems that Japanese architects confront today, and what are the prospects for the resolution of those problems?

First, as I stated at the outset, the Japanese architectural world has been weakened by the recession that has gripped the country since the bursting of the Bubble. This is especially true of all fields of the building industry. Even the large construction companies are no longer in a position to be as generous as they once were. The period of harmony and goodwill between architects and builders that our predecessors enjoyed is ending under the relentless pressure of rationalization. In particular, the fierce competition in private-sector construction that is driving down prices has all the marks of a war of attrition between construction companies. The restructuring these companies are carrying out in the name of rationalization is mostly in departments that are not directly involved in construction work. But design and research departments are beginning to feel the effects of restructuring in diminished size and capability. This will eventually leave even fewer companies in possession of the skills necessary to take on technologically demanding projects. The situation will become only more oligopolistic.

The unit cost of building projects in the public sector, as opposed to the private sector, has been maintained at a certain level. In the prevailing political climate in Japan, construction projects, particularly local construction projects, are apt to be parceled out to a number of small and medium-sized builders. A development with quite serious repercussions for the architectural profession is a new policy adopted by the national government to curtail the traditional power of the architect to supervise construction. The government is increasingly awarding 70 per cent of the supervision fee to offices specializing in construction supervision (although in reality, most of the work these offices do is paperwork required by public agencies). This development is likely to upset the present system which enables the architect to collaborate with the builder, fabricators and manufacturers in conceiving, testing and ultimately implementing design ideas during the construction process.

Has the collaboration between architects and the construction industry in Japan since World War II yielded anything that is exportable to other regions in this era of economic internationalization? The answer is no. Japan may export automobiles and home appliances, but it has nothing exportable in the way of buildings or even peripheral products. For excellent furniture and hardware, for example, we quite often turn to Scandinavian and German products. They tend to be far superior in beauty, durability and price (even when transport costs and patent fees are included). Although I will not go into the details here, many companies in those countries adopt a long-term strategy and view that emphasize steady improvements of products rather than constant model changes. This suggests that we Japanese need to reexamine our own cultural attitude toward manufacturing, especially the manufacturing of durable consumer goods.

I have had the opportunity to visit two recently completed works: the Mediatheque in Sendai by Toyo Ito, and the Art Hall in Kirishima Kogen, Kagoshima Prefecture, by Kunihiko Hayakawa. They embody the concept that Buntrock calls "lead architect–lead users." In particular, the Mediatheque, in achieving a new integration of architecture, structure and environmental systems, is the most innovative high-tech building since the Hongkong Bank by Norman Foster. Hayakawa's Art Hall, on the other hand, is a work in which already-developed elements have been carefully and splendidly assembled. The architect's idea for the cylindrical air-conditioning duct of transparent acrylic that cuts through the exhibition space, for example, was only realized through the joint efforts of people of different trades – engineers, manufacturers and the builder. The object is beautiful not simply because it appeals to the eye but because it represents the product of human collaboration.

Both works are public buildings, and their designs are based on winning entries in open competitions. The chairman of the jury for the Mediatheque competition was Arata Isozaki; I served in the same capacity for the Art Hall competition. The public agency administering the facility to be designed is often the biggest obstacle to the realization of innovative architectural ideas, but that was not the case in these two works. Overcoming differences and arriving at splendid solutions, the architects and the clients have done an admirable job. Although very different in style, the Gallery of Horyuji Treasures, which was completed by Yoshi Taniguchi for the Tokyo National Museum in Ueno last year, is yet another superb public building.

I am frankly not optimistic about the future of the Japanese architectural world. However, works such as these, though few in number, succeed in expressing the spirit of the age and will serve to transmit to future generations our cultural memory. That, I believe, is the ultimate role of architecture. We architects must never allow the flame of architecture to be extinguished.

1 Kunio Maekawa, *Kosumosu to hoho* (Cosmos and Method), Tokyo: Maekawa Kunio Kenchiku Sekkei Jimusho, printing by Toppan Insatsu. pp. 209–10 1985.

Translation by Hiroshi Watanabe

Preface

This book began simply; it was a long time before I even realized that it was becoming a book. While I was still in graduate school in the late 1980s, Japan became the site of a brief, incandescent and ostentatious speculative period now called the "Bubble." There was simply too much money, and as speculation in real estate overheated, architects were increasingly pressured to design almost anything, and to assure it was built as quickly and as flamboyantly as possible. Like many others, I found the dash of that era intoxicating, especially in contrast to the staid commercialism and excessively dull buildings in my own country, the United States. In short order, I was taking advantage of the summer holidays afforded me as a graduate student, and later, a young professor, to shuttle back and forth to Japan. Just as the Bubble began to burst I found myself employed in a Japanese architectural office, Dai'ichi Kōbō.

This was not the bad timing one might think. Watching the effects of an economic roller coaster ride has encouraged me to look at Japan with a long-term perspective. As a result, I have tried not to be overly persuaded by the dynamism of the 1980s nor by the gloom of the 1990s. In this book, both enjoy their due. Yet I treat them as the critically important, but anomalous, periods they seem to be.

Since I was already a licensed architect with some experience in offices, my employer assured me that I would find no difference in the practices at my new office and I was prepared to believe him. However, as I will recount, the opposite was true – the differences in practice surprised me daily, from my very first tasks. I began to keep a notebook of these oddities, so that over beer and *sake* I could amuse my colleagues with what I had found strange, from the fashionable pink *shichibu* trousers worn by carpenters to the way my boss would greet laborers in Chinese. Somehow, my more earnest observations always led to new questions. Ultimately, I began to explore how other architects and contractors worked as well, in order to learn if I had just found myself working in an exceptional situation – which, as it turned out, was to some extent true, as I will explain. I began to observe other practices and study how Japanese trade journals and books represented the profession and to use these as the basis for more accurate generalizations. In the course of this modest volume, I attempt to explore the answers to many of my earliest questions, even as I recognize many questions remain unanswered.

Telling others about Japan is frequently painful; often, people who have never visited the country hold deeply rooted beliefs regarding its culture. Yet in the short time I have known it, Japan has changed a great deal, and the changes are not over. I discuss the nature of architectural practice in Japan – as I saw it yesterday, as it appears today and to some degree how it may be tomorrow. By doing so, I hope readers will derive lessons about practice that can be of value to professionals everywhere, because there is no question in my mind that the result of such practices is that the best buildings built anywhere are built in Japan. It is no coincidence that the country with the second highest number of architects winning the Pritzker Prize is Japan – with three architects to the seven from the United States. This gap between the nations virtually disappears when one recognizes that Japan's population is only half that of the United States. Even more remarkably, many of the US Pritzker Prizewinners immigrated to North America, while the Japanese winners are all native. Although I do not specifically discuss the work of these leaders in any depth, this book begins to suggest how Japan's construction community can foster sophisticated approaches to architectural design.

A note on names: all Japanese names in this text are given in Western order with family name following a person's given name. When conventional English language spelling has been adapted which ignores long vowels, as in the name "Toyo Ito," I have followed that convention. At the beginning of 2001, the names of most Japanese ministries were changed during a reorganization. As this book was already in production, the text retains earlier versions of ministry names.

Acknowledgements

Like any ambitious effort, this book would not be possible without a great deal of assistance. In Japan, I have been extremely fortunate to know a number of good architects; many of them have been generous with their time and thoughtful with their responses to my relentless and occasionally repetitive questions. Three architects have offered long and unstinting aid and earned my deepest gratitude. Tei'ichi Takahashi hired me, then told me that there were no differences between Japan and the US – in doing so, he gave me a whole world to discover. Toyo Ito allowed me to spend so much time on his construction sites that I was accused occasionally of knowing their day-to-day activities better than he. More importantly, he always seemed to anticipate my next questions. Finally, Dr. Terunobu Fujimori gave me a place to think, and shared his remarkable enthusiasm with me. Not surprisingly, buildings by these three designers have a strong place in my text. I show the process of building as honestly as possible, but I hope no reader will take this as a criticism of the truly exemplary work each of these men and their staff have accomplished.

I asked Fumihiko Maki to write the foreword, because his work and international experience held the kernel to this book. There were times when I questioned the value of this book, and he always seemed, sometimes without his knowledge, to be there with encouragement. Many other architects have also accommodated my research. My thanks goes out in particular to Kinya Maruyama, Kunihiko Hayakawa, Hajime Yatsuka, Riken Yamamoto, Jun Aoki, Kazuyo Sejima, and Yoko Kinoshita and Makito "Shin" Watanabe of ADH. All made significant efforts to show me their working process.

Many others have also taken time from demanding work to help me learn and see. To list everyone I interviewed would be impossible, although some are named in the pages that follow. Three should be singled out, however, for putting up with the added strain of a foreign woman visiting their construction sites with a myriad of strange and foolish questions for a full year. Kumiko Inui cheerfully accommodated my visits to her first construction project; the more experienced Toyohiko Kobayashi and Kiyoshi Nishikura were also generous with their time. These three project architects and many other men and women treated me with grace while I got in their way.

I am indebted to Emmanuel-George Vakalo, who taught me to write and, far too young, died before I could share this book with him; Steve Lee, who saw the direction my research was leading; Stephen Kendall and Kinya Maruyama, each of whom asked just the right question at just the right moment; and Roberta Feldman, who kept me on track. Hajime Yatsuka and Tim Porter should also be singled out; with their advice, I opened many doors. Finally, Robert Cole, John Campbell and Jonathan Reynolds all helped me to feel that I could join in the discourse on Japan and gave me the confidence to try.

Colleagues at several universities deserve particular gratitude for making space and encouraging my work. My heartfelt thanks to my friends at Carnegie Mellon, the University of Illinois at Chicago, and the University of California at Berkeley, and to everyone in the University of Tokyo's Institute for Industrial Science, Fujimori research lab. Students at all these places have also been gracious, listening and probing as I worked out my questions about the differences between production systems in Japan and the US.

I am also deeply appreciative of the financial support I have received for this book. The Graham Foundation for Advanced Studies in the Fine Arts supported publication expenses, especially for the translation of Professor Fumihiko Maki's foreword and for including color photographs. This research was bolstered by a jointly funded post-doctoral fellowship from the National Science Foundation and the Japan Society for the Promotion of Science, allowing me to take a year away from teaching and return to Japan. The people representing NSF in Tokyo are the warmest and most encouraging people anyone could ever hope to know, and I found an intellectual center with their help. In particular, Ed Murdy gave me generous encouragement to strive and deserves my deepest thanks.

A number of friends read this manuscript, offering careful and thorough criticism. My sincerest gratitude goes out to Hajime Yatsuka, Howard Davis, Carol Mancke, Catherine Wetzel and Mimi Locher; all offered time they did not have to make sure that at least some of the dumbest things I almost said were cut. Carl Sapers also generously agreed to look over the legal chapters of this manuscript in an earlier form; they are much revised thanks to his comments.

Max Underwood and I wrote a piece, called "Innovation: Lessons from Japan and the United States on Challenging New Technologies," for the Third Annual International Symposium on Asia Pacific Architecture held in April 1999. Small parts of that paper have made their way into this book, but more importantly, our conversations helped me to reconsider the value of my work in a larger cultural context. In addition, many sections of this book were presented in earlier forms at regional, national and international meetings of the Association of Collegiate Schools of Architecture. These include "Outside Currents Strike a 'Small Island Nation': Global Trade and Japan's Contractual Flexibilities," at the international meeting in June 2000; "Customization in Japan: Opportunities and Constraints," at the technology conference in June 1999; "All Work and No Pay: Japanese Architectural Firms' Strategies in Hard Times," at the Northeast regional conference in October 1998; "The Political Economies of Japan's Traditional Craft and Contemporary

Collaborations," at the technology conference in March 1998; "Iemoto and University: Two Japanese Modes of Architectural Education," at the West Central regional conference in October 1997; "The Development and Implications of Post-fordist Manufacturing," and "Material and Ornament in Katsura and Nikko," for the European meeting in May 1996; "Japanese Building Production: Four Models of Design Development and Delivery," at the annual meeting in March 1996; and "Terunobu Fujimori: Working with Japan's Small Production Facilities," for the technology conference in March 1996. An earlier paper that became the basis for this book, "Architectural Production In Japan: Factors that Support Design," was printed in the ACSA's *Journal of Architectural Education*. I am grateful for the comments received during reviews, and for permission to include this material here.

Emotionally, I was fortunate to share with several dear friends the odd circumstances of being a foreign woman who loves both Japan and the field of architecture. Kathryn Findlay, Carol Mancke, Jackie Kestenbaum and Mimi Locher enlightened and inspired me not once but repeatedly. We were all trying to find our way in Tokyo's architectural community, and I confess to being nostalgic for those days. Kathryn, Mimi and Carol have established international practices that reach beyond Japan's shores and Jackie found success outside the field of architecture. I feel as if I was left to tell a story that might have been better told by all of us.

And finally to my husband, LeRoy Howard, who started me on this path because of his own interest in a country I'd barely considered. He listened to my fears, read my drafts, created space for my work, fed me and wrote me daily when we were apart – which was far too often. Each page of this book was a result not only of my efforts, but also his.

Introduction

Social behavior is largely path dependent ... Where a country is now will to some extent always reflect where it has been in the recent past.[1]

Japan's construction industry has consciously made different choices compared with the choices in the same industries in North America or Europe. As one example, Japanese builders can emphasize the importance of craft, even (at times) over economy. More importantly, designers and contractors celebrate common goals in the execution of built work; aesthetic and material decisions are not solely the realm of the architect. Although there is no single model that is universal in Japan, it is possible for the trades to have significant impact on design. Anyone on site may make design decisions, working under the architect's orchestration. Japan's wonderful buildings thus reflect a larger context. They are the product of differences in the opportunities and processes of construction. The results are highly variable: along with many fine buildings and far too many dreary, bathroom-tile-covered blocks. Both arise from the nation's economic, legal and political systems, and from historical norms.

Books on Japan's architecture do exist. Important and widely respected authors such as Kisho Kurokawa and Botond Bognar offer cultural reasons for Japan's idiosyncratic architectural profession, pointing to the influence, for example, that the traditional teahouse may have on current constructions.[2] This is understandable, as the overheated economy of the late 1980s promoted greater eccentricity and public openness to unusual forms and materials. Still, "culture" seems too imprecise to capture the broad set of influences on architectural practice. Furthermore, it offers little succor to the foreign architect hoping to learn lessons from Japan. The result, as Hajime Yatsuka and others have noted repeatedly, is that there has been far greater willingness on the part of Westerners to isolate Japan's accomplishments, focussing

1.1
Fumihiko Maki's 470,000 square-foot Tokyo Metropolitan Gymnasium demonstrates careful detailing throughout.

only on aesthetic character and quaint historical issues.

Whereas most English language discussions of Japanese architecture, especially those written by architectural historians, concentrate on buildings as artefacts, this book intends instead to consider architectural design and construction as processes. In doing so, the benefits that emerge as a result of the opportunities found in Japan's construction industry become more clear. Architecture is not simply a fashionable manipulation of surfaces, reducible to sexy photography. Rather, architecture is the expression of a building culture.

Japanese architects are extraordinarily confident at home: they resolve challenging performance issues, introduce cutting-edge material technologies and achieve remarkable levels of refinement and faultless detailing. Oddly, when the same architects build abroad, many seem unable to produce similar results. Tadao Ando summed up his first venture at building in the United States (a fractious experience that included removing a contractor from the job midway through construction), "When working overseas, *everything* – ideas about design and management, construction techniques, legal regulation – is different from Japan . . ."[3] Japanese architects' overseas buildings lack the crisp finishes and provocative reasoning of work at home, because the designers find themselves working in relative isolation. The reasons that Japan's construction industry works together, and the resulting contributions of many participants, are at the center of this discussion.

In developing the material for this book, I have spent countless hours interviewing archi-

1.2
Toyo Ito's latticed structure for the Yokohama Care Center.

tects, shadowing project teams, and developing a larger conceptual framework to understand the things I observed. Nevertheless, the first step was simply to look at the buildings around me and to wonder: How did these come about?

Fumihiko Maki's modern buildings have the refinement and delicacy of seventeenth-century sukiya teahouses; rich surface patterns and striking details define his work. It is difficult to grasp how his staff achieve the finely scaled complexity of these buildings – especially large structures like the 470,000 square-foot Tokyo Metropolitan Gymnasium – investigating and selecting many elegant finishes, and managing to achieve a high degree of coordination in the way these are used. Maki's office, like many in Japan, continues to design during construction. As the larger gestures of the building are resolved, the staff looks out at the emerging structure and turns to decisions about detail and finish.

Arata Isozaki, in an attempt to blend contemporary and vernacular forms, used roof tiles very much like those found on Japanese houses, on his Oita Convention Center. The tiles have a cleaner look to them, however. They are a combination of half-cylinders (much rounder than traditional tiles) and very flat tiles. These are not for sale in catalogues, and Isozaki only required about 100,000 of them for the project. Many architects, confined to a choice of off-the-shelf materials or handcrafted ones, might wonder how Isozaki justified the decision to customize. However, Isozaki had another alternative: the manufacturer modified the profile of each tile during production, without adding significant expense.

Toyo Ito developed an unusual latticed structure to support the roof of a modest community center in Yokohama. Although Ito is neither an engineer nor a "high-tech" architect, the completed design is effective both aesthetically and structurally. The project architect, who had previously been involved only in a series of unbuilt competition entries and had limited construction experience, marveled at the tonnage of material necessary, but showed complete confidence about his ability to manage the site. His responsibilities included assuring that the surfaces of formwork would yield sufficiently neat unfinished concrete, developing construction details and custom-designing a number of components. He was able to overcome initial concerns raised by the steel fabricator about the very precise tolerances the architects required.

Itsuko Hasegawa, with little experience beyond residential construction, won the competition for the Shonandai Children's Museum and Culture Center in 1987. The project is highly successful: the community embraces it because local citizens contributed to design decision-making, and the building, which includes advanced technology, performs well. Many young architects, facing a shift from residential scale to a complex cultural facility, might join forces with a more experienced firm – and would probably confine detailing to a more conservative palette of materials and forms. Hasegawa saw no need to do so; from the unusual concrete finishes to a range of animal footprints set in tiles scattered throughout the site, the building's surprising detail captivates its young visitors.

As these vignettes suggest, Japan's production process makes possible greater experimentation, greater customization and greater specialization than is thought feasible in many countries. Production flexibilities also affect construction, making it practical for architects to try new materials and components. Furthermore, anyone involved in a building's construction – not only those schooled in aesthetics – can contribute expertise and ideas to design and execution. Few Western architects have been able to experience the opportunities for innovation intrinsic to the Japanese system of building production – and others have not been able to discover how to make such unwieldy groups work effectively. Those that do – and I would count Rem Koolhaas and Frank Gehry among architects who have learned from Japan – dominate the field internationally.

Three international trends particularly suggest why Japan's practices merit scrutiny by architects elsewhere. First, manufacturing has become increasingly flexible throughout the world. Japan was simply in the vanguard of customization trends now emerging elsewhere. Working with both large and small manufacturers, architects have already developed approaches for achieving innovative structural forms, developing new building materials and finishes, and advancing architectural technology. Second, in much of the industrialized world the roles for architects, contractors and construction managers are unresolved, as building has become more complex. Japanese architects, working in an elastic legal context, treat the lack of distinct roles as an advantage, whereas practitioners in many countries fear this signals the end of the professions. Lastly, architectural educators and practitioners today fear that universities are unable to sufficiently teach students the technological information they require to become tomorrow's architects. Japan offers a very different model, where architects, contractors and manufacturers share knowledge and expertise and expect learning to be a part of practice, transcending widely acknowledged educational deficiencies.

In the pages that follow, I explore the origins of architectural and construction practices in Japan, and the opportunities and difficulties architects face today.

1   T.J. Pempel, *Regime Shift: Comparative Dynamics of the Japanese Political Economy*, Ithaca and London, Cornell University Press, 1998, pp. 2–3.
2   Representative of this approach are K. Kurokawa, *Intercultural Architecture: The Philosophy of Symbiosis*, Washington DC, American Institute of Architects Press, 1991, or B. Bognar, *Contemporary Japanese Architecture: Its Development and Change*, New York, Van Nostrand Reinhold Company, 1985.
3   T. Ando, Eychaner/Lee House, *A + U*, no. 338, November 1998, p. 118. My emphasis.

Historical precedents

CRAFT IN EARLY MODERN JAPAN (1590–1868)

Although international recognition of Japan's crafts reached its peak in the latter half of the nineteenth century, the flowering of craft dates from Japan's early modern era, particularly the building construction boom of the early sixteenth century. The Tokugawa era, from the end of the sixteenth century through to the middle of the nineteenth, is sometimes called the "Age of Craftsmen" because of the quality of refinement that was achieved. In earlier periods, Japanese political leaders and nobility relied on the best available labor, often from China and Korea, sometimes even forcibly relocating whole communities of artisans to Japan.[1] However, from the beginning of the sixteenth century, Japan restricted international trade, and it became necessary to encourage domestic labor to take over this role.

During the Tokugawa era, the shogunal government used legal and economic means to grimly maintain a large laboring class and a tiny connoisseur class. Beginning with the 1591 Edict Restricting Change of Status, social classes were prescribed and hermetic, with very limited opportunities for moving between ranks. Society broke down into nobility, warrior, merchant, artisan and peasant classes. Custom and regulation tied families, except for the warrior class, to their communities. Yoked by inflexible circumstances to both location and work, artisans were generally not well compensated. Since trades were hereditary and families poor, there was also a strong incentive to begin learning crafts at a young age. Even so, apprentices spent the initial years of formal preparation in mundane chores, and when training commenced, it was rudimentary. Apprenticeship conventionally took ten years or more. The apprentice learned by stealthy observation over time. This ultimately encouraged an ability to independently innovate, as proficiency advanced through trial and error.

Discriminating consumers of craft actually came from several classes. The nobility, isolated from political power, concentrated on cultural refinement. Over time, the merchant class accumulated much of the country's wealth and consequently its purchasing power. The warrior class, as a group, held political strength – although in practice this usually accrued to individual leaders – but instead of paying for craft, those having greatest power could requisition labor. Still, the pool of connoisseurs was not large. Warriors, for example, accounted for only about 5 per cent of the population; most were poor and they had little political power. The nobility, at the time the system broke down in the middle of the nineteenth century, accounted for less than 2 per cent of the population.

As for material limitations, these were established both by fiat and by nature. Throughout the period, laws that defined consumption by class grew increasingly restrictive. The government specified appropriate construction materials, building size and architectural elements for each class; restrictions also extended to clothing, foods and even the use of picayune materials such as hair combs and tobacco pouches. From the eighteenth century on, the country faced severe depletion of timber and metals; these laws, at least in their most repressive form, may have been a response to Japan's ecological collapse.[2] The result was that crafters learned to parsimoniously exploit a limited set of raw materials. Additionally, the legal restrictions on merchants' consumption encouraged inventive demands on crafters, as the wealthy attempted to outmaneuver these regulations.

The early modern period was also a time of enforced trade isolation, when the Shogunate maintained strong control over foreign goods and information. Western technology, which had begun to move towards industrialization, was not completely unknown. It was, however, politically suspect and dissemination was rare and potentially dangerous. Even outside trade with Asian nations, which continued, was closely watched. Thus, crafts advanced internally, without the introduction of foreign materials or technologies. Architecture, for the most part, remained conservative.

The age may appear harsh: heavy taxes restrained spatial and class mobility, and isolation led to environmental collapse. However, this was also an unusually prolonged period of civic consolidation and amity, following over one hundred years of civil war. Heavy bureaucratic authority maintained political stability from the early seventeenth century through to the mid-nineteenth century; such constancy ensured that the development of craft and the transmission of knowledge remained undisrupted. In the end, then, it is not surprising that sophisticated craft traditions are widely associated with Japan; the environment fostered craft development to a degree rarely found. The isolation and carefully defined political structure also maintained crafts long after the industrial revolution overwhelmed them elsewhere.

DRAWING THE LINE: THE CARPENTER AS ARCHITECT

Before architecture was introduced to Japan, who designed buildings and developed new styles? This is a more difficult question than one might expect.

One of the problems is simply that our expectations of architectural design today would seem odd historically. In his book on carpentry, William Coaldrake makes this

2.1
Shugakuin Villa. Who designed these buildings before architecture emerged as a profession?

distinction when he notes that, "Many of the precise dimensions of the parts of the building were more the natural result of a process of interaction between man, materials, and tools than of arbitrary design will."[3] Another author on Japan's traditional architecture, Heinrich Engel, similarly notes:

> If the word "design," in its contemporary definition, is at all appropriate for that which is drawn with a brush or frequently with a pencil on a single wooden board and which serves as a working drawing, then no architect is needed to "design" a house, or else both patron and carpenter are the true architects.

Engel continues, "While the actual creative work of the design process, i.e., adding and grouping space, is accomplished by the client, the carpenter's part is confined solely to the placement of columns."[4] This ignores a number of decisions that must be made. Most discussions of architecture in Japan argue that the carpenter was both builder and designer, just as in Western pre-industrial societies. Even today, temple, shrine and teahouse carpenters often maintain both roles. However, these carpenters work with little flexibility, constrained to only the most unavoidable modifications of an accepted model.

The character of "design" in traditional Japanese architecture may be significantly different from present-day expectations. Carpenters, working within narrowly established norms affecting the appearance and proportions of buildings, probably saw themselves as making necessary adjustments based on the

2.2
Katsura Imperial Villa, exterior.

specific problems presented by the site or available materials, rather than exerting deliberate choices. Even then, only some were qualified to do this. In reality, there were many words for carpenters, creating a distinction between those skillful enough to oversee a project and those limited to some specific area of a building.[5] This has led to some confusion, even among Japanese scholars, as to whether carpenters were merely subcontracting, or did indeed undertake design.[6]

There is, however, some evidence that the carpenter acted more as an artisan than a mechanic. Kenneth Frampton argues that this is even indicated by the word *daiku* (carpenter), since it is, he says, made up of the characters for "chief" and "artisan." In fact, it is probably more true to say that the characters refer to something "large" or "grand" and to "technology" rather than artistry. More telling than the etymology of the word for carpenter is the simple fact that during the Edo period (1603–1868), carpenters were the only trade that was, as a rule, allowed to sign their work, a privilege otherwise specifically extended only to the most talented crafters.[7]

THE PROBLEM OF STYLE

Many of the stylistic choices informing the design of temples and shrines were made beyond Japan's shores, not by her carpenters. Scholars regularly note the Chinese, Korean and even Indian influences in Japan's architectural traditions. Furthermore, for the most part there

2.3
The Toshogu roofscape.

has been little variation in the appearance of important buildings in Japan over the centuries. Those variations that emerged generally exist in the detailing, rather than overall character, of buildings. Two highly original styles, however, emerged during the Edo period: the elaborately decorative style first introduced at Nikko, and the sensual materiality of the *sukiya*. Two buildings completed around the same time, Nikko's Toshogu and the buildings of Kyoto's Katsura Rikyu, effectively illustrate the characteristics of these styles. They suggest how carpenters, even in the seventeenth century, sometimes took on design decision-making, while at other times elite clients, broadly schooled in aesthetics, shaped design.

Although much about Katsura remains debatable, most experts agree that the villa was probably begun around 1620, and that additions to the complex date to around 1642. Originally built for Prince Toshihito Hachijo, his son, Noritada, undertook significant reconstruction in the 1630s and 1640s, following a series of natural disasters. Near the Imperial seat of Kyoto, it naturally reflected orthodox attitudes to taste and refinement. Furthermore, as members of the imperial household, both princes would have been conscribed by a 1613 edict, the Five Rules for Nobility, which enjoined them to "follow the path of learning and the arts." As a result, Katsura is conspicuous for its subtle imagery and for the way small details throughout appeal to the intellect. Gold leaf, expensive woods, paintings by some of Japan's leading artists and other ornament exist at Katsura; however, gnarled bamboo, thatched roofs and other references to rusticity create an effective foil to the more lavish gestures.

2.4
The interior of Katsura's Shōiken Pavilion, showing a combination of rusticity and refinement.

The Toshogu as we know it today was begun in 1634 and most work was completed by 1636; some work in the complex continued through 1643. (An earlier shrine stood in the same location from 1617.) Thus, both complexes emerged almost simultaneously. Their differences, however, demand attention. The Toshogu is astonishing, made up of over fifty-five structures. Of these, twenty-nine have carved ornament, some to such a degree that Ralph Adams Cram called the buildings "... the last word of religious architecture in Japan ... That they are in a way supremely beautiful is perfectly true – they are the apotheosis of colored and carved decoration; but it is beauty gone mad, and busting beyond all bonds."[8] Kora Munehiro, a woodworker and carver who rose to a bureaucratic position overseeing shogunal construction, probably planned the complex with Kano Tan'yū, a respected painter. Most likely, Kora was responsible for construction oversight and carving, and Kano was responsible for surface reliefs and painting.[9] The gaudy ornament and the significant size of the complex did not come cheap; the Toshogu was "one of the most expensive architectural projects per square metre of building undertaken at any time in the entire Momoyama and Edo Periods" – a period when a number of major buildings were constructed.[10] Its construction absorbed roughly one-seventh of the treasury

Historical precedents   11

2.5
The Toshogu's ornamental exuberance.

left by the prior shogun, Hidetaka, and required over 4.5 million "man-days" of labor, over half of this simply for conveying materials to the remote site. Carpenters accounted for 1.7 million "man-days" and even gold leaf application required 23,000 "man-days."[11]

Although Katsura and the Toshogu have very different characters, they also hold some attributes in common. Both of them are complexes of buildings where attention has been paid to creating a unified sense of design in siting and in the architecture. This reflects technological advances of the time; as the size of projects grew in the early years of the Tokugawa period, carpenters moved beyond simple plans to use large-scale drawings that included elevations and details. They also relied more on the use of a proportional system for construction, contributing to a sense of unity in the designs of the complexes. Interestingly, the renowned painter Kanō Tan'yū also worked on both projects.

Equally notable are the differences between the two compounds, demonstrating a robust and flexible construction culture. Whereas the Toshogu finishes are a riot of ornament, Katsura Villa is understated. The scale of the shrine complex is monumental, with a clear hierarchy based on one's social status informing where each visitor worshipped; but in Katsura, the buildings are anti-monumental, both because of their delicacy and their multiple references to farmhouses and other modest structures. Additionally, expectations of social behavior in the many teahouses may have encouraged visitors to overlook status in their interactions. More useful for the discussion at hand, the clients of these two projects came from different social groups; the Toshogu was built for the warrior classes, whereas Katsura served the nobility. Naomi Okawa argues that the refinement found in Katsura is the result of its design process, which could not be guided wholly by the builders.[12] The discernment in allusions suggested by details throughout the complex indicate a level of education and erudition – and an awareness of the restrictions on nobles – unlikely among even the most advanced constructors. The princes' training, emphasizing traditional aesthetics and simplicity, led them to a very different style than the ostentation and more obvious references found in the carvings of the Toshogu – which could hardly have commanded similar oversight from the shogun.

It is interesting to note that one of the largest construction companies in Japan today, Takenaka Komuten, appeared around the same time as these two buildings were built, although they did not work on either of them. Although the firm did not take up modern contracting methods until 1899, they trace their history back to Tobei Mataka, a shrine carpenter in 1610, leading Takenaka to call themselves the oldest contractor in Japan – and perhaps the world. Several of Japan's other large contractors appeared in the waning days of the shogunate, but it was the values and practices developed in the Meiji era (1868–1912) that followed, that shaped contemporary construction practices, and consequently, the opportunities for architectural design.

A CHALLENGE TO TRADITIONAL TRADES

In the mid-nineteenth century, the context for craft and construction changed. The Meiji Restoration began in response to both international pressures to revive foreign trade and because of internal political collapse. Control shifted back from the shogunate to Japan's imperial household; trading and political exchange resumed with other nations, especially the Western powers. Japan became aware of its own lack of power at a time when Britain was already dominating the much larger nation of China; the government felt that it must encourage Westernization as a way to catch up. Leaders in government, education and business aggressively adopted Western technologies and systems. Naturally, conflicts between craft and manufacturing appeared in Japan as new, objectives related to efficiency were introduced. Historically, labor saving in production and construction was not valued, because the social order maintained a surplus of workers in the artisan class. However, as Japan joined the international community, manufacturing began to supplant handicraft in routine production, just as it had elsewhere during the Industrial Revolution.

There are understandable labor gaps between manufacturing and craft. When a community lacks pervasive industrialization, most materials of daily life are handmade. Thus when manufacturing is introduced, it captures a portion of the original craft market, because basic goods can be produced more cheaply without significant differences in quality. Since industrial production is most efficient in the manufacture of simpler articles, apprentices have less opportunity to rely on mundane work to develop their fundamental skills. Furthermore, the natural education of consumers, developed through interactions with crafters, weakens, and the respect for craft becomes less pervasive.

Japan's restoration of open, international

trade also meant that formidable challenges were no longer resolved by developing new craft technologies. Instead, foreign technologies or materials were mined for solutions. However, Japan remained poor. Although the country sometimes imported new materials or developed the ability to produce them domestically, doing so was costly. A dependence on traditional craft and construction approaches thus prevailed for much of the Meiji era. By the early twentieth century, industrial production and craft would achieve an awkward balance, with industrial production increasingly important in urban settings.

Interestingly, the Meiji government participated in eroding the strength of craft trades. The period of apprenticeship was legally limited to five years or less and an emphasis on universal education caused the average starting age of apprenticeship to rise. Thus apprenticeship became one-half (or less) of its traditional length and occurred later in life, when manual dexterity is more difficult to accomplish. The use of construction and trade manuals also proliferated during the Meiji era, perhaps in response to incomplete apprenticeship terms. These would, however, have discouraged the development of individual resourcefulness common on hands-on apprenticeships. As political will favored manufacturing, the negative effects of these changes to apprenticeship and the craft trades may have been deliberate.

Perhaps the most notable example of the weakness of Japan's indigenous building trades at that time is the early twentieth-century "restoration" of Todaiji, a major temple considered even today to be one of the world's largest wooden structures. Because many of the original construction skills were lost in the latter half of the Tokugawa era, and because there were foreign solutions that offered greater strength and speed, the renovation openly employed steel.[13] Steel framing was also used in several major government buildings, at a time when its use was still rather novel in institutional buildings in the United States and Europe.

At the same time, there were also advocates for craft. Many were Westerners, and their voices offered a challenge to the rush towards Western technologies. In the latter half of the nineteenth century, because foreign travelers were just beginning to freely visit Japan and there was a great deal of curiosity, even the most inelegant observations were widely read. German and English intellectuals were actively attempting to promote the revival of craft in the West; Hermann Muthesius, Bruno Taut and others influenced by the Arts and Crafts visited Japan. Observers wrote favorably of the nation's crafts, in particular pointing to differences between debased building trades in their own countries and evidence of refinement in Japan. Typical of many authors, Edward Morse (in a classic text on domestic architecture written in the early 1880s) stated that, "A somewhat extended experience with the common everyday carpenter at home [in the US] leads me to say, without fear of contradiction, that in matters pertaining to craft the Japanese carpenters are superior ..."[14] Ralph Adams Cram, based on a briefer trip to Japan than Morse's, stated it even more strongly:

> Whatever any [Japanese] workman did, he did it as well as it could possibly be done. Ugliness was ... a sin; carelessness and cheapness of workmanship ... a crime. The fact that the thing was humble in its function was no reason why it should not be perfect in form and fashion.[15]

2.6 & 2.7
Todaiji, elevation and detail of steel strapping.

Not surprisingly, these visitors spawned Japanese intellectual movements – for example, fostering the work of the Japanese White Birch Society, which included Bernard Leach and Soetsu Yanagi. The German Bruno Taut also directly addressed the public with his observations, published in Japanese and widely read. Ultimately, intellectuals came to emphasize the Japanese home as a refuge for crafts traditions (with greater success than similar efforts had in the European Arts and Crafts movements). In doing so, a schizophrenic attitude towards Western innovations emerged: Japanese people eagerly embraced the modern offices, schools and railroad stations that changed public life, while zealously maintaining domestic and religious traditions. Continuing acceptance of craft in residential life and leisure environments creates opportunities for architects even today to utilize a wide range of crafts in building production, a point that I will return to later.

DESIGN IN THE NINETEENTH CENTURY

Because leaders in Japan's new Meiji government felt that it was necessary to adopt many of the ways of more powerful nations in order to be accepted as equals on the political stage, architecture and building production became a symbol of a new political context. This was especially true of buildings related to the reestablished government's attempts to unify Japan through compulsory education, universal conscription and sophisticated transportation technologies. Japan built structures associated with Western technology throughout the country, especially schools, military barracks, lighthouses, railroad stations and government offices. Many of these were, for Japan, new building types, and the Meiji government adopted both foreign planning norms and quasi-foreign architectural styles. The change, at least in the treaty ports where foreigners were first confined, would have been extraordinary. One observer, Basil Hall Chamberlain, summed up the period with the words, "To have lived through the transition stage of modern Japan makes a man feel preternaturally old; for here he is in modern times … and yet he can himself distinctly remember the Middle Ages."[16]

Although a demand for Western-style architecture existed as early as the 1870s, there were no native professionals, and very few foreign architects in the nation. As a result, Japanese carpenter/designers, combining stylistic inventiveness with construction skills, emerged before the imported profession of architecture. Their earliest exposure to Western styles came through foreign enclaves. The emperor's forces originally attempted to confine foreigners to limited, undeveloped areas called "treaty ports"; both Yokohama and Kobe began from scratch. Thus, all foreigners' daily needs, from housing to offices, required new construction. Yokohama, the most sizeable of the treaty ports, was established in 1859, and then rebuilt in 1866 and 1872, following disastrous fires.

Many of the construction companies that dominate the market today emerged or expanded in this period. One of the earliest of Meiji carpenter/designers was Kisuke Shimizu, who began his apprenticeship in 1804, and rose in the Tokugawa bureaucracy. With the government's collapse, Shimizu began independent practice as a contractor in Yoko-

2.8
Yamagata University, Yonezawa.

hama in 1859. However, he continued to have contractual obligations in both communities, and he apparently died from exhaustion and overwork in the same year, while returning to Tokyo from Yokohama.[17] (It is hard not to suggest that the hours kept by employees of Japanese contractors may also date from this period.) Shimizu's adopted son took his name (and the contractual obligations associated with it) and is generally referred to as Kisuke Shimizu II; the firm he went on to found has grown to be one of the world's largest contractors, Shimizu Construction. According to many historians, he was one of the most skillful of Japan's early "Western-style" designers. Two of the earliest Western-style buildings he produced for Japanese clients, the Mitsui Bank and the First National Bank, were both built in 1874, and he later designed the Minato Club for Mitsui, in 1908, said to be a particularly fine example of "Stick style" architecture.[18] However, Shimizu was also constructing buildings designed by others, including the 1891 Nikolai Cathedral, credited to the architect Josiah Conder, and the 1906 buildings designed by a Japanese architect on the Mitsui staff, for Japan Women's College. In addition to his efforts as a carpenter/designer and as a contractor, Shimizu was also supplying lumber and metal goods to other contractors in the early years of Meiji.[19]

As I noted earlier, Takenaka has a history going back to the Edo period, but it was in Meiji that it took the name Takenaka Komuten – "Komu" was understood at the time to refer to design offices, so the name was a clear indication that Takenaka also anticipated offering both design and construction services. Another of the largest contractors in Japan today, Kajima Corporation, also emerged in a similar way. Iwakichi Kajima, the founder, began as a carpenter's apprentice in 1840. When still young, he began to build for the foreign trading firms Jardine Matheson & Company, and Walsh-Hall.[20] The demand for new buildings and for innovative approaches to their materials and construction seems to have laid the basis for most of Japan's major contractors during this period; Taisei Construction and Obayashi also emerged around the same time. Taisei built one of the best-known architectural works designed by a foreign architect in Japan, Josiah Conder's Rokumeikan, in 1883, and also built Ginza's up-to-date commercial quarters, constructed in modish brick. Obayashi, founded in 1892, was one of the last of the contractors to benefit from the Meiji government's policies related to commercial capital,

2.9
Saiseikan (1879) Hiroyuki Haraguchi, contractor. Dallas Finn notes that carpenters competed to work on this site, to learn Western construction practices.

intended to establish large, well-capitalized firms in key markets. As with Shimizu, these contractors had varying roles. On some buildings, they were responsible for both design and construction, whereas on other projects, they worked from designs supplied by professionals. Many of the structures they designed are appreciated today for their fanciful renditions of Western architecture. However, although these early buildings were stylistically naïve, they very often were based on hard-won technological sophistication. Today, Japan's leading contractors continue to emphasize the importance of new technologies in their work.

Other carpenter/designers emerged across the country. Most are said to have learned their skills working in the treaty ports set aside for the foreign community, although as the Meiji government was beginning to build other, Western-style buildings in more remote areas, there were opportunities to learn the new technologies throughout the nation. For one such building, a Western-style hospital in Yamagata, completed in 1879, Dallas Finn notes that, "Carpenters fought to work on this structure . . . so eager were the Japanese to learn how to produce clapboarding with vertical battens, details, properly louvered shutters, king posts, hooded window frames, circular stairs, and dozens of other Western features."[21] Occasionally, wealthy and *au courant* clients sent their carpenters to Tokyo to study buildings in the foreign community, and one carpenter seems to have traveled as far as the United States to study in the years before 1875. In addition, carpenters' manuals had been in use in Japan for quite some time; new publications attempted to explain Western stylistic conceits. As local carpenters began to understand these new approaches to style and construction, they also made use of American design manuals. Publications of designs by A. J. Downing and Calvert Vaux can even be found in the library of a Hokkaido agricultural college.[22]

These carpenter/designers, however, remained at a disadvantage, especially when serving informed clients such as foreigners or government officials with experience overseas. For designers unfamiliar with the new styles and building types, even professional architects, the solution was to order plans from abroad: for the Nikolai Cathedral, Josiah Conder, an architect himself, worked from designs drawn up in Russia, and the Japanese carpenter of an 1880 museum used plans drawn up by an obscure Boston architect. However, these solutions were difficult to implement because they did not engage the particularities of the site or of local construction norms.

The increasing need for professionally trained designers led to the establishment of architectural and engineering practices in Japan, but the result was a gradual and incomplete split between design and construction.[23]

THE EMERGENCE OF ARCHITECTURAL PRACTICE

In many nations, architectural practice emerged from construction. Given time, Japan's carpenter/designers might have traced the same path followed by the early masons and carpenters who acted as designers in Europe, gradually effecting a separation between construction and architecture. Certainly, in 1912 the professional community hoped to establish such a split. A key distinguishing characteristic between craft and the professions remains at the heart of such separations, whether in law, medicine or architecture: whereas skillful building production is based on empirical experience, the professions, such as engineering and architecture, start from theoretic foundations. Historically, however, this disjunction developed not only from within the professional community, but also because the public supported building professionals, as a result of its growing needs for symbolic imagery and sophisticated scientific approaches. In Meiji Japan, the government's wholesale efforts to adopt Western customs and appearance meant that the cultivated styles required for palaces, ministries and even frivolous ballrooms for foreign and Japanese social elites would not wait for the country to develop a native resolution to problems of technology and style.

Initially, the government relied on foreign professionals for its most significant undertakings. Foreign architects designed university buildings, offices for the national government, museums and villas for the rich. Foreign engineers oversaw the construction of lighthouses, railroads and bridges. More importantly, they built professions. The term used for these imported specialists was *yatoi*, a name that explicitly suggested that their employ was to be short-term. There was good reason for the government's reluctance to depend permanently on foreign employees. Japan's first architects and engineers were privileged European and North American professionals, hired at great expense to introduce and promote Western technologies. These employees peaked at 520 in 1875. Over the early years of Meiji, over 3000 people were employed as *yatoi*. In the mid-1870s this meant that the Department of Public Works, which favored the British, paid over one-third of its budget to foreign employees – at a time when the country was also spending heavily to import the tools and materials needed for an extensive railway and telegraph system. Not all *yatoi* were professionals, though. For technologically demanding projects, masons, machinists, plumbers and even painters also came to Japan. However, in time the government replaced the *yatoi* with native artisans and professionals.

On construction sites, British technicians and engineers found that they were often shadowed by native "interpreters" – students in the same field, who benefited from observing how the foreigners worked on site. For the professions, the government used foreign experts to establish educational programs in university settings; the enormous salaries they commanded gave their employers an incentive to train others and replace them quickly.

The first professor of architecture in Japan, the English Josiah Conder, was hired in 1877 to teach at the Imperial College of Engineering in Tokyo and to simultaneously manage a professional practice. While Western colleges and universities offered architecture courses from the 1830s onward, Conder's comprehensive curriculum predated all but a few such architecture programs. It was over ten years later before a similarly complete architecture curriculum would be found in his native country, and only three universities had established architecture programs in the US by this time: Cornell, MIT and the University of Illinois. The early founding of architectural education in Japan was, of course, in part a result of a lack of alternatives. In North America, England and Europe, apprenticeship remained the norm, and, as I discuss later, apprenticeship eventually became important in Japan.

However, education was also attractive for its up-to-date sophistication. There are indications that the nation also made deliberate efforts to take on the most contemporary approaches to professional development. Henry Dyer, who headed the College of Engineering that included Conder's department, argued that his programs were deliberately forward thinking. He claimed that it took many years for, "... all the improvements which we had adopted in the Imperial College of Engineering, Japan, to be found in almost all the colleges in Britain."[24] And Dyer's friend and former professor, Lord Kelvin, noted that the labs in Tokyo were more sophisticated than those found at any educational institution in London.

Conder's earliest students graduated in 1879. By 1884, Conder had left teaching; his position was taken over by Kingo Tatsuno, one of the university's first architecture graduates. Conder's students (and the students they trained) demonstrated the benefits of university education. Rather than narrowly imitating the designs of their talented teacher, students produced a wide range of projects in appropriately eclectic styles. At the same time, only a little more than twenty years after the first treaty ports were established, others already studied abroad. In 1879, the first Japanese received an architectural degree from the Ecole Polytechnique. By 1905, native architects served not only Japanese clients, but also produced some of the banks and villas for Japan's foreign population.

Like many other aspects of Japanese society, architecture was thus imported and overlaid an earlier system, arresting the natural evolution that might have led from one to another. In 1912, a professional association of architects called for the elimination of corporations offering both design and construction services. These architects were not successful, however, and at least one of the contractors, Takenaka Komuten, responded strongly. Initially, in 1913 Takenaka hired their first professionally trained designer, a graduate of Japan's leading architecture school. Then, in 1917, the firm officially and publicly restated their policy of undertaking both design and construction. Finally, in 1921, the company hired two of Japan's most remarkable young designers, who had participated in founding the 1920s *Bunri-ha* movement.[25] By 1927, Takenaka had fifty professionally trained designers on their staff – greater than the design population of any other architecture or construction firm in Japan. Although Takenaka's actions were most assertive, they represented a larger expectation in the construction community: design and construction would not be easily split. Consequently, an uncompromising division between architecture and construction did not arise in Japan. Furthermore, many *yatoi* – including Josiah Conder, one of the most influential – emphasized the importance of builders and architects working together to achieve high standards in construction. Jonathan Reynolds, in a lengthy paper on the early years of architecture's professionalization in Japan, noted that the university system quickly moved to embrace construction. Students were encouraged to visit building sites during a two year "practicum" (what would be called an internship today) and by 1889, courses taught by a master carpenter were a part of the restructured curriculum at Tokyo's Imperial University.[26]

Contractors such as Shimizu and Takenaka continued to offer design services (although they began to hire people trained as architects in order to do so), while architects in independent practice served a privileged few on the most symbolically important projects. Thus, even in the earliest days of the Meiji era, a loose hierarchy was established; the same client might turn to an independent architect for one project, a carpenter/designer for another, and – in the case of the large corporations – in-house architects to design a third building, based on the relative importance of each.[27] Later, local communities operated only slightly differently; whereas architects were called upon to design the most important buildings, it was often professionally trained engineers, employed by local governments, who took the place of the in-house architects employed by Mitsui and Sumitomo. This system remains in place today, and is one of the chief reasons for many of the flexibilities found in Japan's construction and professional communities.

1   One village of Japanese wood carvers I have visited, for example, uses a notably Chinese pronunciation of its name, "Kaminyū," rather than Japanese pronunciations. Although this village dates back over three hundred years, it also is remarkably similar to villages I have visited in Taiwan, and has only one counterpart I have found in Japan.
2   C. Totman, *Early Modern Japan*, Berkeley, Los Angeles and London, University of California Press, 1993, p. 226. Totman's book *The Lumber Industry in Early Modern Japan*, Honolulu, University of Hawai'i Press, 1995, is also recommended.
3   W. Coaldrake, *The Way of the Carpenter*, New York & Tokyo, Weatherhill, 1990, p. 24.
4   H. Engel, *The Japanese House: A Tradition for Contemporary Culture*, Tokyo, Charles E. Tuttle Company, 1964, pp. 84–5.
5   T. Masuda, *Living Architecture: Japanese*, New York, Grosset & Dunlap, 1970, p. 120.
6   Iwashita Hideo, *Nihon no Zenecon: Sono Rekishi to Ima*, Tokyo, *Nikkan Kensetsu Kogyō Shinbun Sha*, 1997, p. 13.
7   C. J. Dunn, *Everyday Life in Traditional Japan*, Tokyo, Charles E. Tuttle Company, 1969, p. 91.
8   R. A. Cram, *Impressions of Japanese Architecture and the Allied Arts*, New York, Dover, 1960, p. 106.
9   *Shogun's Shrine: The Magnificent Nikko Toshogu. Vol. 1: Plant and Bird Carvings*. In Japanese and English, with translations by Jay Thomas. Tokyo, Graphic-sha Publishing Company, 1994, p. 129. All information related to the numbers and types of ornaments found in different parts of the complex are taken from the surveys in this book and its companion volume, *Shogun's Shrine: The Magnificent Nikko Toshogu. Vol. 2: Human and Animal Carvings/Paintings*.
10 W. Coaldrake, *Architecture and Authority in Japan*, London & New York, Routledge, 1996, p. 181.
11 N. Okawa, *Edo Architecture: Katsura and Nikko*, New York & Tokyo, Weatherhill/Heibonsha, 1975, p. 33.
12 Ibid., p. 135.
13 This point is one made by Coaldrake in *Architecture and Authority in Japan*, pp. 245–7.
14 E. Morse, *Japanese Homes and their Surroundings*, New York & Tokyo, Charles Tuttle & Co., 1972, p. 35.
15 Cram, *Impressions of Japanese Architecture and the Allied Arts*, p. 162.
16 B. H. Chamberlain, *Japanese Things: Being Notes on Various Subjects Connected with Japan*, New York & Tokyo, Charles E. Tuttle Company, 1971, p. 1.
17 Iwashita, *Nihon no Zenecon*, p. 42.
18 D. Finn, *Meiji Revisited: the sites of Victorian Japan,* New York & Tokyo, Weatherhill, 1995; p. 126.

19 Iwashita, *Nihon no Zenecon*, p. 43.
20 Ibid., p. 42.
21 Finn, *Meiji Revisited*, p. 38.
22 Ibid., p. 57.
23 Iwashita dates this to about Meiji 20, or after 1887. Iwashita, *Nihon no Zenecon*, p. 90.
24 N. Pedlar, *The Imported Pioneers: Westerners who Helped Build Modern Japan*, New York, St. Martin's Press, 1990, p. 19.
25 T. Muramatsu, "History of the Building Design Department of Takenaka Komuten," *Takenaka Komuten Sekkeibu* [Building Design Department of Takenaka Komuten], Tokyo, Shinkenchiku Sha, 1987, pp. 35 and 37.
26 J. Reynolds, "The Formation of a Japanese Architectural Profession" unpublished manuscript, September 1995. Part of a forthcoming book: M. Takeuchi, ed. *The Artist as Professional in Japan*.
27 The use of in-house architects, employed by firms like Sumitomo and Mitsui, can be dated to as early as the 1890s. I am unsure of the origins of the practice, but it may have been related to the more common practice of maintaining in-house engineers, and the Japanese tendency to commingle the two professions.

Education and the professions

In Japan's traditional arts and crafts, students selected a school of practice represented by a leader, the *iemoto* (literally "foundation of the house"). Each school had an entrenched and specific approach to the subject; they expected students to wholeheartedly embrace the school's entire set of rules and practices. Because learning came through imitation of others following the same path, the schools emphasized training the hand and eye to learn fundamental concepts, in contrast to Western forms of education, which emphasized intellectual study of fundamentals. Although architectural education is sometimes seen as close to arts education in the West, training for Japan's nascent profession understandably followed Western educational patterns at first.

Today, however, Japanese undergraduate education in architecture is notoriously undemanding. After a rigorous and intense education through high school graduation, the pace slackens until the final year of college. Emphasis is not on acquiring learning, but on developing social skills. As a result, graduates from Japan's architecture programs are not as well prepared for the profession as North American students. Consequently, the profession has embraced an *iemoto*-like system of training. Post-graduate experiences, in the office and on construction sites, are undoubtedly the primary way of learning about the profession. This is not the same as a Western internship; learning occurs through direct observation, often without an analytic framework

THE UNIVERSITY

The word commonly used for architecture, "*kenchiku*," is ambiguous. It translates as either "architecture" or as "construction" – and the title *kenchikushi* refers not exclusively to someone who offers design services, but also to constructors. Essentially, the license encompasses

3.1
An intern at work.

architecture, engineering and contractors' licenses. Not surprisingly, Japanese architects do not perceive themselves as part of a discipline distinct from engineering or construction practice – although most recognize that architects maintain special responsibilities regarding aesthetic and social issues. Universities' organizational structures reflect this ambiguity. Whereas a limited number of fine arts universities do include architecture in their curricula, most architects study in engineering departments and receive the same degrees as students who focus on the scientific or technological opportunities of construction. Significantly, many Japanese architects feel this allows for a shared sense of values on the design team later.

The student with an undergraduate architecture degree in Japan is most likely to have been in a program similar to a North American Bachelor of Arts, Bachelor of Science or Bachelor of Architectural Studies program. Undergraduate admissions are extremely competitive, but the schools students enter are not. As far as general education goes, the overall educational system is robust enough to allow for some slack. Much of the material that a North American student might learn in college (e.g., higher level physics and chemistry, mathematics through trigonometry, and the history of Japan and other nations) is simply studied in the high schools in Japan. In fact, because Japanese students in primary and secondary schools attend classes for about 50 days more each year than in North America, they actually have spent the equivalent of three or four more years in the classroom by the time they arrive at college.[1]

Unlike the rigors of Japan's secondary

schools, teaching at the undergraduate level is quite loose by North American standards. Professors frequently cancel classes. Student attendance is customarily low. Undergraduates can sign up freely for classes and drop them even quite late in the term. Moreover, "... almost no one is ever failed."[2] Four-year graduation rates remain high, estimated at 75–79 per cent, and even in 1990, the beginning of a long period of on-again-off-again recession, 81 per cent of all students had jobs right out of college – suggesting that the professional and business communities have accepted the current state of university education.[3]

Since a 1950s reorganization of university education, most specialized programs, including architecture, follow two years of general studies. At some universities, these courses take place at different campuses, further isolating younger students from the potential influence of academically immersed upper-level undergraduates and the few students – less than 7 per cent – who continue on to graduate studies. Technical programs are somewhat demanding because they require students to pass an entry examination at the end of the second year. Nevertheless, even considering the entry exam, architecture undergraduates do face a relatively effortless experience. Not only is the first half of most Japanese architecture programs based in general studies, even for upper level students some general studies courses, especially English language classes, continue to be required.

Consequently, by simply looking at the time committed to professional studies it is fair to say that students graduating from architecture programs are not well prepared for the profession. Furthermore, unlike the situation in many countries, in Japan the four-year degree, combined with two or more years' of professional activity, remains sufficient qualification for taking the licensing examination. A shorter three-year degree from vocationally oriented schools is also possible, though not highly regarded; graduates from these programs must have three or more years of professional experience to take the exam.

THE OFFICE

In a typical North American office, new hires will probably draw standard details for contract documents, working under the close supervision of a senior member of the firm. This is necessary in part because of the large number of details required in current North American architectural practice. However, it is definitively not the most effective way to teach building production, because it begins from the abstract. In Japan, rather than relying on the university as the primary location for training and then shifting recent graduates to document production, architects have embraced learning through direct observation, during the period immediately following graduation. Japanese internship differs in its intentions, breadth of experience, the transmission of values and the ultimate abilities of the architect.

As one author put it, "Today, the apprenticeship system is a work place [sic] environment that touches the lives of only a few contemporary Japanese. However, the values that ... define appropriate behavior for a learner in a new job are still very much present ..."[4] One example is the way simple tasks, intended to teach kinship rather than

3.2
On a *kengakkai*.

encourage efficient production, are a regular part of the apprentice's experience. In a carpenter's workshop, young apprentices traditionally would have been expected to do errands on behalf of the carpenter's household, deliver finished goods and keep the workshop clean. Historically, apprentices could not even touch tools for at least three years. Vestiges of these practices exist in the Japanese architectural office today: firms require interns, during their first year, to make the morning coffee or tea, neatly arrange furniture for meetings, air out the office, or even clean toilets. (The last duties were among those required of young interns in the office I worked at in 1993.) Since interns' production is generally limited to simple tasks such as model building and they are not considered to have productive value, they are often brought along for trips, meetings and other activities where they offer very little in the way of contributions, but begin to develop an appropriate background for later work.

Interns are exposed to a hodgepodge of information, whether appropriate to an individual's skill level and duties or not. In this way staff learn how their work fits into the larger context. Inexperienced staff regularly attend meetings that address advanced topics (sometimes sleeping through these meetings, admittedly), participate in visits to manufacturing sites, and join *kengakkai* (literally "see and learn meetings") to other design teams' construction sites. The offices I have studied also have young staff propose their own solutions for competitions, facing off against everyone from the head designer on down. In the office, design teams rarely discuss senior staff members' proposals at any length, but junior staff receive lavish attention, criticism and encouragement. Generating and reviewing design proposals that are unlikely to be of use is inefficient and uneconomical in the short run, but helps younger staff develop an understanding of the design solutions appropriate within the firm.

Consistent with the apprenticeship model, most offices do not rely on staff to have learned anything elsewhere. This is true even if the intern has a more advanced technical education or has worked for another office. Basic information is "taught" to all recent hires. Westerners who find themselves in Japanese offices often chafe at the simplicity of some of their early assignments.

Oddly, simple assignments commingle with advanced ones in an apparently random way; the progression from learning one set of skills to the next is not necessarily logical. In my observation, offices do not attempt to determine whether an intern can do a particular job well; instead, employers assume that staff should contrive skills as appropriate. As one remarkable example, on my first day on the job in a Japanese architectural firm, I was given the task of using a word processor to write up a finish schedule. By Western standards, this was an absurd assignment. While word processing is not a sophisticated activity, my Japanese was still rudimentary and finish schedules include "Chinese" characters (kanji) unknown by most college graduates. When, after four hours, the machine crashed (taking with it my unsaved efforts), no one in the office gave any thought to reassigning me. Instead, I simply received cheerful and supportive encouragement to keep at my work.

This reassurance, generally warm and profuse, is noteworthy. Some Westerners misinterpret the intent of such assignments as hazing – one of my Australian students who had a military background at first assumed these assignments were intended to "break one's spirit." In my experience, lavishly warm encouragement accompanies seemingly impossible tasks.

My experience at the word processor was not unique; I see similar situations frequently. Architects can confidently delegate to inexperienced staff because juniors have been trained to devise successes even when previous experiences did not adequately prepare them. Interns learn how to contrive skills through watchfulness and imitation. (One Japanese verb, *manabu*, originally meant "to imitate" and now translates as "to study" or "to learn.") Supervising staff rarely pass on information in an explicit way. Instead, since work assignments are unpredictable, interns must be alert observers of their environment. In this way, they prepare themselves to handle any assignment.

One social anthropologist, G. Victor Sogen Hori, refers to this approach as "Teaching Without Teaching," and suggests that its effectiveness lies in creating similar results by members of a team, while encouraging skills useful when no precedent exists and innovation is necessary.[5] The intern does not choose freely from any solution he or she may like; aside from the fact that the construction process reveals impractical efforts, deviations from the office's accepted practices deny the collective wisdom of the *virtuoso*. The results of all staff's work should appear similar – but the manner in which staff achieve these results may vary. In the short term, this training strategy is clearly inefficient. However, as Hori points out, the ultimate result is that staff members are continually and unconsciously preparing themselves to take on new responsibilities without any specific training, rather than simply learning how to complete assigned duties.[6] Such internships also conform to the notion that Japan's educational system values personal development and improvement over acquiring specific skills and credentials, an idea embraced by many anthropologists. Inefficient in the short run, in the long term the approach saves time – especially the time of supervising staff, who otherwise must always explain new tasks to junior staff – and also creates greater flexibility for the office, expanding the number of staff capable of taking on any new assignment, regardless of its potential difficulty.

In this context, interns require more than simple mechanical ability to do their work. As a result, senior staff in Japan must do some assignments North Americans consider appropriate for junior staff, such as drawing details. Before being able to draw a detail, new interns generally spend time working at the office's construction sites, where many of the final decisions about detailing occur. This is most effective when the firm establishes a hierarchy of the systems involved. The customization of unimportant components becomes a training ground for junior staff, allowing them to participate in design development. Typically, interns work out minor connections and, using models, make proposals and undergo reviews with the project architect and contractor – a process that leads to the greater refinement seen in many Japanese buildings.

As people prove themselves capable of coming up with solutions that are appealing aesthetically and in terms of performance, they take on greater responsibilities. At one site, for example, the most senior members of Toyo Ito's staff were concerned with overseeing the design and fabrication of a building's unusual structural system. The youngest person on site, a recent college graduate, generally assisted senior staff, but he was also solely responsible for designing and making proposals for smaller curtain wall connectors. Ito has frequently told me that he is not one to focus too much on details. This is a point I repeatedly questioned, because his buildings suggest otherwise. In light of the hierarchy of responsibilities I have described, perhaps it is not surprising that when I passed Ito's remarks on to an intern in Ito's office, the intern laughed and replied that Ito did not need to consider the details too much, because everyone else did. The staff also emphasized, however, that Ito defined those parts of the building of greatest importance to him, in part to identify the other areas where staff could have greater flexibility in decision-making. For materials or methods of assembly less central to Ito's conception of the project, the staff often took the initiative in exploring innovations. Part of this freedom may also be to do with the fact that for the most part Ito is more likely to reject a poor solution than he is to try and suggest the best direction for his staff to explore.

One result of working out the role of collaboration on site is that staff must perform more autonomously than is the norm in the West, something also noted by engineers and anthropologists observing Japanese manufacturing practices. As Hideshi Itoh states, "Job demarcation in work organization . . . is more ambiguous and fluid . . . More *de facto* responsibility is delegated to the lower ties of hierarchy in Japan."[7] This is true not only of professionals, but of people at all levels of the project. Architectural staff are comfortable pursuing a promising idea quite far before consulting with the firm's principal.

This may in some way compensate for the low pay and long hours. As Judith Blau noted, autonomy and responsibility generally lead to greater satisfaction for architects; Alan Day argues that the quality of work also improves when staff feel they are involved in decision making throughout a project.[8] John Creighton Campbell, however, offers a caution based on his years of research in Japan:

> Many of these Japanese-style techniques include a higher level of involvement by blue-collar workers, engineers, and middle managers than Americans are used to. The common error ... is to imagine that involvement is effective because it makes people happier or more satisfied ... it often does not, it makes people feel more pressured ... Although working in this way is likely to be more interesting for workers and engineers, and thus more fulfilling in a deep sense, it is also more frustrating and stressful.[9]

Interns are under pressure to perform beyond their experience. Many fortify direct observation with published reference works. Japanese publishers produce a variety of magazines and textbooks with surprisingly specific directions on any subject, from managing a construction site to the tea ceremony. Several popular magazines offer precise explanations of specific families of details or the processes common to certain trades, written in an accessible tone and even mixed in with cartoons, making light of the subject. Today's trade journals may be rooted in the manuals that became popular during the Meiji era. However, these publications are clearly not substitutes for direct observation. Barbara Mori's dissertation on the learning of the tea ceremony observed that, "The [published text] books, although heavily illustrated with photos and pictures, are made so some details are omitted. Thus to completely learn ... the student can't rely on the text alone ..."[10] As an example from the construction industry, one text on managing a construction site asks the reader how to weld a box column on all four corners, but offers no solution.[11]

One reason that this system works is that all members of staff see themselves as having a long-term commitment to the firm and thus to each other, although this is being challenged in the current economic climate. If they see themselves as part of a firm for only a short time, employees will want to accumulate a bounded set of marketable skills. With a longer commitment, staff will be open to letting the office teach them in a way that might be harder to package. This is why I favor the term for a quasi-familial structure, *iemoto*, over "apprenticeship." The familial nature of the office reveals itself in a number of ways, but most notable is that time is not the foremost factor in deciding how staff work, any more than it is a factor in child rearing. The system can only work if mobility is low, and indeed low mobility has been, until recently, the norm. There are only a few periods in one's career when departure is acceptable in Japan. In the early years of entering an office, it is still possible to accept that one has made a poor match and move on, although it would be unlikely for someone to do so twice. Later, when in their late thirties or early forties, architects may agreeably set up an independent office, perhaps in part as a result of changes in family responsibilities. They may, as *deishi* (disciples), even expect that the office they have left will send small projects their way, in order to assure a successful start. Later, architects who retire, which may occur as soon as in their early fifties, can set up a small practice without censure. These shifts are so predictable that, for example, a male project architect approaching 40 will be asked repeatedly if he will be leaving the firm after the project winds up. (Women, who still face difficulty as principals, seem to be asked this question much less often, although they, too, consider departure at such a juncture normal.)

As one author on Japanese management noted, "What comes first is getting the job done, not the employee's well-being."[12] This familial structure also means that junior staff must sacrifice their own judgment or goals in favor of the expectations of the *virtuoso* and more senior staff. Shifting responsibility for work quality from the intern, assumed to be too inexperienced to know better, to senior staff also prevents mistakes. If an intern should do a job poorly or overlook a task, very likely the supervising staff member will be roughly blamed for the mistake (if discovered by someone else) or the supervisor will personally rectify the deficiency, perhaps ostentatiously working late into the night to do so. Typically, though, the intern will take note of the burden put on senior staff and put greater effort into assuring that further problems do not occur. Much to my initial astonishment, offices will not even fire or reprimand young staff members who routinely turn up late, use colloquial language in formal settings, or otherwise behave inappropriately. The need for behavioral change may be indicated in a variety of ways, some of which are quite different from Western office practice. Although somewhat extreme, few Japanese were surprised when one of the new staff in the office I worked in was considered promising and ambitious, but tended to routinely take naps on office time – at his desk, under tables or in storage areas. He was scolded – especially when found sleeping in inappropriate locations by the office partners – but there was never any question that his behavior could be rectified with time. Instead, such interns find that their workload remains quite dull and they may be teased until their behavior changes. Individuals only progress to more advanced challenges after demonstrating appropriate skills and character.

Without going into this issue in any depth, I should note that understanding form alone is not perceived as superficial in Japan. The assumption is that to learn forms well is to adopt the embodied wisdom that has led to the significance of those forms. Although intended as a summary of Japanese approaches to teaching Noh theater, architectural educators anywhere can certainly sympathize with Tom Hare's sentiment that, "The process of training is not the same as learning about the art, and a comprehensive intellectual understanding of training is not necessarily a goal in the art; indeed, in the first stages of training, such an intellectual understanding might be considered an obstruction."[13] In North America, the influence of the "Master studio," an outgrowth of the European apprentice system, means that there are strong parallels between the *iemoto* system and some practices found in university-based architecture studios.

It is worth noting, however, that some architects have emerged with virtually no experience as interns in another architect's office, and there are no formally structured internship programs. Tadao Ando is perhaps best known for his claims not to have worked in another architect's office, and Shigeru Ban and Osamu Ishiyama are two other leading architects with no post-graduate experience as interns. To avoid this path is rare, however, and probably will never be practicable beyond a small, talented group. In addition, since the profession benefits by limiting the number of interns during a recession, it is very unlikely that there will be much support for those trying to achieve licensing without a period of apprenticeship. However, today's poor economy and the emergence of new digital technologies have caused architects to see some value in shifting part of their basic education to the universities.

TRANSFERRING KNOWLEDGE FROM THE UNIVERSITY

There is one area where the transfer of knowledge from senior to junior staff was temporarily disrupted; this is computer literacy, especially in the use of computers for drawings (word processing has its own difficulties because of the number of characters in the Japanese language and internet usage only became common at the end of the 1990s). Universities became the sites where basic computer skills first emerged. Where no precedent exists, whether introducing an entire profession or certain new tools, the Japanese university becomes the more efficient location for the initial transfer of information.

That computers were likely to become important in the practice of architecture was widely understood. Although Japanese computer use lagged as system and software developers worldwide struggled to develop a comprehensive strategy that could combine four writing systems (*kanji*, often derived from Chinese, with about 2000 basic characters, many with more than one phonetic reading; *hiragana*, the phonetic alphabet for native words; *katakana*, the phonetic alphabet for words derived from non-Japanese languages in the twentieth century; and *romanji*, the English alphabet), the rapid acceptance of computers in other developed countries was understood to indicate the direction that practice in Japan, too, would ultimately take. With this in mind and perhaps spurred on by the recession and declining employment of college graduates, universities and schools began to offer basic computer drafting courses. These students, in turn, were already in place when contractors or clients in real estate development either offered architects computers or demanded their use. As noted earlier, however, drafting is not generally treated as a routine task in offices, and the use of green staff to produce drawings inverted existing hierarchies. Most firms have begun to send mid-level staff out for commercial training, allowing them to re-establish their position as seniors to the new interns. It is my suspicion, however, that computer use is by its nature not a skill easily learned through observation and that it will, to a certain degree, remain contrary to the normal approaches to skill-building that exist in offices. In this way, a Western technology may be increasing the importance of Japan's reliance on Western systems of learning.

In addition, as small offices are increasingly pressed to make their staff efficient as quickly as possible, the level of technical and graphic skills expected from recent graduates seems to be rising. In larger offices, one or more experienced staff have remained with the office through their mid-fifties or longer, to guide recent college graduates in the manner I described. In the current economy, however, one approach to economizing has been to move retirements earlier and earlier. In an extreme case, a leading designer told me that he was trying to limit the new staff to an average of three years in his office, during which time they would be responsible for the construction of a single project. More commonly, project architects are leaving firms in their late thirties or early forties. These architects start their own firms, but the end result is that there are more firms with fewer layers of staff – reaching a high of 87,634 registered architectural offices in 1998, up over 20,000 in ten years.[14] Instead of a principal overseeing design and bringing in work, complemented by senior staff who can manage design development and train younger members of the firm, many offices today have one or two principals who are trying to do all of these tasks. Many have told me that the poor quality of architectural graduates' skills is a burden in this context, and that they would like to see the universities play a larger role in training. They are, however, often too harried to do much more than complain. The costs of training staff are especially high when staff turnover is deliberately kept high, although the low salaries for entry-level employees may offer some balance.

Schools today are changing, however, and after a long period of stability, most are experimenting with new curricula and new educational approaches. One of the difficulties of preparing students for the profession, however, is the greater diversity in architectural practice in Japan.

1. T. P. Rohlen, "Education in Japanese Society," in T. P. Rohlen and G. LeTendre, eds., *Teaching and Learning in Japan*, Cambridge and New York, Cambridge University Press, 1996, p. 25.
2. E. O. Reischauer, *The Japanese Today: Change and Continuity*, Cambridge, Massachusetts & London, The Belknap Press of Harvard University, 1977, p. 193.
3. The 75 per cent graduation rate and 81 per cent employment rate are given in *Japan, An Illustrated Encyclopedia*, Tokyo, Kodansha, 1993, s.v. "Universities and colleges." The 79 per cent graduation rate is given in Ellington, *Education in the Japanese Life-cycle*, p. 145.
4. L. Ellington, *Education in the Japanese Life-cycle*, Lewiston, Queenston & Lampeter, The Edwin Mellon Press, 1992, p. 165.
5. G.V. Sogen Hori, "Teaching and Learning in the Rinzai Zen Monastery," in T. P. Rohlen and G. LeTendre, eds., *Teaching and Learning in Japan*, Cambridge and New York, Cambridge University Press, 1996, p. 29.
6. Ibid., p. 34.
7. H. Itoh, "Japanese Human Resource Management from the Viewpoint of Incentive Theory," in M. Aoki and R. Dore, *The Japanese Firm: Sources of Competitive Strength*, Oxford and New York, Oxford University Press, 1994, p. 238. See also J. C. Campbell, "Culture, Innovative Borrowing, and Technology Management," in J. K. Liker, J. E. Ettlie and J. C. Campbell, eds., *Engineered in Japan: Japanese Technology Management Practices*, New York and Oxford, Oxford University Press, 1995, p. 318.
8. J. Blau, *Architects and Firms: A Sociological Perspective on Architectural Practice*, Cambridge, MIT Press, 1984, p. 53. And A. Day, *Digital Building*, Oxford, Laxton's, 1997, p. 80.
9. J. C. Campbell, "Culture, Innovative Borrowing, and Technology Management," p. 318.
10. B. L. Rowland Mori, *Americans Studying the Traditional Art of the Tea Ceremony: The Internationalizing of a Traditional Art*, San Francisco, Mellon Research University Press, 1992, p. 46.
11. H. Yō and T. Furusawa, *Zusetsu Kenchiku Sekō Nyūmon: Sekō Purosesu to sono Jitsumu no Kaisetu [Architectural Construction Book of Learning with Explanatory Graphics: The Construction Process and Practical Business Affairs Explained]*, Tokyo, Shokoku-sha, 1992, p. 57.
12. P. Herbig, *Innovation Japanese Style: A Cultural and Historical Perspective*, Westport, Connecticut and London, Quorum Books, 1995, p. 185.
13. T. Hare, "Try, Try Again: Training in Noh Drama," in Rohlen and LeTendre, *Teaching and Learning in Japan*, p. 324.
14. "Kenchikushi no Ikiru Michi [The Road for Licensed Architects' Existence]" *Nikkei A-kitekuchua* [Nikkei Architecture], no. 666, 15 May 2000, p. 102.

Architectural practice today

In 1993, the International Union of Architects commissioned an international study of change in private practice. The UIA report on Japan, written by Weld Coxe and Mary Hayden, argued that architectural practice there "... runs the *entire range* of options found elsewhere in the world."[1] It is not that Japan offers a completely different model for practice. Rather, it encompasses a range of opportunities for designers, some more familiar to readers in one community than another. The breadth available to architects, however, is notable and worthy of study. There is no single accepted model for practice; the organizations that offer architectural services have a number of different corporate structures and support a diversity of approaches to practice. Construction firms handle about 40 per cent of all building design in Japan, from detached single-family homes to soaring office towers, as part of design-build packages. Independent architectural firms, ranging from small, single-principal studios to some of the field's largest corporate entities, do the remaining 60 per cent.

On average, Japanese architectural staff spend around two-thirds of their time on building design and one-third in construction supervision, but, understandably, the amount of time and the nature of construction supervision vary widely, depending on the approach taken by the architect. Moreover, the point at which design stops and construction supervision begins is often difficult to establish, since much design development may occur simultaneous to construction supervision and on the construction site. Nevertheless, it is possible to describe four major models of practice, each defined here by the level and degree of control architects exert. These models range from the architect supplying a very simplified conceptual design, allowing the contractor to be responsible for all areas of detailing, design development and execution, to the architect commanding such a high degree of customization that he or she is able to impact not only on-site construction decisions, but areas of the manufacturing process as well.

FOUR MODELS OF DESIGN DEVELOPMENT

There is a new kind of practice in Japan. They do a different kind of hand-off. The architect is the conceptualizer and maybe goes through schematic design. The contractor has the responsibility for design documents, and he builds from his design documents.[2]

(Peter Eisenman)

Foreign architects who have built in Japan are probably most familiar with this simple approach: architects and contractors sever design from detailed development, production and supervision. Usually in this model, the architect produces only a conceptual design and basic design drawings, with perhaps a small model. The contractor is responsible for producing all construction documents – including working out any detailing – and managing construction. There are several reasons for employing this model, and this can result in differing levels of care in the latter stages of design. The approach is not limited to foreign architects, but it is desirable in these cases because clients assume that the designer would find it difficult to work in Japan, because of language and cultural differences. Clients overcome these difficulties by having a contractor manage the construction phase. The contractor has the added bonus of increasing prestige and motivating in-house design staff through the relationship with a world-class architect. In such cases, the contractor aims for excellence. Foreign practitioners generally report that the level of development and the quality of construction are higher than they have experienced at home.

In contrast, many Japanese architects try to avoid this model, since contractors and clients may propose it as a cost-saving measure. When this is true, the assumption, often correct, is that the caliber of design development and construction detailing, if not under the architect's control, will be diminished by the contractor for budgetary reasons. Thus, the design architect has little authority over the final result, yet may find the project affects the reputation of the firm if it is obviously of the architect's *oeuvre*. One such example is the "Physic 2B" building, designed by Edward Suzuki and prominently located on the heavily traveled Yamanote train loop in Tokyo. Trade journals and guidebooks do not list it as Suzuki's and it lacks the sophisticated use of materials evident in much of the architect's work. However, it is clearly recognizable as being of his hand, and indeed, is a rather clumsily executed project for which he generated the concept. Suzuki himself seems to have recognized too late the impact of taking this approach in such a prominent location.

One architect who has at times been particularly comfortable using this model is Arata Isozaki and oddly enough, his most prominent example, the Globe Theater, is also located on the Yamanote line. At the time of the Globe Theater's construction, Isozaki was doing quite a bit of work abroad, relying on "associate architects" – local "production" architects – for design development and supervision. Isozaki considered this Japanese model as similar; he also explored the pairing of young foreign architects with small contractors in the public works programs he coordinated in Toyama and Kumamoto Prefectures. The fact that he is comfortable working in this way may be one of the reasons that Isozaki has been more successful in building abroad than many of his Japanese colleagues, in that his approach at home is already drawing on the skills and expertise more likely to be available in architects from North America and Europe. Notably, today, Isozaki has taken back much of the responsibility for the latter stages of design, signalled in the publication of a special issue of *Japan Architect* called *Arata Isozaki: Construction Site*.

> By sending the drawings and instructions to the site by telefacsimile, the construction of [the Karaza Theater] is easily accomplished anywhere. By reducing architecture to information we can transmit it to any location around the world.[3]
>
> (Tadao Ando)

This model is similar to the norms of North American practice; design development and administration remain the architect's responsibility. Often, design staff work primarily from the main office and use drawings as the principal means of communicating with the contractor. However, since design development still occurs simultaneous to construction, opportunities for consultation and adjustments remain. Because the architect retains control of design, buildings constructed under this model are generally well detailed. However, decisions involving construction tend to be conservative, since the relative lack of give-and-take between architect and contractor rules out experimentation. Often there is little evidence of inventive material use or technical experimentation on buildings produced in this fashion.

Architects frequently employ this model for small projects that are close to the main office and do not justify a separate, site-based office. Nevertheless, Tadao Ando seems to favor the approach in larger projects as well, even when the commute between the site and office seems excessive. (This is probably one of the reasons that, more so than most architects, Ando has favored publishing working drawings and as-builts of his projects.) For example, Ando's project architect in charge of construction of the *Chikatsu'Asuka* Museum remained based in the Osaka office through completion of the project, even though going from the office to the site required more than a one-hour commute. More recently, Ando worked without a site office on the Awaji Island "Yume Butai" – at the time the largest active construction site in the world, at 214,000 square meters (2.3 million square feet). Five contractors met with Ando once a month and with his staff somewhat more regularly, but all design development was done out of Ando's Osaka office, well over ninety minutes away by car.

Although this method surely allows Ando to maintain tighter control over the office's work, another explanation for the firm's reliance on this approach is their choice of materials. When using extensive areas of unfinished concrete, there is little flexibility to make decisions during construction. Planning the pour takes place in advance and off-site – regardless of the designer – simply because of the level of calculation and advance preparation involved.

This model is effective where the office wants to maintain control over design; since decisions take place at the office, staff are in regular discussions with senior partners. Architectural offices may also choose this model or call staff back to the office for at least part of each week when the project architect has less than ideal experience or confidence in managing design development and site supervision.

This will assure that the contractor's influence does not overwhelm other goals. With new technology, variants of this approach exist. For example, Kunihiko Hayakawa felt that the contractors on a project in southern Japan, all small local firms, might not be able to produce work of the same quality he demands in Tokyo. This meant that Hayakawa could not delegate design decisions to the contractors; greater responsibility for detailing fell to his project architect, who was skilled but, for budgetary reasons, working alone. (In fact, the public agency contracting the work had initially pressed to do the construction supervision internally, an approach Hayakawa refused to accept.) To overcome these limitations, the main office and the site office sent detailed faxes back and forth daily and frequently sent packages by courier with photographs and drawings. In this manner, Hayakawa maintained control over the project, although working remotely.

As the Hayakawa example suggests, another benefit of this model is that it is less expensive than other, subsequent models. Site-based facilities for the architect (which the contractor supplies at their own expense) are minimal, and the architectural office can simultaneously use staff in the planning or proposal stage of other projects.

> The Japanese building construction site is not just the place where a structure is erected but also where the construction process is managed and final designs are completed. Many tasks that are usually tackled at the home offices in the US, including construction planning, drafting of many details and checking shop drawings, are performed on the building site.[4]
>
> (Anthony C. Webster)

In both of the remaining models, design development shifts to the construction site during construction, and detailing and construction overlap in a manner that is something like the North American "fast-track" approach.

The contractor supplies prefabricated offices for staff from architecture and engineering firms, and for the contractor's and subcontractors' staff. Depending on the size of the project, these can begin to resemble mid-rises or small villages in their own right. Professionals commute daily to the construction site, living, at least temporarily, somewhere nearby. (Often this means moving to a new town for the duration of the project.) Depending on the size of the project, additional staff join the project architect. Three to five people from an architecture firm or consultant is probably the norm, although a relatively simple project may require the attention of only a single individual. Projects over $500 million often require twenty or more architectural staff on site, and similarly high involvement from consultants' offices.

Being on site has the advantage of allowing staff from different organizations to meet easily, even several times each day, and to find opportunities for casual interactions, such as having a drink together at the end of the day. People employ informal ways to communicate, such as sketches and three-dimensional models or mock-ups. In my experience, such models are not treated as the sole property of the office that fabricated them, another reflection of the less formal territorial distinctions between groups. Contractors or laborers are as likely to use models in consultations as architects, and widely used models are usually stored in common meeting rooms.

Since decision-making takes place on site, this model encourages fine-tuning in response

4.1
Shizuoka Granship site office, 1997.

4.2
The structure to the rear of this construction site is a particularly large site office complex, made up of modular offices.

to circumstances. The architect is able not only to study seasonal change, views or light, but also to make adjustments to construction that is already underway, resolving mistakes or pursuing unexpected opportunities. Because many suppliers employ the "just-in-time" system, architects choose building components and finishes comparatively late, supporting this relative spontaneity. Design development is expected on site, and the documents used to bid for a project are not treated as binding, but rather as the basis for establishing the rough cost estimates on a project. Because construction and design development are simultaneous, architects and contractors do not consider many modifications as "changes," as they would be in North American practice. These cost-free alterations may be as modest as revisions to the size or finish of materials that have not yet entered production, or as significant as resiting buildings. For example, in the case of a theater complex nestled into the hills of Shizuoka, Isozaki's office resited some buildings as many as ten times between letting the contract and breaking ground. Minor modifications – accommodating revisions or correcting earlier work – are often referred to as changes by the contractor, but not, tellingly, by the architect. Regardless of terminology, such expenses are normal and are bundled into the original bid on a building; they are not seen as an opportunity to make up for unseen expenses elsewhere, as is sometimes the case in other countries. This is probably because the small number of dominant firms making up the construction industry in Japan means that groups will work together repeatedly, over time, and it is important to maintain trust. Naturally, changes that are more expensive will be negotiated, sometimes at the end of construction.

The difference between this model and the one that follows is really the degree to which the architect shares control over the design development process with other members of the production team, and thus is able to exploit team expertise, manufacturing opportunities and new technologies. Younger architects, who have understandable concerns about their ability to negotiate effectively with contractors having more experience, generally carry out decision-making independently or in limited consultation with other members of the production team. Thus, these architects innovate conservatively. Generally in this model, designers limit their experimentation to components such as handrails, door pulls, skylight and window shapes, panel elements and prefabricated stairs, since these alterations can result in significantly different aesthetic qualities without affecting performance criteria. Nonetheless, the opportunity to work on-site tends to yield a greater awareness of *techne*, yielding low construction tolerances and finer detailing.

> Subtlety of detail is explained by the Japanese industrial context. Industrial production, as organized in Japan, allows constant adjustment in the course of manufacture. Almost any prefabricated element can be modified, in its technology of construction or in its dimensions, at the moment of ordering or even in the course of manufacture.[5]
>
> (Sere Salat)

By far the most interesting model for Western observers involves the work of Japan's best-known designers. Leading architects willing to commit the staff and attention are able to customize extensively. When there is firm support from clients, architects can conceivably produce buildings where virtually every component, crafted or manufactured, has been customized – although most, understandably, concentrate their efforts on specific effects. By collaborating with manufacturers, crafters, subcontractors and contractors in a carefully orchestrated development process that draws widely on the team's overall expertise and resourcefulness, architects can achieve very high levels of innovation and customization. In many cases, collaboration even precedes taking bids for a project. Many designers rely on manufacturers to test ideas during schematic design; the result is greater refinement in execution.

Architects using this model allow other members of the team, including constructors, to propose ways to achieve desired effects and may in fact no longer maintain a central position on the team. Representatives from the architect's office, the contractor and consultants will commonly go together to manufacturing facilities to observe the plant and what flexibilities exist before making their decisions about development. Architects and contractors also exhaustively consult subcontractors specializing in particular materials or techniques. This level of collaboration can be very demanding and requires more time and effort than non-collaborative approaches. Designer and constructors use shop drawings extensively to revise and refine a design; models and full-scale mock-ups also become production "documents." Without consistent, clear goals and an openness to risk – even failure – designers can literally become overwhelmed by the options available to them.

Furthermore, under these conditions construction costs are estimated at two to five times higher than average costs for comparable buildings in the United States. This strategy is clearly one that is not always appropriate, but such a highly collaborative approach allows constructors with relevant expertise to determine the best way to fabricate and execute construction, making experimentation and innovation more economical and practical. In this way, the process allows a level of production and design that is unparalleled, and certainly appropriate for consequential buildings anywhere.

LEADING ARCHITECTS AS "LEAD USERS"

What justifies the decision to use one kind of approach instead of another? These four models define a range of strategies that demand increasing involvement on the part of the architect. Architects' choices and the models they become most comfortable with affect not only the execution of specific buildings, but career trajectories and influence. Rising architects move smoothly from the third to the fourth model, as experience on site allows them greater confidence in managing the contributions of other members of the production team. In this way, the designer is able to take on larger, more complex projects with minimal difficulty. By contrast, the first and second models, when used exclusively, appear hermetic; the successful architect using the second model may find it harder to manage large-scale projects or those where clients demand inventive features.

Designers who tend towards the first two models are often unwilling or unable to dedicate the time, staffing and commitment to intense negotiation of design decisions. The relative inflexibility of the Japanese architectural firm exacerbates this problem. It is only with difficulty that companies will lay off permanent employees, since doing so makes adding staff later more difficult. Forms of temporary staffing do exist, but these staff rarely handle the responsibility of design development. Additionally, architects dispatch temporary staff to the job site only for routine work, such as computer drafting or model building. Under the circumstances, expanding an office to take on a larger project is not as feasible as it is in the United States, and even the best architects may choose the less collaborative models when staff are stretched thin.

The choice between the latter two collaborative models, though, seems to reflect less a question of commitment to the production process than confidence in the strength of one's negotiating position and a belief that the project warrants greater attention. The final model I outline above is available only to a limited set of architects who have both practical experience and the strong support of clients. Under these conditions, there is an opportunity to successfully manage a design team with a broader range of skills and knowledge and to achieve unusual levels of refinement. However, in both of the latter models, collaboration and responsive constructor–consultant relationships allow for greater innovation or more careful detailing. It is my belief that these approaches allow architects to make better buildings, and because of this, I pay particular attention to how and why these models are possible.

Eric von Hippel, a professor at MIT's Sloan School of Management, coined the term "lead users" to describe a population that recognizes needs in their market months or years before their competitors and that hopes to benefit by finding solutions to these needs.[6] In my research, I concentrated on architects who are lead users. The materials and systems used as examples in the discussions that follow are often completely new. Fumihiko Maki, Toyo Ito and Kazuyo Sejima (to name but a few practitioners who will appear in the following pages) not only design buildings that are beautiful, but also regularly exploit the opportunities of Japan's construction systems to demand building systems and materials that are innovative.

Lead users do not, and perhaps cannot, work alone in a market as technologically diverse as the construction industry. Manufacturers also benefit from working closely with these designers, as their input can encourage innovation and help industry to project future demand more accurately. Furthermore, since developing new materials is also one of the strategies for economic advancement promoted by Japan's Ministry of International Trade and Industry (commonly known as MITI), Japanese industry is more inclined to identify and support lead users. Thus, Japanese architects who utilize flexibilities in production more easily influence the products and materials to be available for a wider market. Even without industry support, lead users can be identified among the architects of any country. These are the architects whose work again and again seems to create solutions that become, over time, common and unremarkable: Mies worked with Kawneer to develop curtain walls for his Lake Shore Drive apartments, but today such curtain walls are unnoticed and perhaps even banal; the Eames' ubiquitous glass fiber and molded plywood were similar prototypes, and there are many others from the history of architecture. In the time I have studied Japan, Fumihiko Maki has developed a stainless steel roofing material now in general use, and that and other examples are discussed later.

The pages that follow will tell the story of how Japan's construction industry developed, and how architects fit into this industry. I began with a historical overview, because history informs architects' and builders' expectations today. From there, I turn to a look at contemporary practice, and finish with a discussion of the legal and political context that allows Japan's leading architects to act as lead users. Finally, in my conclusion, I will argue that Japanese practices, while they occur in an unusually flexible context, offer architects in other nations a provocative challenge – one we have allowed ourselves to overlook simply because we did not understand its implications.

A CLUSTER OF INNOVATIONS

Sendai Mediatheque illustrates how Japan's construction industry uses groundbreaking prototypal buildings as an opportunity for market innovation. This is particularly true of public works – especially those awarded through competitions, where a conceptual approach is of primary importance. Such buildings are economic engines where the process of construction and the impact of innovation on employment have high value.

The design, by Toyo Ito, working with the structural engineer Mutsuro Sasaki, won a national competition in 1995. One of the landmarks of the new century, 3,500 people visited the building while it was still under construction. To execute this innovative structure, the interactions of the design team were so complementary that frequently architects seemed to be protecting engineering decisions and contractors seemed to be emphasizing design.

Mediatheque's team described their intent as working with "today's technology plus alpha," a term that suggests going far beyond the baseline. Innovations fall into four groups: structural innovations, new systems for daylighting and air handling, new material applications, and new construction processes necessitated by these other breakthroughs. The structural innovations are the most successful and often linked to developments in the other areas.

Le Corbusier's Domino system, sketched as a thin, flat slab supported by slim, regular columns, inspired Mediatheque's structure. Mediatheque is a seven-story building, with several floors housing relatively high live loads such as book stacks and an auditorium. Ito and Sasaki's solution was to support thin, beamless "honeycomb" steel floors on thirteen lattice-like tubes. The floors are generally less than 400 millimeters (15 inches) deep although some are 650 millimeters in depth (26 inches). In much of the building, the distance between tubes is more than 12 meters (39 feet), and in some locations, it is 14 meters (45 feet) or more. (The longer spans yield a depth to span ratio of 1:35, almost double a normal depth to span ratio for conventional steel frames.) The steel floor is not only structural: in many areas, the steel is also the ceiling

4.3
Toyo Ito's Sendai Mediatheque, exterior.

finish. Ito's office went to a great deal of trouble to assure that the interior honeycomb ribs read through the steel plate, clearly indicating it as a structural plane.

The tubes range in size from 2.3 meters (just under 8 feet) in diameter to 8 meters (about 26 feet) in diameter. The four large tubes are bulkier because they carry lateral loads; the slender tubes only carry gravity loads, and so the designers have been able to make their steel pipe lattices increasingly thinner towards the top of the structure. These tubes resemble irregularly shaped tree trunks, visually referring to the tree-lined street that runs in front of Mediatheque. To assure precise construction, they were built at the fabricators and trucked to the site. Smaller tubes arrived on site in two-story sections, whereas the larger tubes were broken up into one-eighth diameter sections. Equipment inside the tubes, especially the self-supporting steel shafts used for vertical air movement and the elevators, required particular care in planning.

At the foundation, Sasaki designed a cast steel joint intended to break away in large earthquakes, isolating the structure. There is no precedent for the system in Japan, although other Japanese designers have concurrently developed similar ones.

The pipes that make up the tubes are "fire resistant steel," a steel made with about 1%

4.4 & 4.5
Sendai Mediatheque structural tube and floor section at fabricators.

alloy content: chromium, molybdenum and nickel. This higher alloy content makes the steel more expensive, but allowed the architects to avoid using any kind of fireproofing in many areas of the building. (Local officials allowed the architects to zone spaces according to their potential heat load and fire danger.) In other areas, the architects used an intumescent paint for fire protection, and in the library, officials required the architects to use fireproofing over the steel. A plaster-like ceramic fireproofing follows the shape of the structure. (This material has been given the name "Taika-Arock" in English.) Hand applications are common in Japan, but this was the first time the material was cast into a half-pipe form, which allowed it to maintain the precise shape of the steel structure below.

Fire-resistant glass walls surround the tubes in many areas. The architects used two types of fire-resistant glass, one able to absorb heat so effectively that it can be touched while a fire rages on the other side – Pilkington's "Pyrostop." Nihon Ita Glass produces a less fire-resistant material that is also rated, and this was used in less crucial locations. The firm began manufacture of large panes of unusually shaped "PyroClear" glass especially for Mediatheque. Because of the complexity of the glass shapes, the contractors ultimately decided to put up the curtain wall frames and then field measure the locations of each piece of glass

4.6
Architectural staff and subcontractors explored running conduit through a thin precast wall, but were not able to bring this idea to a satisfactory resolution. Note the number of full-scale models in the site office.

4.6a
"Rockwall" in place.

44 Japanese Architecture as a Collaborative Process

before ordering; only one piece of glass had to be rejected. In addition to the glass, these frames are also notable; they are more slender because the curtain wall supports the glass in tension.

For the skin of the building, the architects developed a double skin curtain wall; the south facade received particular attention. In the winter, solar gain tempers the air, reducing heat loss through the wall on sunny days. In the summer, outside air rises through the wall by natural convection. The curtain wall itself is "frameless," and Ito's office worked with consultants to develop a way of supporting the glass panes at their edges, rather than penetrating the glass with holes, as was seen in Peter Rice's original frameless system. The sheets of glass are about 2 meters by 4 meters (6.5 feet by 13 feet). Glass engineers said even this can be considered an innovation, in that sheets of glass of the strength and precision demanded for the system were limited to much smaller sizes until quite recently. Although the size of the sheets required robotic equipment for installation, Ito's design does not appear to have pushed these new technologies so much as simply taken advantage of them.

One of the main justifications for the structural tubes is flexibility; this system allows for easy replacement of telecommunications cables and fiber optic lines. The competition program for this building was set without a clear understanding of what activities might occur in a "Media Resource Center." Even today, the architects would be hard pressed to make confident projections regarding necessary infrastructure more than a few years in the future. Ito expanded the concept of electronic flexibility in the tubes to a range of vertical movement systems: stairs, elevators, vertical ducts, water and even transmitting daylight to the lower floors. The self-supporting ducts required special production. The system of reflective louvers used today, which the design team called a "light extractor," is a relatively unsophisticated system. Original plans to use lenses and fiber optics were abandoned in light of some of the additional costs of earlier work.

Not all the innovations Ito's office considered were implemented. The steel fabricators floated the hope that they would do 80 per cent of the welds on site robotically, but I saw no evidence of this. For some time, Ito's office also explored running conduit inside the open core of a very slender precast panel system, but they were unable to get regulatory approval. Most intriguingly, Ito considered a new *locally* photochromic glass for the curtain walls. He said that where a tree's shadow fell the glass would be transparent in the exact shape of the tree's shadow, while the rest of the pane would become milky where the sun struck it.

In a way, these innovations are as important as those that succeeded. They demonstrate that Japanese architects are not afraid to reach beyond currently available technologies and dream. Even without having achieved all of the project team's goals, the building as completed demonstrates the extraordinary possibilities accommodated in public works projects.

1. W. Coxe and M. Hayden, "UIA Project Work Group: Trends in Private Practice. Report from Japan," unpublished report dated 20 March, 1993, p. 12. Emphasis mine.
2. "Peter Eisenman: Interview," interview with G. Simmons, *Practices 1*, Spring 1992, p. 8.
3. Ando is quoted in K. Frampton, "Tadao Ando and the Cult of Shintai," *Tadao Ando: the Yale Studio & Current Works*, New York, Rizzoli, 1989, p. 9.
4. A. C. Webster, *Technological Advance in Japanese Building Design and Construction*, New York, ASCE Press, 1994, p. 37. In his book, Webster is primarily addressing the design-build side of the industry, although he does not make a clear distinction between design-build and work by independent architects.
5. S. Salat with F. Labbé, *Fumihiko Maki: An Aesthetic of Fragmentation*, New York, Rizzoli, 1987, p. 101, footnote 2.
6. E. von Hippel, *The Sources of Innovation*, New York and Oxford, Oxford University Press, 1988, p. 107.

The roots of collaborative practice

> No architect can presume to be so well-rounded as to be competent in all aspects of architectural work . . .[1]
>
> (David Leatherbarrow)

Today in North America, design and construction have become isolated fields and architects fear they hold only a marginal place on the team. In one vivid statement, a trade magazine noted, ". . . architects are running the risk of being treated as design subcontractors. Rather than being the spouse, many architects are becoming like the household chef, respected for technical and artistic talents, but nevertheless part of the downstairs kitchen staff and paid accordingly."[2] These statements focus on perceptions of power and financial compensation, and neglect the question of what is effective in architectural practices. Another author presents a more balanced perspective, and one that suggests perhaps architects have been too hasty about loss of leadership:

> Collaboration has been seen by many architects as the greatest single threat to their long established position as the "natural leader" of the team. The view is often expressed that designers must provide leadership and that if they do not the quality of building, in both functional and aesthetic terms, will suffer. The weaknesses in this argument were provided by a plethora of studies which suggested that the traditional method of independent practice was equally susceptible to considerable criticism for inadequate performance of buildings, not only in functional and aesthetic terms, but also in technical, management, and cost control aspects.[3]

In a symposium intended to celebrate the establishment of the Center for the Study of the Practice of Architecture, North American panelists instead returned repeatedly to the dilemma of how to control production.[4] For many, the increasing complexity of practice leaves architects with little choice but to limit participation to *either* design *or* production, although which role a firm plays varies from project to project.

The contraction in architectural services is related not only to the increasing complexity of architecture and construction, but also to stricter definitions of liability in the United States (a topic I address in my chapter on legal issues). North American architectural practice has retreated from activities that hold greater risk, such as construction supervision or detailing. Standard contracts used by the AIA note that, "The architect will not have control over or charge of and will not be responsible for construction means, methods, techniques, sequences, or procedures ..."[5] In capitalist economies, compensation is tied to risk and to clearly necessary skills. The profession's emphasis on aesthetic and programmatic issues over technical strengths has caused architects to lose authority in the marketplace.

When architectural practice was introduced to Japan, building trades were already powerful and offered a comprehensive range of services, including design. Japanese architects thus have no presumption of leadership and have never really been perceived as directing the building team. (I should note, however, that the architect is most likely to sit at the head of the table and conduct the site meetings between consultants and constructors – but even this modest suggestion of greater power is not universal, and the firms most interested in collaboration often seem to take pains to avoid having anyone at the head of the table, or to locate someone clearly peripheral to the process – such as a foreign researcher – at the end.) There is no distinct center of responsibility on Japanese building teams; the Japanese architect has an interdependent relationship with constructors and can, consequently, share decisions about design development with them, during construction.

Whereas architects in North America most commonly team up with professional consultants (including other architectural offices), with supportive constructors, Japanese architects may share supervision within a larger production team that includes contractors, subcontractors, manufacturers, professional consultants, and even clients, in the case of public works projects.

DESIGN TEAMS

The segmentation of the building industry in North America has led individual organizations, whether constructors or professional consultants, to hold diverging goals, ones that are often in conflict. As a result, notes Howard Davis, "there may be a common vision of what will be built [but] it does not reflect a common, positive understanding of what *should* be built."[6] This is not true in Japan, where loyalties to the underlying craft of building seem to dominate. More than once, I heard teams on site use warm phrases such as "all of us together ... everyone around this table ..." to underscore commonality over differences. The flexible, site-based organizations and a lack of clear job demarcation – in spite of very clearly defined titles and roles – create opportunities for the design team to establish reciprocity.

Through frequent meetings, often with models or mock-ups to facilitate consultation, collaboration unfolds between the trades and professions responsible for a building's execution. Generally speaking, professionals – especially architects and structural engineers – set the tone by defining the conceptual goals of a project, and they rely on other members of the production team for support. However, it is not uncommon for the contractor, fabricator or even industry associations to have a role in setting conceptual goals. As examples in this book suggest, contractors may have new construction technologies they hope to exploit, manufacturers may have new patents or fabrication processes they want to employ, and industries may subsidize work in order to develop new markets. In the broadest sense, the design team – individuals and groups who share a concern not only for a building's cost, safety, stability, but also for its aesthetic and material qualities – may include:

- the architect and architectural staff;
- the contractor and major subcontractors, such as the mechanical and electrical subs;
- consultants from the disciplines of engineering, cost and project management, and specialized areas such as acoustics;
- craftspeople or skilled subcontractors who have experience with specific materials;
- fabricators or manufacturers who are able to respond flexibly;
- clients' representatives, who may act as construction managers and even take over detailing, especially in the case of public works;
- and industry organizations which offer subsidies and other support.

Many of these parties play a role in design in other parts of the world, too. However, in Japan, contractors, subcontractors, manufacturers and fabricators are better prepared and under more pressure to contribute to design decision-making. Not all do so extensively, but each can play a significant role in areas of the project that they are responsible for, and – as I discuss later – even areas beyond their responsibility or expertise. I will explore the reasons for this in later chapters.

These teams do not engage in the kind of bargaining that has sometimes led to jokes about the results of "design by committee." Successful teams recognize that a vision for the building must inform their work, and quite often, it is the architect who establishes this vision. However, such a team can be unwieldy, and it is a rare and experienced architect who fully exploits the potential of collaborative teams. Broad collaboration in design and construction is an effective but demanding method best used for particularly important or innovative structures.

Architects who have experienced it, speak of Japanese construction with rare warmth. Cesar Pelli said simply, "there is no more satisfying experience than building in Japan."[7] Rafael Viñoly is quoted as saying that the Japanese system "works incredibly well" and that "... design professionals and construction managers cannot isolate themselves from the process ..."[8] Kathryn Findlay, whose practice is based in Japan and the United Kingdom, describes her early experiences in Japan with warmth, saying:

> When I first began working on the construction site, the process was relatively smooth, [and I thought] Japan's contractors more accommodating, compared to England, where even a small building required detailed, difficult drawings to be completed ... [In Japan] we're able to get substantive changes implemented on the site, after construction has begun ...[9]

And Tadao Ando, reflecting on his recent experiences building in Chicago and preparations for the Modern Art Museum of Fort Worth (an addition to the Kimbell Museum), is quoted as saying:

> After all, Japan is blessed to be small and geographically isolated, I think. In architecture, too. The design consultant and the contractor work collaboratively, so it is easy. The contractor says "leave this to us" about some area, and the architect is happy to do so.[10]

These comments indicate some of the essential conditions that promote successful collaboration. As Viñoly observed, architects are not isolated from construction – so architectural staff quickly recognize and respond to construction-related problems. Similarly, contractors learn which issues are important to architects and can support designers' efforts. Findlay reinforces this point, and, as she notes, the process is flexible. An architect is not confined to communicating with drawn media. Rather, through models and countless hours of discussion, the architect and contractor cooperatively engage in design development. Furthermore, this flexibility continues during construction and allows the team to respond to the building in context and at full scale. Finally, Ando not only points out that designated design development is often encouraged by contractors, he suggests these collaborations are successful because of Japan's isolation. In my mind, it is not so much geographic isolation, as Japan's economic isolation and oligopolic economy, that are important.

Why would contractors promote collaboration? When construction and design are separate, important communications between the architect and contractor are primarily by abstract written and drawn documents. Yet these cannot clearly communicate many of the concerns each side holds. The contractor thus indicates problems with staging, safety, ease of fabrication or uncertain labor supply crudely, through pricing. Western architects try to resolve this split by relying on consultants and the accumulation of personal experience – imperfect mechanisms in a volatile and increasingly sophisticated context. Problem solving occurs internally: an architect, unsure about how to resolve water problems in a detail, may choose a more conservative solution. Von Hippel has noted that *where* the boundaries between tasks occur will often affect how design problems are resolved.[11] He argues that problem solving can be improved by reducing these boundaries, allowing the team to identify potential drawbacks early enough in the process to make adjustments.

The breaking down of boundaries can also encourage members of the design team to share tacit knowledge, something not possible when architects and contractors struggle to communicate their goals through explicit documents. In my experience, the most effective teams not only represent a wide range of experience and ideas, but also seem open to speculation in discussions, opening the way for one member of the group to build on others' suggestions. Many economists argue that these teams can thus develop their own kind of efficiencies, by recognizing the potential for problems and addressing difficulties at an early stage. Von Hippel points to one study where the costs of teamwork on a $30 million engineering project were assumed to add $50,000 to implement – but to have resulted in savings of close to $1 million.[12]

Incertitude is a natural outcome of not only

the complexity of contemporary construction processes, but also of unpredictable conditions such as soil strength, weather and the variable results of manual work. In this environment, it is impossible to predict all the potential problems that may arise, and prepare sufficiently without unnecessary expense. Cooperation and mutual trust between members of the team allows resolution to occur when problems arise.

LINKAGES BETWEEN PROFESSIONALS

Some parts of the design team in Japan will be familiar to architects in other parts of the world, although even here there are some differences worth noting. Fumihiko Maki has turned to the research labs at Keio University to do wind tunnel tests of his ventilation grille designs, and Jun Aoki consulted with a professor from Hokkaido when designing a cooling system that utilized stored snow. In general, scholars argue that applied research in Japan generally comes out of the laboratories of private corporations, and it is true that Japan's contractors have large and sophisticated research facilities. However, architects in Japan seem more willing and able to draw on the universities as a resource than I have witnessed in the United States. This may be in part because Japanese universities are more comfortable with applied research, but I also suspect it is the result of a greater willingness on the part of private industry to overlook any potential competition from these collaborations.

Shigeru Ban's development of paper tubes for use as structural components, walls and even small "cubicles" in both high-end and low-cost constructions did not come from alliances with manufacturers, but from the confidence that working with an esteemed engineer offered. Ban found his greatest support was from the pioneering engineer Gengo Matsui, who also had cost-free access to testing equipment at Waseda University. The two professionals developed the vocabulary of connectors; the fact that constructors have not been involved in developing the system explains the details' simple, even crude, character. Nonetheless, Ban needed to achieve structural consistency and acceptable finishes for exterior construction. He also investigated fire- and waterproofing techniques. However, manufacturers have not been enthusiastic supporters of these innovations, for the simple reason that Ban's work has, to date, yielded no imitators. As I explain later, this may partly be because Ban is interacting with an economically viable industry, not one in decline. Without substantial market incentives, manufacturers see less value in the collaboration, and, therefore, Ban has had to shift his work from one producer to another over time.

However, it is fair to say that Matsui's willingness to work with Ban in this way was partly the result of Matsui's long experience in a variety of collaborations, the most notable being his post-war work with Kiyonori Kikutake. To date, Ban employs the tubes, in varying sizes, for both furniture and buildings. Lined up vertically, the tubes constituted structural walls in both a gallery for Issey Miyake and a temporary structure for refugees who lost their church in the Kobe earthquake of 1995. Ban also used the tubes to build outside walls offering insulative value for homes for

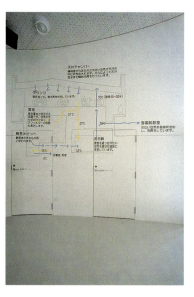

5.1 & 5.2
Jun Aoki's "Snow Village Future Foundation," stored snow for summer cooling. The exterior shows the door to the storage area for snow. At right, a promotional diagram explaining how the space is cooled.

5.3
Shigeru Ban's inventive structural use of paper tubes is seen in his Miyake Design Studio Gallery.

the same refugee community and used large single tubes as toilet compartments for a temporary exposition building. Smaller, structural components of the same material have been shipped to sites inside the large tubes. Recently, opportunities to explore these innovations have emerged abroad. Working with Vitra, Ban developed the tubes as a replacement for aluminum tent supports used by UNHCR, achieving significant economies, and in 2000, Ban built a cardboard tube structure in the courtyard of the Museum of Modern Art in New York. Ban worked briefly in Arata Isozaki's office and may have developed a bias towards professional collaborations there, as Isozaki also tends to favor professional consultants over constructors.

In Isozaki's own collaborations, both in Japan and abroad, the level of professional support and experimentation is notably high: for a concert hall, for example, Isozaki reports that the design team used detailed 1/50 models, and later ran a listening test involving eighteen samples of differing floor constructions, with musicians from the Kyoto Philharmonic Orchestra. For his Team Disney building in Florida, Isozaki similarly drew on the expertise of the Florida Solar Energy Center. Obviously, many architects throughout the world work with a variety of professional consultants, and in fact some of these specializations may be less well represented in Japan than elsewhere. However, what is notable about Isozaki's work with such consultants is that the designs that emerge are extensively tested with constructors, not merely in simulations.

When disciplinary boundaries are more ambiguous, the contributions of each team member may also not be what one expects. A structural engineer may suggest a finish he or she has just seen, a mechanical engineer may propose a structural approach or the contractor may suggest a new lighting technology. One scholar calls this the "garbage can model" of innovation: rather than a fixed problem-solving sequence, the process allows for "... a confluence of changing streams of problems, solutions, participants, and change opportunities."[13] Consequently, the individuals I observed generally seemed more confident, more secure and more willing to take risks. They saw the entire construction team as committed to successfully executing their ideas, rather than feeling pressure to personally assimilate essential information. Instead of pursuing answers in meetings, teams were often testing proposed solutions.

This is also expressed in many of Japan's architectural publications. Western architects often feel that the evaluation of practice requires them to play down the contributions of other consultants and constructors. This can prevent the architect from making counterparts feel that a partnership exists. In Japan, on the other hand, the profession recognizes partners' contributions. *GA Japan Environmental Design* and *Shinkenchiku* [the *Japan Architect*] index information on the design team as part of an extensive body of data published on each project. The data include not only lists of the various engineering consultants specialized consultants, and the general contractor, but also the major subcontractors and materials suppliers, often filling several columns of text. Furthermore, the names of all staff who have been closely involved with the project are listed – not only the architect's project team, but the project supervisor from each group and other key staff. In both magazines, interviews or explanatory articles by mechanical or structural engineers associated with highlighted projects are also common. Structural engineers receive particular attention in the architectural press, perhaps because the *kenchiku* departments in universities still tend to be sited in engineering schools. In the past few years, both *Shinkenchiku* and *Kenchiku Bunka* have come out with more than one special issue on leading structural engineers. In *Nikkei Architecture*, the architect–contractor relationship holds greater weight. Recent articles have addressed evolving relationships between architects and general contractors; photographs during construction are also not uncommon. More detailed fabrication information is routinely included, e.g., small photographs and drawings showing three alternative profiles for holes in punched metal (a clean cut, or with the lip rolled inward deeply or more shallowly) and discussions on how these features affect the building's performance and appearance.

TEAM PLAYERS

In the period before World War II, architectural practice throughout the world tended to incorporate some level of design development by constructors and crafters. Today in North America, however, the opportunities for builders to offer feedback to architects has eroded. This separation did not develop in Japan.

Architects who are inclined to rely on a design team that extends beyond professional consultants collaborate most effectively by building up an increasingly larger set of frequently utilized suppliers, constructors and consultants. Firms may participate in more than a single project, learning how to work together over time. This is especially true of the relationships that architects develop with other professionals and with fabricators, where they have the greatest potential to choose to work together again. In these situations, there is a conscious willingness to test out the attitudes and perspectives others hold, as a way of investing in the relationship.

Riken Yamamoto has a tight-knit group of designers who work with him on the customized fabrics, furniture, signage and other interior design. Most have been introduced to Yamamoto by Akane Yamazaki, and she sometimes takes responsibility for coordinating the activities of the group. This team is responsible for the bright, cheerful character of interiors at Iwadeyama Middle School, Saitama University and Yamamoto's latest university, in Hokkaido. Yamazaki represents a number of designers, so she is able to smoothly introduce new candidates to the group. These kinds of networks effectively expand successful teams; at least some members of the team recognize that new participants hold compatible interests or values. Nonetheless, sometimes consultants first join teams as unpaid advisers, on a trial basis. Usually early participation is brief or occasional, but it allows the team to assess the contributions of prospective team members. This is because:

> There is room for the relationship to work itself out over a series of transactions over a long period of time, rather than have each transaction pay for itself. This approach lowers the overall risk associated with the relationship because individual events or episodes do not become make-or-break.[14]

Additionally, as a working relationship advances with one contractor, manufacturer or engineer, these new participants draw other organizations into the team, relying on their own networks. Toyo Ito, for example, has an effective working relationship with Mutsuro Sasaki, a structural engineer, and this team has, over time, grown to include a steel caster and a steel fabricator. Together, this team has designed and produced the remarkable structures for Sendai Mediatheque, based on the earlier work by Ito and Sasaki: the Ota Ward Guesthouse, the Notsuhara Village Offices and the Taisha Cho Culture Center.

Architects also recognize how team makeup affects design. When Ito decided to use aluminum for the structure of a small house, he also made a point of working with a different structural engineer, Masato Araya, on the project. Araya earlier explored structural curtain walls in the Kasai Rinkai Park Visitors Center, designed with Yoshio Taniguchi, and his influence is seen in the Ito building's curtain wall, which is also structural. Each team thus develops aims, materials and a formal vocabulary that carries over from one project to the next, rather than simply reflecting the architect's aims.

Such insularity can lead to cronyism and is therefore under attack by Western politicians, since it acts incidentally as a barrier to trade. However, this is not its justification; enduring relationships are preferred because they have their own set of efficiencies. Through collaborations, individuals develop an awareness of the values, tacit knowledge and opportunities offered by their counterparts.

Based on much written about Japan, it is easy to assume that these teams succeed because harmony is intrinsic to Japanese culture. Yet John Creighton Campbell notes that although Westerners assume that the Japanese "deal with one another easily because they trust one another," the opposite appears to be true. Surveys of Japanese and Americans, for example, show that *Americans* see themselves as more trusting and loyal. Campbell's point is that "... the reason that Japanese talk about harmony all the time is that they see it as desirable, perhaps vital, but as quite unnatural ... if consensus came naturally, the Japanese would not have to work so hard at it."[15] I frequently see painstaking efforts by architects to encourage teamwork between all partners in design and construction, and I hear architects' concerns when some part of the team performs unsatisfactorily. Many times a member of the team may ignore or fail to meet goals set by the larger group. Architects or contractors will counter less-than-satisfactory performance by agreeably adding pressure, perhaps offering to work more closely with the recalcitrant, setting tighter deadlines or otherwise increasing oversight. This is frequently effective at achieving minimal standards, but understandably does not encourage innovation with the reluctant supplier. Design decisions related to low performers follow a path of least resistance, and innovations will not develop in this area. As an extreme response, when a subcontractor or fabricator shows less than enthusiastic support on a crucial component, the architect or contractor may suggest that the indifferent firm can be replaced – which might also be desired by the subcontractor, as they become aware of their difficulty in meeting project goals. There is little likelihood that such an unwilling subcontractor will be on subsequent teams.

Rather than attempting to establish a comprehensive body of knowledge, each participant's efforts are coordinated to effectively identify and access helpful information held by their counterparts. Overlapping territories of responsibility also allows team members to learn responsibility in areas that go beyond their expertise. Although the contractor holds the greatest liability and may have the greatest resources, most times, approvals will involve a number of professionals and constructors. This is true not only of shop drawings, but also of formwork and other areas that, in the United States at least, are conventionally the contractor's responsibility. On one project, welders were approved through samples of their work reviewed by the steel fabricators that employed them, an independent testing agency, the contractor, the project engineer and the project architect. As it turned out, the architect's staff discovered problems with a sample overlooked by other reviewers.

It may be easier to encourage successful teams when there are no clear territorial boundaries. Instead of focussing on professional status or conventional lines of skirmish between groups, everyone can attend to the tasks at hand. Architects see their greatest impact as bringing together trades or consul-

5.4, 5.5
Ota Rest House by Toyo Ito and Mutsuro Sasaki (exterior and interior views).

5.6
Kasai Rinkai Park structure by Yoshio Taniguchi reflects a different approach to engineering.

tants with specialized interests and challenging the team to produce unique results. In this vein, Kazuyo Sejima noted:

> Companies can provide a lot of knowledge and technology. We meet with them constantly throughout the project and learn from experiments. Everybody involved is specialised in a particular field. The glass producer has no knowledge of the possibilities in steel production, and vice versa. But the architect is the one who connects the different fields in order to come up with new solutions.[16]

Her partner, Ryue Nishizawa, further elaborated on this point with a lengthy tale about the design of a curtain wall:

> We were making this seven-meter-tall curtain wall . . . I was asking the curtain wall manufacturer about a back mullion, where I wanted to use a steel flat bar. Well, anyway, if the vertical bar faces perpendicularly, it is pretty efficient, but if it faces parallel to the glass plane, there is not much [lateral] resistance. So the curtain wall guy, it's his business, says it is no good to do it that way . . . I started asking other people what they thought, and the structural engineer had an idea. If you compare steel and glass, the steel is stronger, but with the spacing of the back mullions on the curtain wall of the Pachinko Parlor, well, then a pane of glass and a single mullion had about the same strength, according to him. And because they are equal strengths, the flat bar was not

The roots of collaborative practice 57

really carrying any weight – because of the strength of the glass, there was no lateral load being transferred. Since it could carry the same lateral weight itself, he said . . . When I told all this to the curtain wall rep, he was surprised, and began to say, "Well, if the structural says it's okay . . ." And then the contractor began to say that if the back mullions are directly sealed, well, all the seals aren't going to break at the same time . . . And everyone began to say "that's right, that's right."[17]

BUILDING COOPERATIVE TEAMS

Most architects confess that they do not initially have a clear sense of the opportunities to collaborate on any given project – even with contractors they are familiar with – until supervising staff have had some experience working together on site. The team's personality will emerge in the early stages of construction, based on the expertise and interests of each participating organization and the building's character or program. Even with firms that work together over time, the relationships between team members vary from project to project. Teams that have worked together in the past will still be affected by the client's budget or timing and by external factors, such as construction and labor markets. These factors may be more or less compatible with the core values represented by the various trades or professions and by each firm involved.

Nonetheless, architects consider some contractors, subcontractors and suppliers to have greater flexibility and a willingness to work out problems in a team setting. This may be because some organizations draw on a broader range of expertise and interests (especially the largest contractors), but it may also be because the goals or production norms of some organizations are more in line with the goals that the architects themselves bring to these teams. Some companies, for example, put a higher value on aesthetic issues, or on the quality of craft, than do others. Voluntary collaborations between manufacturers and architects, an area I discuss further in the chapter "Architects and Industry," commonly emerge from interdependent or like goals. These can make for a smoother collaboration. It also seems that voluntary collaborations, which begin in the basic design stage, are more effective than collaborations initiated later, perhaps because both parties hold less commitment to mutually established goals or approaches. Finally, each individual's inclinations lead to variation, even within a firm: experience allows team members greater confidence and a broader expertise to draw upon in discussions. Personal attitudes about responsibility, persuasiveness and even charisma play a role in negotiations. Over time, the individuals directly involved in a building's production develop an understanding of the biases and experience held by their counterparts. It becomes easier to draw on tacit knowledge and establish trust, which may expand the information known by the group or the willingness to collaborate.

Most architects spend the first few months on site attempting to shape an effective team. It is possible to construct a refined building under acrimonious conditions, and I have seen at least one highly refined complex concluded in spite of constant back-biting on the site, simply because the contractors continued to maintain high standards for construction. However, most architects will acknowledge that their best work results from the cooperation of a sympathetic construction team. The architects' own investment is also higher on those projects where the team is enthusiastic and architects, especially principals, grow less involved in those buildings where they battle indifference. To work effectively with teams, especially because there are no set roles, architects must have specific skills. For example, the architect must be able to draw out tacit knowledge and expertise compatible with their design intentions and must be able to communicate goals in a way appreciable by the trades. Architects do not explain their concepts for the building in depth, but they must indicate specific formal goals clearly, e.g., getting a wall as thin as possible or keeping an elevation clean and uncluttered. (This may be one of the reasons that Japanese architects will often begin by discussing their buildings using formal terms, rather than starting with theoretic constructs, program, inspiration or urban context, as architects in many other countries do.) In some negotiations, a misunderstanding on the part of the trades has led them to suggest that the architect had abandoned earlier, agreed-upon principles, while the architectural team see their efforts as consistent refinement. Unless these disagreements are resolved, the level of trust can erode, affecting the character of teamwork. Architects must also be able to communicate a respect and openness to the contributions constructors can offer, while keeping the discussion focussed sufficiently to find a solution. This is reflected best when the team is comfortable ending meetings with questions unresolved, but a clear sense of purpose. At times, this may mean that between meetings individuals have specific tasks that they will report to the group, but it is also important that the team be able to occasionally accept that they must all sleep on an idea. If architects feel that each meeting must end with clear action, then they may not be allowing the team to develop shared responsibility. Architects do not so much try to control the constructors, but instead rely on different mechanisms to promote quality.

Every project team holds weekly meetings of professional staff and the constructors (usually representatives of the general contractor/s and of major subcontractors). General contractors direct all points discussed in these meetings and independently manage a meeting of the subcontractors that anticipates the weekly meeting of all members of the design team, but final decisions are made in the larger meeting – with the consultant team – even on relatively minor points. Thus, a balance of power does exist between the contractor and architect. In any collaboration the involvement and discernment of the contractor's site supervisor is a significant force in the success of the project. Contractors must be able to communicate a concern for design quality to subcontractors, and often (though not always) participate in discussions architects hold with fabricators and subcontractors. If the contractors are unwilling to engage in speculation or to develop problem statements as part of a group, this will also affect the effectiveness of the team.

The trades, too, may inadvertently affect the quality of construction at crucial locations, in part because the architect has put them in a greater position of trust through less specific documents. The North American architect may reject difficult details or finishes *a priori*, because of the transfer of responsibility involved.

Instead, on the Japanese construction site, architectural staff accept that they must respond to finish failures or problems in material coordination.

Still, architects in Japan will often propose the use of entirely new technologies or materials with complete – and to the outsider, audacious – confidence. One project that I visited, the Saitama Arena, includes a curved, 15,000-ton moving wall that adjusts to accommodate various seating configurations. Several years ago the American partners on the project stated, "Probably the most unique thing about this building is the money being spent on technology that really doesn't exist ... Technology is being developed especially for this building."[18] Today, the necessary technology to move the wall is in use.

Anyone with a passing knowledge of Japanese architecture can think of other examples where an architect without sufficient expertise to assure success floated an idea: designs with unproven technologies, with audaciously long spans, or with questionable new materials. Foreign professionals in Japan also take advantage of the unusual interactions between architects and contractors: this is where Zaha Hadid completed her first built work, where Tim McFarlane developed a cantilevered glass structure, and where Foreign Office Architects, the relatively young architects Alejandro Zaera-Polo and Farshid Moussavi, hope to build their competition-winning proposal for the Yokohama Port Terminal, an unusual undulating structure that even the Japanese consider challenging.

TRADE-OUTS

On the other hand, at times, ambitious proposals are not what they seem. Sometimes architects will include expensive innovations as a potential trade-out, dropping these from the project in favor of something else when there have been too many changes or unforeseen costs. (Such a strategy is more likely in a community where the costs of change orders that add to construction and the costs of removed items are treated similarly.) Which items are expendable is not immediately clear to the contractor. Some untried materials or components may be central to a project's concept, while on the same site the architects include other elements intended to allow for negotiating space. Often the most easily deleted elements are stand-alone pieces that can be cut without having too great an impact. In negotiations, the decision by an architect to relinquish such components in favor of work more central to the project is not as explicit as I suggest here. Such trade-outs may not be planned; in his design for a house in Tokyo, Jun Watanabe felt forced to accept what he considered an inferior bathroom slate because of time constraints, but in exchange he required the contractor to encase a key column in Carrara marble. Nonetheless, architects will often introduce a series of trade-outs by noting that they have decided to abandon specific expensive components, moving quickly to a discussion of another area where they need additional effort or funds. Several designers have acknowledged to me that such decisions were linked, and that they expected the contractor to recognize this fact, but that openly acknowledging it would suggest the piece traded out was frivolously included. In fact,

5.7
A relatively large weekly meeting.

very often these expendable pieces reflect ideals that the architect recognizes are only likely to be attainable under the best circumstances. When components seem potentially difficult to produce or expensive, but the architect is not giving the area much attention in meetings and document production, experienced contractors already recognize that the material may be deleted and should not receive too much attention. The point is not to maintain the original materials list on a project, but to maintain the original costs. As long as changes do not increase total costs on a project, contractors tend to be supportive.

Even this goal is not entirely fixed. This is why one recent report noted that, "There is a strong sense of social obligation beyond the conditions of the contract [in Japan]. It is important to sustain a good and long-term relationship. If a loss is sustained at the end of a contract, often there will be negotiations to secure an adjustment to the fixed price."[19] I would say that final price adjustments are the norm on construction projects in Japan, although as the poor economy has increased pressure on contractors, the margins for these adjustments have been tightened.

Collaboration does not come without costs; the investment of human capital is high. On projects that are large or complex, the weekly "general" meeting alone may involve thirty or forty people in free-ranging discussions about scheduling and execution. These meetings routinely stretch seven or eight hours, especially in the early stages of construction. Furthermore, this is only one meeting; on projects of any size, meetings can average close to forty hours of the project architect's time each week. In order to respond to the decisions made in these meetings, most architectural staff on construction sites (as well as the other professional consultants and contractors' staff) will work fourteen- or fifteen-hour days, including Saturdays, and will work around the clock during crises. It may be worth noting that in Japan I have never seen the kind of focussed attention on billable hours common in the United States. Since the costs of collaboration are not made explicit to clients, they in turn are less likely to attempt to rein in this inefficiency.

Because of diffused control, contractors and consultants are also able to influence architects in ways they might not in other countries. On one site I observed, for example, the contractor pressed the architect to use ISO 9000 series certification, although the highly bureaucratized process is burdensome. Under the North American system, where document production is essentially complete before construction begins, such efforts would be moot.

However, these disadvantages may be balanced by the benefits found in collaboration.

Although many consider mutual trust and obligation to create inefficiencies, some economists suggest that there are also genuine efficiencies created by avoiding the conventional skirmishes between business partners.[20] By allowing the trades to be involved in conceptualization and determining how work will be done, there are economies in the construction process. Furthermore, the constructors' participation in design development may encourage pride in their work, and thus better quality.

WORKING IN THE MIDST OF CONSTRUCTION

A survey of design and construction periods in Japan (as reported in *Shinkenchiku*) shows that about 20 per cent of projects report overlapping design and construction phases. Yet this number is almost certainly low, since the process of design development and construction supervision is not distinctly separated. Often, project supervision must of necessity include design development, although it may not be reported as such. On all but the smallest projects, the builders and professional staff work together on site, during construction. This is in marked contrast to the norms for design and construction in most countries. In the UK, the chairman of the National Vocation Qualification working group on architectural technology once stated baldly, "The job of the architect is complete within the initial third of the design process."[21] Robert Gutman, an anthropologist studying a 400,000 square foot site in the UK, concurred, reporting that during construction, "No architect ever appeared."[22] The United States is no better; Robert Greenstreet, Dean of the School of Architecture and Urban Planning at the University of Wisconsin-Milwaukee, in an essay entitled, "What Do I Do on Site Anyway?" said, "The short answer is, of course, relatively little, although there are numerous instances of architects acting, often in good faith, beyond the limitations of their contractual obligations and getting in all sorts of trouble."[23]

In Japan, the contractors are on site from the beginning, and most professional staff move to the site about the time that the building's foundation is completed. The representatives of each group are in frequent (often daily) contact and focus almost exclusively on the project at hand. Meetings with other relevant groups, including manufacturers and suppliers, also occur on site or in the factories and plants producing materials for the project. Fumihiko Maki portrays the site as a refuge, "The field office is not only a place for the liberation of the work of the architect from the world of thought, but also is a place where many people participate in the effort towards its crystallization."[24]

The site offices and much of the equipment – even servers connecting all organizations on

5.10
Mock-ups of duct and part of the structural system for Sendai Mediatheque by Toyo Ito.

5.11
Mock-ups will continue to be used throughout construction. Here, a welder works while others from the contractor and a subcontractor look on.

5.12
Staff also use the mock-ups to test ideas; Ito's office tries out a proposed lighting grille using a simple foamcore model. (The author is at the left in this photograph.)

the materials and detailing under consideration by the construction team. Architects have the opportunity to use the mock-up to test proportions, relationships between parts and even the colors of materials. Where there is a concern about the weatherability of the proposed design, larger contractors also have the research facilities necessary to expose the mock-up to various conditions to assess performance – and are sometimes even required by the government to do so. Sometimes this coordination may seem unnecessary to an outside observer: architects routinely require large prototypes of quite simple elements, even those utilized on earlier projects easily observed in situ. Isozaki, for example, described the necessary mock-ups of a concrete panel as requiring that the contractor "... vary the type and size of stones in the aggregate, the proportions of the mix, and the surface finishing."[28] Furthermore, the design team will often decide that these submittals are unsatisfactory and use them as the basis for design development. This may have as much to do with defining the larger goals of the team as it does with the acceptance of a specific material or assembly.

Mock-ups include modest 1:1 models of lighting, handrails and door pulls, built by the architect out of foam core or cardboard and sometimes attached to other mock-ups of facades several bays in length, built by the contractor of the materials that are under consideration for use in the building. Manufacturers and subcontractors also furnish prototypes and full-scale assemblies. Mock-ups are of course used in the United States as well, but the extent of use and the range of applications is much greater in Japan. If one includes the relatively simple full-scale samples produced by contractors to demonstrate material finishes and detailing options, (usually ranging from roughly a half meter square up to 1 × 2 meter panels) there is literally not a project directed by architectural firms that does not rely on full-scale mock-ups. Larger mock-ups can be quite elaborate; one project I observed in 1993 was a relatively uncomplicated ten-story research facility, a project that would not normally call for mock-ups in the United States. The largest mock-up on the project was used to assess the composition of exterior elements and included wall panels and fenestration, a narrow exterior walkway with handrails, and solar panels. It extended over six meters in length and was one-and-a-half stories high.

The mock-ups, prototypes and samples supplied by constructors are collected adjacent to the construction of the building itself, making it easier to envisage the transition from structure to window sash or the role a component plays in the overall scale of the building. Mock-ups may offer little opportunity for further development, however, unless the construction or manufacturing process allows the architect to respond and fine-tune the design. These flexibilities will become more evident in later chapters.

1. D. Leatherbarrow, "Apart and Together: Vicissitudes of Architects in Practice," *Journal of Architectural Education*, 45/4, July 1992, p. 203.
2. D. Maister, "Lessons in Client-Loving," *Architectural Technology*, p. 49 as quoted in Gutman, *Architectural Practice: A Critical View*, Princeton, Princeton University Press, 1988, p. 45.
3. T. Muir, "Introduction to Collaborative Practice" in T. Muir and B. Rance, eds., *Collaborative Practice in the Built Environment*, London, E & FN Spon, 1995, p. 15.
4. See *Journal of Architectural Education*, 45/4, July 1992.
5. This from the 1987 Doc 201. This point is made by Renee Cheng, "Wielding a Bigger Hammer: Scaling up the Instruments of Construction, *Association of Collegiate Schools of Architecture Technology Conference Proceedings*, March 1998, p. 413.
6. H. Davis, *The Culture of Building*, Cambridge, Cambridge University Press, 1999, p. 129.
7. N. Turner, "Japanese Sense and Sensibility," *World Architecture*, no. 60, November 1997, p. 11.
8. J. M. Dixon, "Urban Showplace," *Progressive Architecture*, vol. 76, no. 9, September 1995, p. 74.
9. K. Findlay, "*Ruiji de ha Naku Sai wo* [Not Similar, Different . . .]," *GA Japan: Environmental Design*, no. 30, January/February 1998, p. 169. My translation.
10. An interview with Tadao Ando, by M. Kawamura. "*Digitaru to no Tatakai no Zenyō: Fo-towa-su Gendai Bijutsukan* [Digital and the Fight for the Whole Picture: Fort Worth Modern Art Museum]," *Nikkei A-kitekuchua* [Nikkei Architecture], no. 623, 5 October 1998, p. 114. My translation.
11. E. von Hippel, *The Sources of Innovation*, New York and Oxford, Oxford University Press, 1988, p. 6.
12. Ibid., p. 6, referring to "Integrating Construction Resources and Technology into Engineering" *A Construction Industry Cost Effectiveness Program Report*. New York: The Business Roundtable, August 1982.
13. L. H. Lynn, *How Japan Innovates: A Comparison with the U.S. in the Case of Oxygen Steel Making*, Boulder, Colorado, Westview Press, 1982, p. 6.
14. J. K. Liker, R. R. Kamath, S. Nazli Wasti, and M. Nagamachi, "Integrating Suppliers into Fast-Cycle Product Development," J. K. Liker, J. E. Ettlie, and J. C. Campbell, eds., *Engineered in Japan: Japanese Technology Management Practices*, New York and Oxford, Oxford University Press, 1995, p. 179.
15. J. C. Campbell, "Culture, Innovative Borrowing, and Technology Management." In J. K. Liker, *et al.*, *Engineered in Japan: Japanese Technology Management Practices*. Surveys are cited on p. 312, the quote is from p. 316.
16. C. Hageneder, "Parallel Architecture (An Interview with Kazuyo Sejima)," *Plant/TJ Supplement*, Tokyo, May 1999, p. 6.
17. Y. Futagawa, *Sejima Kazuyo Doku Hon, 1998* [Kazuyo Sejima Reader, 1998], Tokyo, A.D.A. Edita, 1998, pp. 283–5.
18. D. Meis of Ellerbe Becket, Los Angeles, quoted in "Saitama to Build State-of the Art Arena," *Japan Times*, 5 July 1995.
19. Hanscomb Associates, "Construction Fact File," *World Architecture*, November 1997, p. 33.

20 R. Dore, *Flexible Rigidities: Industrial Policy and Structural Adjustment in the Japanese Economy, 1970–1980*, Stanford, California: Stanford University Press, 1986, p. 4.
21 P. Smith, "Comment," *Perspectives in Architecture*, September 1995, p. 7.
22 R. Gutman, *Architecture: A Clinical Practice*, Princeton Architectural Press, 1988, pp. 35–6.
23 R. Greenstreet, "Laws and Order," in A. Pressman, *Profession Practice 101: A Compendium of Business and Management Strategies in Architecture*, New York, John Wiley, 1997, p. 210.
24 F. Maki, *Kenchiku to iu Genzai – Genba kara no Ripotto* [A Presence Called Architecture: Report from the Site], Gallery Ma Shōsho no. 5, Tokyo, Toto Shuppan, 1996, p. 37.
25 T. P. Rohlen, *For Harmony and Strength: Japanese White Collar Organization in Anthropological Perspective*, Berkeley, Los Angeles and London, University of California Press, 1974, p. 30.
26 D. Normille, *World Architecture*, November 1997, p. 30.
27 B. Colomina, *Privacy and Publicity: Modern Architecture as Mass Media*, Cambridge, Massachusetts and London, M.I.T. Press, 1994, p. 65.
28 *Arata Isozaki: Construction Site, The Japan Architect* 12, Winter 1993–4, p. 150.

Contractors

Collaborators and competitors

In a country report on Japan, the trade journal *World Architecture* stated:

> First, the Japanese genuinely appreciate good architecture; secondly, their builders are the very best in the world – there is no more satisfying experience than building in Japan. . . . The "Big Five" . . . see no distinction between architecture and building . . . They all exhibit genuine pride, responsibility, and commitment to their work.[1]

Japan's contractors are an unusual resource for architects. There are over half-a-million licensed contractors. Many of these are quite small; according to statistics published by Japan's Ministry of Construction for 1998, almost half of all contractors billed under 5 million yen (approximately $48,000) a year.[2] Nonetheless, only about one-third of the licensed contractors are estimated to operate as general contractors. Furthermore, Japan's largest contractors operate at an entirely different level from their smaller brethren; in the early 1990s eighteen of the world's twenty-five construction firms with revenues over $5 billion were Japanese.[3] Although revenues have since fallen, the country's biggest contractors remain among the largest and most sophisticated in the world, and six – including Sekisui House – were among the top ten contractors in the world in the most recently aggregated figures, from 1997.[4]

In Japan, large contractors are called *zenecon*, a word adapted in the post-war period from the English term "general contractors." The *zenecon* and other "special contractors" hold licenses that permit them to subcontract work out, allowing them to take on larger and more complex projects. The largest firms operate nationally, which requires special registration; less than 1 per cent of all contractors are licensed by the Ministry of Construction to operate in more than one prefecture.[5]

These contractors offer a broad range of construction and professional services, do in-house research and development in facilities that are the envy of any university, carry the financing on some projects during construction, and hold economic power that demands pliant support from subcontractors and suppliers. Architects can and do benefit from such resources. Few able to compare Japan's contractors with those in other countries deny that Japan's contractors are more supportive and cooperative. Architects also tend to have more confidence in the large contractors; although negotiations can be more trying, most designers believe that the largest contractors are capable of higher construction quality than small, local counterparts.

Building construction also remains more significant for *zenecon*, compared with their overseas counterparts. With the shifting economy, there has been some inclination to reduce building construction in favor of civil engineering projects. The top six contractors directly fill a quarter of all Japan's construction orders (down from a third reported by Fumio Matsushita in 1994), and their involvement covers an even higher proportion of total construction because they often share revenue and construction projects through joint ventures.[6] In addition, the largest contractors have a much greater presence on high-end work, which is also where architectural involvement is highest. Even so, the four major publicly traded contractors report that 63–79 per cent of their orders were for building construction in 1999, down only slightly from the 72–83 per cent of a few years earlier.

Of greater concern is the massive debt Japan's largest contractors hold today, preventing them from investing in professional services and research at the same level they did a decade ago. The Taisei Corporation's consolidated debt was the most extreme, peaking at an extraordinary 1.2 trillion yen ($11.3 billion) in March of 1999, with an operating profit of only 43.6 billion yen ($410.5 million), and causing the firm to begin selling many of its best assets, including its corporate headquarters in Tokyo's commercial center, Shinjuku.[7] Other firms in the construction sector acted more quickly to reduce liabilities, but nonetheless were weakened considerably by their debt. However, to date the size and significance of the construction industry protects the largest firms, and Japanese banks, with government support, have been unwilling to act harshly. Thus the long-term impact of this debt is unpredictable, but will certainly have an effect.

For the most part, general contractors in Japan also have not operated under the same economic pressures as do contractors in other countries. In the early 1980s, before the speculative Bubble and subsequent recession, Japan's five largest contractors reported obtaining more than 50 per cent of their orders through non-competitive negotiations (where negotiations were conducted with only one contractor) from the private sector.[8] At the time, Takenaka was actually reporting that only 23 per cent of its construction orders came through competitive bidding.[9] In the current economy, there is much greater emphasis on competitive bidding and the government has shown an interest in shifting some awards from limited pool bidding to open bidding. However, it remains to be seen whether these new practices will remain in place when Japan's economy begins to recover – much of the answer is based on how recovery will reshape the industry and how soon it will occur. To date, there have been ardent and expensive governmental efforts geared at preserving the industry as it is, with more modest counterbalancing efforts at trying new approaches perhaps only intended to bridge a difficult period.

Today, it can be safely said that contractors in Japan seem to have a larger share of the design market than anywhere else in the world. Although the number of licensed individuals continues to climb, the balance of design by contractors and by architects has stayed relatively consistent for much of the post-war period. Architects designed only the most symbolically significant buildings: public institutions, cultural facilities, buildings for the fashion industry and private residential work. Even with these limitations, during the late 1980s architectural offices were strained to capacity and construction companies absorbed much of the excess demand for design; estimates of the contractors' share of architectural design commissions during this period ranged as high as 45 per cent. More opportunities for foreign designers also emerged.

Since the 1920s, architects have been employed by and integral to the *zenecon* corporate structure. Matsushita reports that about 40 per cent of all persons holding the *ikkyū kenchikushi* license are employed by contractors. Not all, of course, are designers, but the ambiguity allows the *zenecon* to offer design-build services as a way of bringing in construction contracts.[10] In fact, each of the five largest general contractors employs more people holding licensing than the total number of licensed individuals at Nikken Sekkei, one of the world's largest architectural firms, where 700 people hold licensing. Takenaka actually employs more people with licensing than the top eight architecture offices in Japan combined.[11] (This is even more remarkable when you recognize that Nikken Sekkei, Japan's largest architectural firm, is also consistently ranked as the largest, or one of the largest, architectural firms in the world.) Historically, Takenaka has shown a particular commitment to integrated packages, and normally 50 to 60 per cent of its work has been design-build.[12] This is reflected in the number of Takenaka's *ikkyū kenchikushi* on staff: 3,133 people in 2000, down 317 from 1995.[13] Although Takenaka may not be wholly representative, the other contractors in the "Big Five" each employ between 2,400 and 2,900 people with *ikkyū kenchikushi* licensing.[14]

Both architecture firms and construction companies can offer any of the range of normal architectural services, including basic design, design development and construction supervision. The profession has split between "design" architects and the more commercially minded in-house architects working in developers' offices or for contractors. Contractors offering design services reinforce and exaggerate clients' goals: some highly refined work is produced by construction companies, but clients who simply want to get something completed at a minimum cost are more likely to do so without being challenged with a larger set of professional concerns for aesthetics, context or public role. Much of the work contractors produce in design-build packages is dull and pragmatic: factories, boxy apartment buildings and modest offices. The lack of common values held between architectural firms and the design service providers housed in contractors affects the face of the city. Designers offering their services as part of a construction package frequently ignore the contextual role of a building or its appearance,

6.1
An elegantly detailed office building in Tokyo, designed and built by Takenaka Komuten.

simply shooting for maximum envelope, minimum maintenance and similarly pragmatic objectives. (Oddly, these buildings are frequently inefficiently organized in spite of otherwise practical goals.) Architectural offices design most of the higher quality buildings and public works, as well as projects that the contractors consider to have unusually demanding and unprofitable aesthetic or programmatic goals. Nevertheless, contractors are capable of high-end design; each year the design yearbooks include one or two projects designed and built by Japan's largest contractors.

In prosperous times, instead of perceiving themselves as competing, architects and contractors embraced this overlap, since it allowed them to adjust design services based on the specific character of each project. Because of this range, when an independent architectural studio does work with a major contractor, it is possible for the two to draw on common experience and for staff from both organizations to share goals and language related to design development and execution. This is one of the reasons that Tei'ichi Takahashi, Tadao Ando, Sei'ichi Shirai, and even a recent chairman of Nikken Sekkei were all able to command respect in the profession without having become licensed – less remarkable when you consider that the licensing of architects in Japan is still quite recent.

The situation is underscored by professional expectations and by legal definitions of architects' responsibilities. While American architects are responsible for health and safety, the Architects Act of 1950 (which established the first definitions of licensing) defined Japanese architects as simply being responsible for the "quality of the building."[15]

The antagonism between architects and contractors witnessed in most markets has been generally absent in Japan. As Sidney Levy rather amusingly stated in his book on Japan's contractors, "The adversarial relationship prevalent in most labor-management negotiations, as well as between some general contractors and their subcontractor and often between contractors and architect-engineer . . . is not fully understood by Japanese builders . . ."[16] I do not think that most Japanese architects would encourage builders to develop this understanding.

On the other hand, the recession has made contractors more willing to compete with architects for design commissions. The comfortable splitting of design services between architects and contractors is eroding as the industry faces dwindling demand for new buildings. Today, competition for work is intensifying because architectural ateliers often lack any marketing staff or even an understanding of how to market professional services. In the past, the profession relied on the conditions of a commission to determine whether architects would be consulted and did little to educate the general public; a clear distinction was usually believed to exist between the production of architectural offices and the output of design-build packages in Japan, and only a few clients were able to demand that the contractors rise above a relatively pragmatic approach.

Today, however, bright young designers have gravitated to the safety of contractors, or large architectural offices. Contractors have also been less willing to pass on even some tiny design commissions, and the quality of design in their design-build packages, at least in major urban areas, is rising. This may have long-term effects on how and where architectural design is supported, or it may be that, as in the 1980s, temporary economic conditions cause temporary changes in the balance between design by architectural offices and design by contractors.

Design and construction – the office and the site – are not separate territories, but instead fluidly intermingle. Builders' involvement in design work is complemented by architects' involvement in construction and the resulting understanding of production constraints. Simply looking at the number of people holding the equivalent of architectural licensing is provocative. Kisho Kurokawa claimed that Japan has the highest number of architects per capita in the world, a point of truth only if you accept that the licenses of various nations are equivalent. But in reality, there is little emphasis on design in the Japanese licensing exams. Today, there are close to a quarter of a million people holding *ikkyū kenchikushi* licensing, two and a half times the number of licensed architects in the United States, a country with twice Japan's population.[17] Per capita, twice as many people are employed in Japan's construction industry, but even these relative figures do not justify the higher number of licensed architects. Embedded in this population is a group that shifts back and forth between design and construction, as their responsibilities require. Many employees of contractors' design departments may act as architects on one project and then be sent out to represent the builder's interests on the next. Contractors are particularly willing to use this approach on challenging designs, where they are most concerned about understanding the architects' goals. In effect, the contractor supplies a liaison.

The line between architect and contractor can grow extremely blurry; there does not seem to be any consistency in where and how these construction company architects fit into the design development team. In one project I researched during 1998, many of the architect's site-based staff were actually on loan from the contractors, with desks in the same room and sitting with architectural staff in meetings. At other times, these people will be on the other side of the table, remaining in the uniforms of the construction company. In one unusual case, a retired employee of a large contractor acted as an adviser to an architectural firm during an ambitious project's basic design. He was in the architect's office one day a week, as a consultant. Younger staff repeatedly told me how valuable this consultant had become and the firm was able to move from relatively simple approaches to construction, toward challenging new technologies and more sophisticated exploitation of existing technologies. Such liminal staff also exist in Japanese manufacturing alliances, where the term "guest engineer" has been coined. As Liker points out, these individuals serve as a "... two-way conduit of information flow ... [and] may be able to influence specifications for the subsystems" in a way that benefits the contractor.[18] Contractors with design skills also expand the way the team can communicate: I have seen architects resort to model-building during meetings, but more often contractors produce very creditable three-dimensional sketches while talking. These contractor/designers often play an important role in linking the goals of architecture and construction. Through these individuals, the design team is often able to see itself as united rather than divided.

In addition, other normative practices also work to bring together architectural staff and contractors. Inexperienced architectural staff sometimes find themselves responsible for project supervision. Usually, these are small buildings, so the project architect will be further isolated because he or she is alone in the firm's site office. Inevitably, the project architect turns to the contractor's representatives on site for advice, since the contractor's and architect's representatives will meet at least daily to discuss design development, whereas the project architect may not see people from the home office more than once a week, when senior office staff meet with them to check on the project. In each of the cases I have observed, the contractors advise green project architects scrupulously and with good will. There is usually greater effort to map out the potential pitfalls of decisions, and schedules for decision-making often seem to be more conservative. Quite naturally, the younger architect develops an appreciation and gratitude towards the contractor/mentor.

Furthermore, many studies on Japanese firms argue that employees consider the work environment to be equally or more important than their families and personal needs. People who work together socialize together, and look out for each other in a variety of large and small ways. In my experience, some of this loyalty is transferred to the site-based work community. In particular, staff from the contractor's and architect's offices can fall into patterns similar to those seen within firms: they develop a sense of identity related to their perceptions of the quality of the organization on site, and on longer construction projects they also sometimes have year-end parties and "company" trips together. The alliances that develop on site do not supercede loyalties to the home firm – for one thing, the site-based organization can do little to advance its members after a building has been completed. These work communities nonetheless have the potential to develop deep and important bonds.[19]

These kinds of interactions establish relationships that allow the site-based design development team to take on greater risk. Elsewhere, new technologies are only slowly integrated in the construction industry, based on an understandable tendency to be conservative in volatile conditions. However, in Japan, the interdependence of stakeholders allows trustful relationships to lead to greater willingness to introduce new technologies. Contractors also place a great deal of emphasis on maintaining up-to-date expertise in construction technologies, even participating in projects with no short-term economic justification in order to advertise their innovative capacity. Thus, they have both the opportunity and the motive to bring new technologies to the industry. Not surprisingly, the largest contractors have explored a range of approaches not yet seen in other nations: lift-up construction, robotic support and site-based fabrication are only some of the technologies where Japanese contractors remain unrivaled.

CONSULTANTS AND CONSTRUCTORS IN ALLIANCE

Many of the decisions a Japanese contractor must make affect the architect's decision-making. Conventional design-bid-build approaches often suggest that the architect, as the client's agent, has greater authority (even if the realities are not so clear). In Japan however, contractors, working with the client, propose the construction schedule (which also affects the schedule for design development), produce drawings of standard details, guide the project through governmental regulation, and write up detailed technical documentation on formwork or other production systems that affect finishes. They may even take the initiative in locating fire exits in buildings. The contractor holds liability and can thus challenge any poorly developed technical proposals from the architect. Contractors save money, reduce risk and promote technical skills.

Architects also make decisions that rely on the contractor for success, and have for some time. Many architects have mentioned to me the stance that Kunio Maekawa took to working with contractors during the post-war period, using minimal sketches and relying heavily on contractors and fabricators to accomplish his precedent-setting designs; for many, this apparently remains an ideal. When architects expose bolts and screw heads (perhaps even pressing to have the slots in the screws all vertical), they implicitly share responsibility for aesthetic success with the contractor.

The best contractors can push architects to be better designers. I have been struck more than once by the way contractors working with the least experienced project architects often ask the kinds of questions other professors and I ask our students in studio. They will gently probe intent or suggest possible problems with use ("it might be kind of small – can you get your hand in there?"). Frequently, these conversations end with the young architect agreeing to rework a proposal to strengthen it. I would say that no contractor expected young architects to have a grasp of the technical constraints and process issues that would affect design choices (although they were happier when architects did). However, the builders did expect professionals to listen and recognize the importance of these issues. On a site that is going well, an architect like Ito or Maki may take advantage of the contractor's supportive stance to propose more challenging materials or formal strategies. In this case, the dialogue between the architect and contractor deepens, resulting in advances that show off the technological sophistication of both the designer and the builder. On the other hand, commercial firms may decide that a good contractor allows them to reduce their supervision and time on site, an approach I have seen in the work of Nikken Sekkei. They most likely choose to do so when they are under pressure to pass savings on to clients through reduced costs for professional services.

As with any relationship, however, architects and contractors find things to complain about in these alliances. Contractors grumble that architects will sometimes take unfair advantage of them, ignoring the contractor's advice and insisting that the contractors make unnecessary efforts to back up their claims. Architects, on the other hand, are quick to note that contractors sometimes claim materials or information does not exist, and that they must repeatedly prod before getting the support to investigate something they know exists. It is also my experience that the biggest, most demanding projects are more likely to fray the relationship between the architect and contractor. There are several possible reasons for this. By their nature, most contractors are conservative in their solutions. Architects will try to prevent the contractor's concerns from leading to overdesign, but if the project is an innovative one or extends for a long period, then the architects are repeatedly pushing the contractor out of their comfort zone, and this may damage the relationship. In addition, larger projects take longer, and financial risks are magnified. On those occasions when the alliance does begin to break down, interdependence can be a genuine hindrance even on small matters. One project architect, for example, griped to me that in response to his desire to use a white finish, the contractor kept proposing "one color sample, and it's ugly." When the relationship does breakdown, contractors can make life very difficult for architects, refusing to participate in crucial decisions, establishing a firewall between architects and crafters, and dragging their feet when supplying crucial information.

In the United States, an architect may need to ally with a local architecture firm on a project, in order to more appropriately address the demands placed on a project by political requirements, weather or by local variations in production and supply. These sorts of pairings may also occur when there is a need for specific expertise, such as in hospital or sports facility design. (Local alliances in the States also overcome differences in codes and other regulations, but in Japan these are nationally consistent.) Japanese architects have only rarely used this approach and with mixed success. For the most part, it would appear that the local architectural firms find very little advantage in the relationship, and reflect their lack of commitment to the work through poor construction supervision. Contractors, on the other hand, may actually be the more suitable choice for such a local partner, since many of the issues locals address are related to production – assuming, as in the case of Japanese contractors, they are capable of sharing and respecting design decision-making. Furthermore, the largest contractors represent complex organizations including a range of expertise and research. These firms are often able to assist the small architecture studio on projects requiring specialized knowledge. That contractors and architects share pride in the results of their alliances is best demonstrated by the fact that, during construction, contractors actively participate in promoting technologically sophisticated projects. They cover the costs of architectural exhibitions and also borrow models and presentation materials for display in their offices or communities.

The wisdom of sharing decision-making with contractors, especially as it concerns production and detailing, is perhaps most evident in the simple fact that shared decision-making has frequently been utilized on exemplary buildings. Louis Kahn's careful collaborations with contractors are well known, as is the more recent success seen in Frank Gehry's Bilbao. Today, as the complexity of building production challenges most design teams, a legal framework for shared decision-making is emerging in other nations. The Royal Institute of British Architects has allowed some responsibility for detail design to be passed on to the builder since 1980 and the American Institute of Architects, the largest professional organization in the United States, opens the possibility for designated detail development by the contractor in its agreement form B141, although to date this contract form has not been ratified by the Association of General Contractors – a crucial step for acceptance. Still, in both nations there is ample evidence of a growing interest in design-build alliances. One-quarter of all construction work in England is now design-build, and in the United States about one in ten projects are done as design-build.[20]

Just as contractors should appreciate the values and obligations architects bring to a project, architects acquire an understanding of the problems and requirements of construction. Conditions require Japanese professionals to pay attention to the relationship between art and building, but this is easier because of the site-based interactions between architects and contractors. On their most important projects, Japan's architects inspect and approve formwork and concrete pours, check levels with surveying equipment, raise questions about worker safety on site, visit plants and approve or arrange the production and delivery of materials (e.g., the length of time taken to travel from a concrete plant to a pour) and directly interact with manufacturers' production staff, areas conventionally considered the domain of contractors in the West.

In addition to making the contractor's work potentially easier and raising the quality of construction by working together, collaborative design development has also been shown to be faster and to offer important cost savings. In one survey of Western clients, over half felt that design-build, applied to simple, easily clarified projects, offered significant cost savings; half expected construction time to be shorter as well.[21] Delays occur predictably at several points in the traditional design-bid-build sequence. Because architects are not reliably linked to the construction industry, for example, a project may require significant redesign because the bids have come in too high. Moreover, because the process is sequential, a delay in any stage can delay completion – perhaps magnifying the delay as the subsequent stages take longer to bring back into succession. These problems can add significant costs to a project. One of the most remarkable estimates I have seen suggested that mistakes and delays account for $200 billion of the $650 billion spent on construction in the United States.[22] In Japan during the Bubble era, the high costs of land caused many developers to consider any innovation that had the potential to get a building into use more quickly, and this may well have cemented private developers' commitment to the architect and contractor working in alliance.

Thus, architects and contractors share many of the activities that define design development and construction supervision. This supports Robert Gutman's predictions for the practice, "... architects will have to learn to share responsibility with other professions and organizations in the building industry."[23]

SEJIMA'S SHOPPING BAG

A site visit I made with Kazuyo Sejima illustrates how architect/contractor alliances lead to fine-tuning a building in ways that ultimately add up to greater overall refinement. In August 1996, I visited the Gifu Multimedia Workshop (sometimes called "Media Academy") with Sejima and her staff. At the time, demands on the office staff had them stretched pretty thinly, and Sejima made the point that, while she felt a site office was desirable, they were too busy to keep someone in Gifu full time. Sejima started in Toyo Ito's office; she understands the potential value of alliances with contractors and fabricators and, as I note elsewhere, she attempts to exploit these opportunities when possible. However, a young office is still building the connections and relationships that allow collaboration to occur, and often does not enjoy the same kind of support that established architects do. The contractor was also under pressure; the 873 square meter (about 9,400 square foot) building, mostly set below grade, went up in six months. A hurried schedule hardly allows much time to explore new relationships either.

In her work, Sejima rethinks the fabric of each building, mixing unusual finish materials to create an unexpected character. This eclecticism means that Sejima's inclination is to begin by considering many surface finishes and then narrow down her choices. Her approach makes it difficult for her to begin by working with fabricators and suppliers, because the broader set of choices she starts with mean that some will inevitably be cut. Even asking for large samples was still a problem in 1996; she was young and the firm had a limited portfolio of mostly small projects. Working closely with her office would not make economic sense for suppliers. An on-going relationship with a curtain wall manufacturer's representative was promising, but he was under some pressure to stop paying the same attention to her orders, because the collaborations were making less money for the fabricator.

Sejima knew she could ask contractors to supply the finish materials she was considering, but doing so would mean that she would be using up political capital at an early stage of decision-making. Her solution was to send staff over to Tokyu Hands, a large store with a hardware section that seems like something *Wallpaper* magazine might have dreamed up. For the site visit, Sejima brought a large shopping bag to Gifu, containing three kinds of oriented strand board (OSB), three good-size pieces of Astroturf, a sheet of whitish vinyl and some wood flooring. Sejima and the staff laid these out and looked at them in the context of the project, essentially draping the building with possible finishes. Ultimately, two materials the team brought that day, a white vinyl and a varnished OSB, turned up in the Media Workshop. The Astroturf did not make it into the mix, although a crushed velvet eventually did. (As an aside, I saw another architect – also a woman – who resorted to buying a switch from an Akihabara electric wholesaler when she was in a similar position. It may be that women architects do not always get the same support in initial negotiations, but it is also possible that early socialization makes some women inclined towards beginning indirectly.)

Once the architectural team decided on materials, Sejima turned to the contractor. Earlier, they had made a provisional determination to use polycarbonate over the concrete

6.2
Kazuyo Sejima at the Media Academy construction site, considering finish alternatives.

6.3
The completed interior at Media Academy.

walls. The main reason for our trip was to review several possible ways these sheets would come together, so that the contractor could figure quantities for the order. He made the point that the polycarbonate needed to go into production by the following day, in order for him to meet his schedule, and Sejima confessed that she had been holding him up as she reconsidered the other surfaces. As we looked at Astroturf and OSB, several laborers attached polycarbonate sheets to a wall in different configurations: two sheets were butted, two sheets overlapped, and two sheets were butted together with a narrower strip running over the seam.

After these polycarbonate sheets were up, Sejima and her staff joined the contractors. All made a quick decision to butt the sheets, but Sejima was already on to smaller points. The fasteners stood out strongly against the polycarbonate and she was not sure that that was the effect she wanted. Were there other types

6.4
Small mock-ups of fastener and finish joint alternatives supplied by the contractor for Sejima's Media Academy.

of screws that could be used in this situation? One of the laborers said he thought there were, and the contractor put in an unsuccessful call to his suppliers. They briefly discussed painting the screws in some way, but agreed that first he should look around a bit more. The washers, too, were an issue. They were a thick, black doughnut shape, and Sejima wondered if perhaps they came in white – or perhaps colors? The contractors responded unenthusiastically, but they agreed that other washers did exist for use with glass fiber, and were perhaps acceptable in this installation. They made more telephone calls and said they would investigate their options.

In the completed building, the final result is a slightly more discrete fastener, but one that is still noticeable; the washers have become part of a vocabulary of dots and circles stamped across floor and wall surfaces. The detail is tiny, trivial – and yet in the aggregation of these details, a young Japanese architect worked with contractors, not only developing a design, but a theory of construction. Even on more established architects' sites, these kind of details are frequently the source of much back-and-forth between architects and constructors. Whether to overlap film sheets on glass or the allowable margin for punched metal panels is negotiated in many teams that have established a high level of care and refinement.

INNOVATING THROUGH TEAM EFFORT

A project that powerfully illustrates the pressures on architects and contractors to collaborate on the development of innovative architectural and construction solutions is the Park Dome Kumamoto, designed by the Tokyo architectural firm Dai'ichi Kōbō and Fujita, one of Japan's top construction companies. Few architects would propose a structural system that required lifting a 2,500-ton roof 19 meters (62 feet) in the air in order to construct it, but this was only one remarkable feature of the Park Dome. The building was the result of a competition strongly biased towards technical innovation. Arata Isozaki and Hajime Yatsuka, then responsible for selecting architects for many public works projects in Kumamoto Prefecture through a program called Kumamoto ArtPolis, randomly matched five preselected architects with five contractors in order to assure the most technically sophisticated proposals possible. Each team officially incorporated as a joint venture for the competition. This practice seems to be true of many competitions for sports domes held during the 1990s. Yoshiharu Kanebako, an emerging leader among structural engineers, noted that, "Starting a few years ago, there can be said to be something of a 'dome boom' involving large-scale domes being constructed in many regional centers. In particular, architectural studios and contractors make up teams, and the team to carry out construction is selected from these. For this purpose, new unique designs and the technological skills of large contractors are combined ..."[24] For the Kumamoto competition, the other competing architects were Kisho Kurokawa, Yoshiro Ikehara, Kiyonori Kikutake and Kijo Rokkaku.

The audacious winning proposal was possible only because the architects developed a conceptual design working closely with the contractor's design, engineering and construction staff. In fact, Tei'ichi Takahashi, the principal of Dai'ichi Kōbō made a point of splitting the team along very clear lines. Right at the start he indicated that he thought it was his responsibility to come up with an idea that could win, while the contractors were responsible for convincing themselves and others that the idea could be built. At project completion, an interviewer asked Takahashi if he was responsible for all design decisions. He explicitly rejected this, noting, "That's how designers think, isn't it? There are many different approaches: being 'carried piggyback' by the contractor, making a variety of proposals for the contractor to choose from ..."[25] I later asked Takahashi's project architect how he could feel confident when there were so many aspects of the project where he could not draw on his own experiences. His simple answer was, "I was not working alone." He went on to point out that his work always requires him to learn about new materials and new building types, so that he was accustomed to seeking out advice from other members of the design team.

Cloistered in a hotel for several days, forty people worked on the basic design proposal, not only those from the architect's and construction offices, but also leading engineers from Tokyo brought in as consultants. Takahashi presented them with a simple, but compelling endeavor: he suggested a "floating cloud" shelter for the sports field. Beneath, diffused natural light and soft breezes would define the character of the space. Takahashi said later that the team's first response was an

6.5
Dai'ichi Kōbō's Kumamoto Dome, exterior.

"uproar." Then a mechanical engineer from Fujita suggested a double-skinned Teflon roof might be the answer, and the esteemed engineer Toshihiko Kimura agreed with the idea.

The team ultimately determined that a "cloud" of Teflon fabric could shelter the field, with a central aperture to increase interior light. The idea spawned a series of innovations. Unusual structural solutions were the first to draw attention: the design team developed a double membrane supported by internal air pressure and reinforced with steel cables; cables stretched from the internal ring to an outer compression ring that allowed the roof structure to stand on only eight clusters of columns, so that the playing field extended visually and experientially into the landscape; and beyond the compression ring, an amor- phously shaped steel structure softened the form of the building and made a gentle transition from the height needed for a sports field to a more human scale. The team also expended a great deal of effort to make the mechanical performance of the building successful and reduce running costs, thus assuring the national government bore greater initial costs and the prefecture, responsible for running costs, carried less expense. In addition to the light introduced through the central aperture, double-glazed roof panels with an aluminum honeycomb insert (developed earlier by Takahashi), allowed the transmission of indirect light at the compression ring, and the Teflon itself brought in some natural light. Mechanical systems were designed to support natural ventilation; the central opening became

6.6
Dai'ichi Kōbō's Kumamoto Dome, view of ring at grade.

an exhaust in the summer, and a perimeter of tall, lightweight polycarbonate doors could be entirely opened up, allowing cool breezes to blow through the building. Each of these solutions illustrate the manner in which architects and contractors can work together to innovate, but the construction process itself may best demonstrate the potential of such collaborative teams. The contractor felt confident of their ability to execute the solution, but it was one that required significant effort and the implementation of new processes. In fact, the most remarkable reflection of the contractor's sophistication, the lift-up itself, was not developed until after the team won the competition.

Somehow, the structure had to be built in a way that was not only safe, but affordable. The ring truss was an ideal solution aesthetically, structurally and in terms of illumination. However, it was 128 meters (420 feet) in diameter at its widest point, infilled with "honey-comb glass" panels weighing 5 tons each. To accommodate a range of sports, the base of the truss is 21.5 meters (70 feet) above the ground. Fujita deemed assembling the glass panels and the truss in place unsafe; for aesthetic and structural reasons, it is around 20 meters (64 feet) from the base to the top of the truss – over 41.5 meters (134 feet) from the ground to the top of the truss. This is too high to use many cranes to move the toplight panels into place at the top of the truss – although using cranes is a conventional approach to large-scale assembly on Japanese construction sites. Instead, Fujita decided to fabricate the ring truss and panels on the ground and then lift the entire assembly into place, in spite of the considerable weight and size of the construction. In seismically active Japan, this was an audacious idea, and the engineers relied on the most advanced technologies, including braking the jacking system with technology developed by NASA. They further simplified their task by breaking down the ring truss into units; they built these in sixteen sections weighing between 37 and 44 tons each.

By using a lift-up system, the contractors were able to fabricate these large components on the ground, reducing the danger to workers and requiring less expensive cranes. The construction team developed a small "factory" for the truss, with an integrated support structure and rain protection, rotating it from one segment of the ring truss around to the next. Crane-based assembly, dropping the panel components into the ring, also allowed speedier

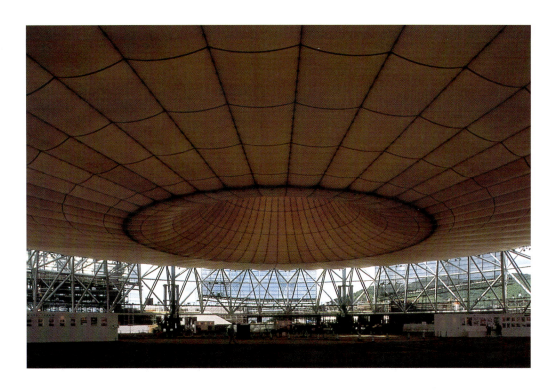

6.7 & 6.8
Interior, Kumamoto Dome, before and after lift-up.

construction – another competition requirement, because an international tournament had been scheduled only two years and three months after the conclusion of the competition. Construction of the stadium, with a total floor area of 26,938 square meters (almost 290,000 square feet), took twenty-one months, from June 1995 to March 1997. Some additional work followed during the three months after the tournament.

The double-skin roof was attached to the ring truss and inflated, then the whole structure lifted into place. Lifting a roof into place had been tried in the construction of a small building in Osaka. The firm responsible for engineering the effort, Miyaji Construction, also used a "push up" system on smaller buildings, but this was generally described by the press as the first large-scale implementation of the lift-up system. They sent only one representative to supervise the process, who supervised Fujita employees. Contractors value the approach because of its safety and cost effectiveness on large-scale projects; others have explored related lifting or push-up technologies, such as sophisticated versions of lift slab construction or self-climbing concrete pouring machinery. More recent systems raise structures into place in a matter of days, but the team at Kumamoto chose a longer period in part to allow differential settlement to be addressed during the lift-up process. Over a three-week period in July and August of 1996, computer-coordinated balancing systems controlling eight jacking mechanisms raised the assembly about 7.5 feet per day. The system included a set of two cross bars, which in turn were inserted through components that made up a central, temporary column, built up in units. Once the ring and the column cluster were firmly linked, this central support was removed. This combination of permanent and temporary structure offered significant savings.

Several years ago, Fumio Hasegawa of Shimizu Construction, looking at the context for practice in his country, said:

> It has become difficult to boost orders merely by building structures according to design and time schedule demanded by the client, and only those construction companies capable of offering new technologies and services through research and development will continue to exist.[26]

This was clearly the case with the Park Dome: the competition teams were initially paired to assure technological sophistication and the time period for construction was ambitious. Nonetheless, the design team took the time for extensive wind tunnel testing, designing the roof for 500-year winds, and also built a 1/10 scale model of the project for weight testing. Lamentably, even with these efforts, Kumamoto Dome also demonstrates how contractors and architects, under pressure to innovate, can find the complexity of the problems they take on and the speed at which they must be resolved too great a challenge. Two years after construction of the Kumamoto Dome ended, a particularly powerful typhoon struck the area. There was extensive damage to the building. After the storm passed, the roof lay in tatters, and shards from shattered polycarbonate doors and the honeycomb glass toplights covered the site. The typhoon damaged other buildings in the area, but none as severely as the Park Dome.

An investigative team reviewed the reasons for the failure and attempted to determine whether the designers were at fault. It decided they were not. Instead, they blamed the failure on an accumulation of unforeseeable events: a particularly powerful storm, a door blown open that allowed unusually high stresses from winds to be applied simultaneously to the top and bottom layers of the roof, and a power failure that prevented fans from compensating for these pressures within the roof structure. A representative from Fujita noted that the contractor did a variety of simulations and calculations to consider possible damage from internal air pressure failure and high winds, but that none of these had included a scenario where wind forces exerted pressure at both the top and bottom of the structure because of an open door or window – a surprisingly frank statement that probably would never have been published in the United States.[27]

The national government, based on these reports, released over 1.5 billion yen (about $14 million at the time) in disaster relief funds for repairs to the building. Notably, however, these funds did not cover the costs of many repairs recommended by the review board: reinforcing door and window locks, building a battery-based back-up for fan systems to maintain air pressure in the interior of the double-skinned roof structure, improving monitoring equipment, and improving the strength of the fabric, glass and polycarbonate. Funds for this work were unnecessary. The contractor, Fujita, had already made it clear to the prefecture that it would bear these costs. Park Dome Kumamoto's architect, Tei'ichi Takahashi, also continues to work with the prefecture. He succeeded Isozaki as commissioner, and selects designers for public works projects awarded as part of Kumamoto ArtPolis. (Takahashi is, in fact, credited with greater attention to public outreach and renewed popular support for ArtPolis in the community.) The building, too, is heavily used and well liked, in spite of its trying history.

To a certain extent failures like this one are an inevitable result of the constant pressure on architects and contractors to push beyond known technologies. Today, similar problems hold true in Britain as well: the Norman Foster-designed Millennium Bridge across the Thames was closed almost immediately after opening, to allow for structural adjustments expected to take months, and flaws have been revealed at the Millennium Dome and London Eye. There is no question that both Takahashi and Fujita got a black eye in this venture – and yet, because Fujita has stepped in to resolve the damage, this is a temporary setback that can be overcome through successes elsewhere. Not all contractor–architect alliances end like the Park Dome – and only some projects demand such a high level of experimentation. The Dome demonstrates the degree to which architects can work with contractors – and, in its failure, suggests how teams handle the risk associated with innovation.

---

1 N. Turner, "Japanese Sense and Sensibility," *World Architecture*, vol. 60, November 1997, p. 39.
2 *Kensetsu Hakushō, Heisei 11 Nen [Construction White Paper, 1999]*, Tokyo, Ōkurashō Insatsu Kyoku [Ministry of Finance Printing Office], 1999, p. 505.
3 NIST [National Institute of Standards and Technology], *Innovation in the Japanese Construction Industry: A 1995 Appraisal*, Washington, DC, US Government Printing Office, 1996, p. 19.
4 In 1997, Kajima was ranked third, Taisei was ranked fourth, Shimizu fifth, Takenaka seventh and Obayashi eighth, by sales. The ninth largest contractor in the world by sales volume was Sekisui House; sales were slightly inflated by Japanese private demand for housing construction to begin prior to the application of a 3 per cent sales tax. These are reported in *Industrial Groupings in Japan, 13th edition*. Tokyo, Brown and Company, 1999.
5 F. Matsushita, *Design and Construction Practice in Japan: A Practical Guide*, Tokyo, Kaibunsha Ltd., 1994, p. 23.

6. Annual construction figures are taken from *Kensetsu Sōgō Tōkei Nendo Hō, Heisei Jū Nendo*, Tokyo, Kensetsushō Keizaikyoku Chōsa Jōhōka, 1999. Revenue for the construction firms was determined using published annual revenues and the ratio of building to total sales, as published in *Kaisha Shikihō, 2000 Nen I Shū: Shinharugō* [Company Quarterly 2000, 1st Quarter: Spring], Tokyo, Tōyō Keizai Shuppan, 2000.
7. Y. Makino, "Massive Debt Burdens Contractor," *Nikkei Weekly*, 10 July 2000.
8. Y. Hippoh, *The Construction Industry in Japan: A Survey*, Asian Productivity Organization, n.d. (c. 1983), p. 274.
9. T. Muramatsu, "History of the Building Design Department of Takenaka Komuten," *Takenaka Komuten Sekkeibu* [Building Design Department of Takenaka Komuten], Tokyo, Shinkenchiku Sha, 1987, p. 33.
10. Matsushita, *Design and Construction Practice in Japan,* p. 85.
11. "*Kenchikushi no Ikiru Michi* [The Road for Licensed Architects' Existence]," *Nikkei A-kitekuchua* [Nikkei Architecture], no. 666, 15 May 2000, p. 105.
12. Muramatsu, "History of the Building Design Department of Takenaka Komuten," p. 33.
13. "*Kenchikushi no Ikiru Michi* [The Road for Licensed Architects' Existence]," p. 105.
14. Matsushita, *Design and Construction Practice in Japan*, p. 179. W. Coxe and M. Hayden, "UIA Project Work Group: Trends in Private Practice. Report from Japan," unpublished report dated 20 March 1993, p. 3, states that about 40 per cent of architectural design is done as part of design-build packages by contractors.
15. Matsushita, *Design and Construction Practice in Japan*, p. 65.
16. S. M. Levy, *Japanese Construction: An American Perspective*, New York, Van Nostrand Reinhold, 1990, p. 4.
17. K. Kurokawa, *New Wave Japanese Architecture*, London, Academy Editions, 1993, p. 13.
18. Liker, et al., "Integrating Suppliers into Fast-Cycle Product Development," in J. K. Liker, J. E. Ettlie, and J. C. Campbell, eds., *Engineered in Japan: Japanese Technology Management Practices*, New York and Oxford, Oxford University Press, 1995, pp. 166–7.
19. Carol Mancke, in reviewing an earlier version of this text, noted that she was invited to the sixth annual anniversary party for those involved in the design and construction of a large hall in Yokohama. Invitees include the contractor's site supervisor, the architect's staff, Ministry of Construction officials, some subcontractors, and even workmen.
20. UK statistics, see S. Ganeson, G. Hall, and Y. H. Chiang, *Construction in Hong Kong: Issues in Labour Supply and Technology Transfer*, Aldershot, Avebury, 1996, p. 69. US statistics are from *Building Design & Construction*, vol. 39, no. 97, July 1998, p. 11.
21. C. Arnison, "An Introduction to the Design/Build Method," in T. Muir and B. Rance, eds, *Collaborative Practice in the Built Environment*, London, E & FN Spon, 1995, p. 86.
22. "New Wiring," *The Economist*, vol. 354, no. 8153, 15 January 2000, pp. 68–9.
23. R. Gutman, *Architectural Practice: A Critical View*, Princeton, Princeton University Press, 1988, p. 42.
24. Y. Kanebako, "*Saikin no Wadaisaku wo Megutte* [Going through Recently Topical Works]" *Kenchiku Tokyo*, February 1998, pp. 12–13. My translation.
25. "*Pāku Dōmu Kumamoto ga Kansei Shite* [Completion of Park Dome Kumamoto]" *Compe & Contest*, May 1998, no. 58, p. 12.
26. F. Hasegawa and the Shimizu Group, *Built by Japan: Competitive Strategies of the Japanese Construction Industry*, New York, Wiley, 1988, p. 160.
27. A summation of the damage to the dome and the report on the reasons for failure can be reviewed in "*Taifū de Kūki Maku Kōzō no Jakuten ga Rotei* [A Weakness in an Air-Membrane Structure is Exposed by Typhoon]," *Nikkei A-kitekuchua* [Nikkei Architecture], no. 664, 17 April 2000, pp. 90–3.

Selecting subcontractors

Also appealing to my particular tastes is the combination between the amazing finesse of certain details and then the terrible air conditioning parts sticking out of it, all with an extraordinary collage of the extremely refined and the silly, the inventive and the kind of "My God, how did it get like that?"[1]

(Peter Cook)

Architects visiting Japan often notice that subcontracting yields variable results. This is because the relationships between firms vary from tight, on-going alliances to one-time business dealings, and the nature of the relationship will have a great deal of impact on quality, cost and even a firm's willingness to accept risk.

The word *keiretsu* has become notorious in the West, but it simply refers to grouped corporate alliances, both those that involve subcontractors and others. Some of these relationships are "horizontal," meaning they happen between companies of similar size or playing similar roles within their industries. Some *keiretsu* are unofficial alliances, and their numbers vary widely in surveys. Others are defined by corporate ties, e.g., cross-holding stocks. There is a great deal of debate over whether these coalitions affect day-to-day operations; most economists and business scholars believe that horizontal relationships have less significance today than they did in the past. However, it is still true that members make a commitment to information sharing and to at least modest support for the value of other member firms' stocks. Banks in the *keiretsu* will also lend more generously. Until banks forgave Kumagai over 450 billion yen in debt, a whopping 70 per cent of its debt was carried by Sumitomo Bank and 11 per cent was carried by Sumitomo Trust, both part of the same *keiretsu* as Kumagai. These connections may also cause a bank or trading company to offer lower costs on loans and supplies. Other members of the *keiretsu* may be inclined to turn directly to a general contractor for design and construction, rather than pursuing competitive bidding. Occasionally, architects may find a client encouraging them to use a certain component because of the relationship between client and supplier. Clients are also more willing to allow an architect to use new or experimental products if these are being produced by other corporate members of the *keiretsu*, since they can assume that any problems that emerge will be resolved, in light of other on-going ties.

In Japan, the largest of these horizontal *keiretsu* are reinforced by loosely organized presidents' clubs, bringing together the presidents of banks, trading companies and other major corporations in monthly meetings. Presidents' clubs include three major contractors: Taisei, Obayashi and Shimizu. Two of the six largest contractors are not in these clubs, but Kajima and Kumagai have looser links to *keiretsu* organizations. Notably, Takenaka Komuten, which has shown the greatest difficulty weathering the current recession – in spite of a reputation for the high quality of its work – is not generally regarded as being part of a *keiretsu* – a point I will return to below.

Other kinds of *keiretsu* also exist. Most important within the construction industry are vertical coalitions, where a contractor, fabricator or supplier orders repeatedly from the same subcontractors or parts suppliers. These alliances are sometimes reinforced with price breaks, greater efforts at quality control to maintain the relationship, cross-training and other kinds of support between firms – all of which can be found between frequent trading partners in other nations as well. Corporate alliances seem to be equally prevalent in Europe, and far less so in the United States, where a Congressional Budget Office study on collaborative linkages in the US found that, "Direct approaches to suppliers . . . are against company rules."[2] The Fluor Corporation, however, stands as one example of a successful vertical *keiretsu* within the US construction industry. Japanese coalitions, nonetheless, seem to be more institutionalized and firms act with greater awareness of the benefits of alliances.

In spite of the fact that there are formal structures and many published reports on corporate affiliations in Japan, the precise numbers of firms in each group are difficult to establish. This is because the vertical *keiretsu* involve not only subsidiaries and affiliates, but also companies where there is no ownership, but simply an on-going demand. Further, since the cluster of firms may extend several tiers, those at the lower levels of the family may be unaware of their connections to the parent firm. Reported figures for vertical alliances linked to Taisei, Shimizu, Obayashi and Kajima range from as low as 21 firms to "over a hundred" – both figures given for the Shimizu *keiretsu*.[3] These allied firms include steel fabricators, concrete suppliers, precasters, formwork installers, equipment leasing firms (including both construction and the office equipment required for site offices), furniture production offices, design firms, real estate offices, panelized housing builders and specialty contractors. Suppliers will also have their own *keiretsu* networks, especially in basic industries such as glass, cement and steel. Very often, these are small companies, which can offer only regional support. Some do not even have any employees – companies sometimes invest in small firms started by retiring employees, and it is unclear if these investments are intended to yield a profit or are simply a golden parachute.

Because lay-offs are still uncommon and mid-career employment changes are rare, general contractors in Japan use subcontracting to address employment fluctuations, and they will tend towards on-going relationships with a higher level of trust. Thus, there is a greater reliance on subcontracting in the Japanese construction industry than in other nations. Although subcontracting costs are potentially higher, inflexibilities in the Japanese labor market allow subcontractors to pay lower wages, so subcontracting is not as expensive as it would be in a more flexible labor market. The problem with this structure is that not only wages but also the potential quality of labor declines in the lower tiers. Sub-subcontractors, extending even four or five layers, are not uncommon; some of these lower tier companies may not be licensed and frequently exploit day labor. Even among established and licensed entities, many subcontractors are so small that the question of wages versus profit is sometimes moot. In 1993, 37 per cent of the 515,000 "contractors" licensed in Japan were individuals and an additional 15 per cent were two-person operations; all would normally operate as subcontractors.[4] Together, these one- or two-person operations account for over half of all licensed contractors in Japan.

There is a specific licensing category for contractors allowed to subcontract work worth over 10 million yen; these firms are legally responsible for supporting and nurturing their subcontractors.[5] Western observers are inclined to take the stance that bonds with subcontractors are more sentimental than pragmatic and that restructuring is necessary. Critics of these kinds of alliances tend to fall into two camps, raising concerns about the inefficiencies of non-competitive alliances – such as lower pricing – or noting that costs often shift to "captive" subcontractors. In fact, there are advantages and disadvantages to both sides in these relationships, and it is difficult to claim that *keiretsu* are inherently bad or beneficial. It is valuable, however, to be aware of how these differences affect practice.

THE BENEFITS OF OLIGOPOLY

Bennett Harrison notes, "One thing on which there is general agreement among scholars and business analysts studying the Japanese *keiretsu* is that so long as markets place a premium on quality and (therefore) on the ability to coordinate within complex systems, *keiretsu*-like big firm-led production networks will continue to have a significant competitive advantage."[6] Some subcontractors can find themselves with as much as 70 or 80 per cent of their revenues coming from one corporate organization. While dependence varies within different sectors of the industry, one report also noted that 50 per cent of electrical subcontractors' work "derives from a continuing alliance."[7] In such cases, subcontractors succeed only if the upstream contractor continues to utilize them, and this places an emphasis on the quality of work and a willingness to work collaboratively. These high standards benefit the architect but are potentially onerous for subcontractors. *Keiretsu* ties can also assure that subcontractors place a greater emphasis on responsiveness and speed – clearly two areas that are of special concern in the construction industry. Finally, when each project essentially brings a new set

7.1
Subcontractors desiring on-going relationships with leading contractors will offer higher care in the work they do. This man hand-sanded the exposed face of several thousand concrete columns for Yamamoto Riken's Saitama University.

of demands and a new context for construction, using a consistent set of subcontractors who are able to learn how to coordinate with the contractor has clear benefits.

Contractors also have the power to demand higher technical performance from their subcontractors, although this can require investments from the upstream organization. Essentially, the subcontractor is able to take on the risks involved in purchasing new equipment or supporting additional training because corporate affiliations offer some assurance of on-going demand. In such relationships contractors and consultants can confidently transfer some aspects of design decision-making to the subcontractor, a point I further develop in my subsequent sections on crafters and fabricators. One concern voiced regarding this system is that over time the contractor becomes dependent on the flexibility and special skills possessed by small firms, while subcontractors become captive. Both sides develop a greater dependence on organizations beyond their control.

Such dependency, however, is also the reason that banks and the Japanese government have been reluctant to place too much pressure on Japan's construction companies, in spite of their recent, sizable debts. If one of the "Big Five" contractors were to go bankrupt, it would not only be the contractor itself, but also a significant cluster of smaller subcontractors and suppliers that would fail. The potential impact on employment is hair-raising. By some estimates, the construction industry is linked, directly or indirectly, to as much as 20 per cent of the working population. This is the reason that, in a 1994 book called *Keiretsu*, Ken'ichi Miyashita and David Russell note,

> There is a well-known adage in business circles . . . "Japanese companies do not go bankrupt." Of course, this is nonsense. Many thousands of companies fail every year, but almost 100 percent of them are smaller firms . . . What the phrase means is that big, important companies do not fail.[8]

Today, even this explanation is no longer entirely true. It is, however, true that firms heading *keiretsu* are less vulnerable. There are clear advantages to being a part of the convoy, but dependency also carries conditions.

In his studies of corporate alliances in Japan published in 1992, Michael Gerlach shows that "the proportion of transactions taking place with firms in the same group is over ten times higher than average with firms in other groups."[9] Client firms who are part of a *keiretsu* will tend to purchase from members of the same group even where costs are higher. As a result of such ties, one rogue steel supplier, who noted that although his prices were about 50 per cent lower than materials supplied by the large steelmakers, struggled to find buyers because he was not part of a *keiretsu*.[10] On the other side, contractors are often interested in purchasing cheaper, imported materials, but feel that dependence on corporate alliances prevents their use. The costs of standardized or common services and goods make up for the higher levels of service and risk the subcontractor or fabricator takes on elsewhere. Because this standardized work otherwise balances the costs of special services, contractors will try to break out low-cost work into separate contracts for allied firms. Architects frequently complain that they have developed a set of specialty components or related interiors working with only one manufacturer, only to have those that have the potential to be less expensive peeled off and subbed out to a different, and potentially unsatisfactory company.

Contractors in joint venture relationships are sometimes able to draw on the advantages of *keiretsu* relationships without the responsibilities. In one project I studied, for instance, two of the "Big Five" contractors were building separate areas of a project. A furniture supplier had *keiretsu* ties with one, and that contractor was more flexible about cost estimates because of these ties. However, when it became clear that the non-allied contractor was inclined to take a tough position in negotiations, the *keiretsu* contractor was happy to allow them to negotiate a lower price for materials used in the entire project.

Some scholars believe that corporate alliances assure contractors consistently lower costs, although my example suggests that is not always the case. Even more interestingly, in some markets, costs have been so mutable as to be unpredictable even following a building's completion; until the mid 1990s flat glass makers were pricing their materials up to one year after delivery. It would be more fair to say that where contractors discover a significant cost difference between prices quoted between allied firms and those outside the *keiretsu*, they are in a position to demand adjustments from allied companies. Furthermore, at the bid stage, contractors will sometimes set the price on special construction, and it is the subcontractor's responsibility to work within this price. On the other hand, subcontractors do benefit from the greater certainty of an ongoing relationship and can sometimes implement production economies on this basis, allowing them to reduce costs. Architects, however, are at a distinct disadvantage if they hope to impact costs, since so much depends on factors beyond their control. It is frequently impossible to make credible predictions in Japan's construction market.

Neoclassical economists argue that government protection for oligopolies reduces pressure to modernize, to engage in research and development, or to improve the quality of materials produced. In short, market demand forces manufacturers to behave competitively. However, although many of Japan's markets are oligopolies, modernization, research, development and quality enhancement remain important policy choices. This is in part because the Japanese government maintains incentive programs intended to counter inefficiencies, promoting the introduction of new technologies, upgraded facilities and higher levels of research and development than might otherwise exist. More significantly, both the contractors and suppliers are often operating in oligopolies. A limited number of dominant agents directing demand keeps this system in balance. As Jeffery Liker notes,

> Suppliers would not be willing to invest the amount required, give in to customers' demands for aggressive target prices, and respond to the pressures of aggressive development cycles if the customers could choose from a large group of competitors at any time.[11]

Most economists agree that in Japan's basic materials markets, especially in those crucial to the construction industry such as concrete, steel, aluminum, ceramics and pane glass, there are clear oligopolies, with at least 90 per cent of the market dominated by five or fewer firms and where international competition is insignificant.[12] Companies are each individually large enough to have an impact on the market, but small enough not to have monopoly control, although corporations most often form cartels. Even outside *keiretsu* alliances, the limited number of major contractors, suppliers and fabricators in the construction industry creates some important differences in how firms work together. In this context, repeat opportunities for firms to work together are sometimes deliberate and sometimes simply a matter of coincidence, because of the small number of organizations in the industry.

Furthermore, many of the larger firms associate with allied subcontractors that make up the remaining "competition." The larger facilities are generally highly efficient, automated plants supplying standardized products, whereas older subsidiary plants work in a crafts tradition. The small companies will often supply the bulk of their output to the parent company, primarily making materials that require greater effort or short, expeditionary runs. Although there is a degree of flexibility in the automated plants, most often architects find that the greatest flexibility is in the more primitive facilities. Nonetheless, they access these through the larger companies; this further encourages market concentration. The potential for these groups to manipulate the market is countered by the fact that their demand is also defined by oligopolies, most importantly the dominance of Japan's largest general contractors.

The quality of design may benefit in some ways from this extreme behavior. I found that customization was more evident in declining – and thus diversifying – industries and almost non-existent in industries such as paper or plastics, which were economically more robust

7.2
Staff representing the architect, contractor and subcontractor struggle with a problem.

and had a broader customer base. Demand for many construction materials has been affected by the bursting of Japan's speculative Bubble and the consequent drop in construction orders, and also by a drop in domestic automobile production, which has reduced demands for steel and glass. It has been a roller coaster ride. From 1984 to 1989, the Japanese construction market expanded 27 per cent.[13] More recently, construction orders dropped for eleven consecutive months in 1997 and 1998, and dropped by 21.3 per cent in one month, November 1998.[14] This has made producers more aggressive about pursuing new markets; the excess capital in manufacturing today has made fabricators hungry enough to be open to the riskier work associated with increased innovation.

Notably, one of the chief characteristics of corporate ties is stability. Growth rates, profits and losses are all less variable within keiretsu organizations.[15] This is why it is not surprising that Takenaka, with no such ties, has seen the greatest drop-off in orders during the current recession, although as I note later, the contractor's reluctance to pursue public works contracts has also had an important impact. Parent companies share profits, finance equipment purchases and engage in training for favored subcontractors in good times. In short recessionary periods, the leading firms will also support members of keiretsu by financing debt, acting as a guarantor or by advancing payments. Equipment leasing, technical guidance, advance warning about shifts in the parent firm's activities and personnel exchange can also allow subcontractors to be more competitive in downturns, when all companies in the alliance – but especially those in lower tiers – are expected to share in cost-cutting. This may be one of the strongest reasons that there has been relatively slow change in the construction industry, in spite of the severity of today's economic slump. Its length, however, has exhausted conventional support and less valuable subcontractors are a growing burden, increasing numbers cut from coalitions. Change, although slow, does exist.

Keiretsu ties also offer an advantage in reorganizations of the construction team. The elasticity embodied in the use of subcontracting allows new technologies to be easily drawn into organizations. Thus, ship- and bridge-building organizations are much more integrated into the Japanese construction industry than they are elsewhere. The contractor can also access new materials, such as ceramics, or new construction approaches, such as automated concrete pours, while avoiding much of the risk of development or the costs associated with less-than-frequent use.

One scholar, Donna Doane, notes that the stability of these groupings allows time for suppliers of indigenous technologies to adjust to new demands and offer innovations that respond to modern technologies.[16] This fits with my observations on the continuing use of handicraft in the construction sector. In areas such as carpentry or roof tile production, where a sufficient background market remains, demand may continue to exist, but be inadequate to maintain a healthy pool of subcontractors or crafters. With the support of upstream contractors (in economically comfortable periods), crafters can develop approaches compatible with market needs. When keiretsu support becomes insufficient to maintain special crafts expertise, architects and contractors respond differently. As I noted earlier, contractors will encourage retraining and retooling, and often will explore new materials or techniques that can adequately replace the original craft. Architects, on the other hand, value the responsive character of the craft industry. Many actively support crafts through design decisions, recognizing that they will not otherwise be able to draw on these skills in the future.

1. "Learning from Tokyo: Academy International Forum" *AD, Architectural Design*, Japanese Architecture III, no. 107, 1994, p. 13.
2. As quoted in B. Harrison, *Lean and Mean: the Changing Landscape of Corporate Power in the Age of Flexibility*, New York and London: The Guilford Press, 1994, p. 181.
3. Reports consulted included *Tōyō Keizai: Nihon no Kigyō Gurūpu 2000 [Asian Economy: Japan's Industrial Groupings 2000]*, Tokyo, Tōyō Keizai Shuppan, 2000; *1999 Industrial Groupings in Japan, 13th edition: the Anatomy of Keiretsu*, Tokyo: Brown and Company, 1999, and *Kogaisha, Kanren-gaisha Sōran: Keiretsu no Kenkyū*. [Small companies, Allied Company Survey: Keiretsu Research], Tokyo, Keizai Chosa Kyokai, 1990.
4. *Japan Almanac 1994*, Tokyo, Asahi Shimbun Sha, 1993, p. 158.
5. Although there is a tendency to overstate Japan's case, a good discussion of the types of contractors defined by the Japanese Ministry of Construction can be found in Levy, *Japanese Construction: An American Perspective*, New York, Van Nostrand Reinhold, 1990, pp. 69–71.
6. Harrison, *Lean and Mean*, p. 162.
7. NIST [National Institute of Standards and Technology], *Innovation in the Japanese Construction Industry: A 1995 Appraisal*, Washington, DC, US Government Printing Office, 1996, p. 11.
8. K. Miyashita and D. Russell, *Keiretsu: Inside the Hidden Japanese Conglomerates*, New York, McGraw-Hill, Inc., 1994, p. 51.
9. M. Gerlach, *Alliance Capitalism: The Social Organization of Japanese Business*, Berkeley, Los Angeles and London, University of California Press, 1992, p. xvii.
10. J. Sterngold, "Exclusive Price Cuts Intrigue Japan," *New York Times*, 9 November 1994, p. C1.
11. J. K. Liker, R. R. Kamath, S. Nazli Wasti, and M. Nagamachi, "Integrating Suppliers into Fast-Cycle Product Development," J. K. Liker, J. E. Ettlie, and J. C. Campbell, eds., *Engineered in Japan: Japanese Technology Management Practices*, New York and Oxford, Oxford University Press, 1995, p. 182.

12 See T. J. Pempel, *Regime Shift: Comparative Dynamics of the Japanese Political Economy*, Ithaca and London, Cornell University Press, 1998 or M. Tilton, *Restrained Trade: Cartels in Japan's Basic Materials Industries*, Ithaca, Cornell University Press, 1996. This serves as a major point in each of the books cited.
13 B. Woodall, *Japan Under Construction: Corruption, Politics and Public Works*, Berkeley and Los Angeles, University of California Press, 1996, p. 29.
14 A. Harney, "Japan Sees Fall in Construction Orders Again," *Financial Times*, 7 January 1998, p. 6.
15 K. Miyashita and D. Russell, *Keiretsu: Inside the Hidden Japanese Conglomerates*, New York, McGraw-Hill, Inc., 1994, p. 197.
16 D. Doane, *Cooperation, Technology, and Japanese Development: Indigenous Knowledge, the Power of Networks, and the State*, Boulder, Colorado, Westview Press, 1998, p. 22.

Two paths to customization

The mix of subcontractors and suppliers selected in response to a specific building project offers a high degree of specialization. Post-fordist manufacturing has begun to directly supplant craft – not only for basic production needs, but also in customization. Architects have learned how to work with crafters, but through these alliances, they have also discovered the most effective way to exploit the opportunities offered by contemporary manufacturing equipment.

ARCHITECTS AND CRAFT

> Detailing was born when craftsmanship died.[1]
>
> (Edward R. Ford)

Where architects simply rely on conventional approaches to including handicraft in a building, they halt market erosion. They may not, though, help crafters to establish practices that are successful adaptations for contemporary demand. Rather, by only using details and materials that are conventional, the profession concentrates on a few accepted practices and allows many crafts skills to atrophy. This in turn causes the crafters to neglect overall versatility. However, some Japanese designers do mirror the traditional role of a connoisseur, by creating new challenges to crafters in the context of on-going collaborations. Over time, and because of the work of these architects, some crafters have also come to target architects in their work.

In my historical discussion, I noted conditions that encourage crafts to flourish in an economy. Today, many of these circumstances no longer survive – and certainly many people would consider these economic changes to be for the better, even if they have a negative effect on construction practices. Japanese society is no longer composed of a small elite and a large laboring population; since World War II there is instead a broad middle class. By international standards, this middle class is wealthy – but, as I noted earlier, connoisseurship requires both wealth and judgment. Consumers develop an understanding of the quality and opportunities of craft through interactions with crafters; opportunities for these interactions dwindled as the purchase of manufactured goods increased. Although the middle classes may not be discriminating, they support a diffuse, continuing acceptance of traditional craft in houses and leisure facilities. Trade organizations in Japan have reacted to the disappearance of a connoisseur class by attempting to educate middle-class consumers and foreign tourists. Many of these organizations employ crafters to demonstrate their work in shows and exhibitions. This strategy can enrich the trades by increasing opportunities for inexperienced apprentices to practice routine, basic skills. Yet as a strategy for maintaining a market, the approach seems ineffective.

Architects have become the chief connoisseurs of construction-related craft. In Japan, there is a more liberal professional attitude towards incorporating traditional materials or forms into contemporary buildings. Japanese architects whose work is decidedly modern feel comfortable employing roof tile, plaster or tatami, and a more catholic professional community allows them to do so without endorsing craft as an on-going focus in their designs.

Even while architects may play some role in replacing a connoisseur class, changes in class structure still have a profound impact on craft trades because poverty has declined. Most of the population chooses work that is, in comparison with crafts, more profitable, less interminable, and where expertise is not so elusive. Today, most crafters tend to be people who trained around World War II. Many are approaching old age and few young people are taking their place.

The different responses by architects, crafters and the construction industry to the effect of these changes are not coordinated. Established crafters are most concerned with the values they consider core to their traditions: skill and versatility. They tend to see dwindling demand as their most important problem, particularly because a more limited and conventional market relates to an acceptance of lower skills and unchallenging production.

The construction companies focus on assuring a steady labor supply well into the future. Because of shifts in education, apprentices do not take on a trade until they are in their late teens or early twenties – a time when people are impatient to begin families and establish independence. They naturally have a strong inclination towards shorter training and expect higher pay even in the early stages of their apprenticeship, when productivity is very low. The national government and large contractors have responded with efforts to improve apprenticeship. Wages are becoming competitive because of these efforts. Subsidized vocational programs now teach basic skills, shifting the costs of training from small workshops to the industry as a whole.

Architects usually work from a critical position, celebrating the value of individual contributions to a whole or drawing on craft because of an interest in materiality. Some Japanese designers encourage artisans to evolve through on-going ties to specific crafters. In this way, the architects promote both demand and flexible application of skills. To effectively work in collaboration requires trust, long-term knowledge of a partner's ability, and an openness to diffused responsibility. Not surprisingly, one of the organizations most committed to such alliances is Team Zoo, which is itself a cooperative, including architects, landscape architects, planners, furniture makers and graphic designers. Established architects push craft; examples of traditional handicraft are frequent in Tadao Ando's and Arata Isozaki's work and have been successfully employed by many young, cutting-edge designers.

What kinds of crafts trades have architects in Japan been exploiting? As in North America, carpenters who are comfortable working collaboratively and flexibly are most common. This may be because the higher volume of wood used for both finishes and framing continues to support a range of skills and a healthier trade. Tatami mats are also frequently used because they are necessary in certain settings. In the next section, I discuss two craftsmen who have had a notable impact on contemporary architecture and represent other trades that have been encouraged by architects: Akira Kusumi, a plasterer who has worked on projects ranging from the replastering of the seventeenth-century Katsura Imperial Villa to Itsuko Hasegawa's award-winning Shonandai Culture Center, and Shuji Yamada, a tile maker allied with Team Zoo.

THE ARCHITECT AND CRAFTER IN ALLIANCE: SHONANDAI BUNKA CENTER

The design community, although not a historical source for craft demand, offers a strong alternative to the connoisseurs of yesterday. Many architects are clear on this point, and see the profession as responsible for on-going access to Japanese crafts. One example, a project by the architect Itsuko Hasegawa, demonstrates how integrating traditional crafts informs contemporary architectural design in Japan.

The Shonandai Culture Center, a small public facility in a bedroom suburb of Tokyo, was a competition-winning scheme designed by Hasegawa in 1989. During construction, she effectively incorporated both handiwork and manufactured customizations into the original design proposal. The overall effect has been to make the building more accessible to the community through the variety of individually executed details; children and older adults particularly appreciate the complex. The project remains unusual in Hasegawa's work. In subsequent designs, she moved away from customizations.

Hasegawa relied on the contributions of Shuji Yamada, a prominent ceramist, and Akira Kusumi, an award-winning plasterer. Yamada has aggressively developed new uses for materials used traditionally to make roof tiles, particularly focussing on creating paving for sidewalks and areas for light vehicular traffic. In an earlier work designed with Team Zoo, the Yoga Promenade in Tokyo, Yamada pressed household articles such as combs into tile surfaces and inscribed *haiku* poetry. In the Culture Center, Yamada made tiles stamped with animal and human footprints and shaped to fit in a stepped amphitheater. He had a hand in creating new tile shapes, working with Hasegawa to design the central element of the complex, a very effective artificial brook that runs through the plaza. At the brook's source, Yamada's tiles become building blocks embedded with children's

8.1
Shonandai Culture Center by Itsuko Hasegawa.

8.2 & 8.3
Shonandai Culture Center tile "river" designed with Shuji Yamada and concrete finish showing Akira Kusumi's input.

glass marbles. Further along the bed, they take on varying profiles to direct water much like stones in a stream. This was not a case of Yamada simply generating shapes developed by Hasegawa's staff. Rather, architect and crafter worked together to create materials that performed effectively. Yamada then took responsibility for execution within that framework.

Similarly, Akira Kusumi has an interest in developing new materials through a combination of traditional and contemporary technologies. He focusses on the composition of plaster-like materials and on how they might be manipulated or applied. At the Culture Center, Kusumi created new finish contours and walls embedded with pieces of tile, marbles and mirror. For the community, one of the most deeply meaningful gestures was a concrete finish that included some of the earth from the site. Kusumi brought knowledge and experience to the project, from an understanding of the potential for failure created by unusual materials in a mix, to novel ways of applying mortars to achieve unusual profiles. He was not directed by Hasegawa, who in any event did not yet have the experience to do so. Rather, Kusumi's expertise was engaged as the two discovered ways that the materials he understood could complement her architectural ideas. Kusumi's experiences in Germany, where he has taught at universities, and in Italy, where he sponsors an exchange between Japanese and Italian craftspeople, have led him to believe Japan enjoys a level of expertise unmatched in other industrialized nations. His own contributions demonstrate that the inclination to collaborate with architects in expanding this knowledge is also notable.

It is worth noting that the nature of the materials Kusumi and Yamada employ require different levels of collaboration. Yamada's tiles, an autonomous finish, required far less coordination than Kusumi's work in concrete.

The benefit of these collaborations is seen in the popularity of the complex. This is not only one of Hasegawa's best-known works, both at home and abroad, but it is also full of neighborhood children from early in the morning until quite late at night – even when the more conventional park adjacent to the site is empty. The tiles and plaster bring a human scale to the complex, by virtue of their inherent variations and also because of the playful range possible in handicrafts.

Hasegawa used the familiarity of traditional handicrafts and the accessibility of their production to encourage participatory design, and for a short while, she was Japan's most vocal advocate on the subject of public involvement in design. Her subsequent international popularity took her away from the office and site for long periods and called for less time-intensive approaches. In her recent Niigata Concert Hall, however, there are tentative signs that Hasegawa may be turning back towards the inclusion of craft and community participation in her work. Most critics would welcome this, as these techniques led to her greatest success.

Shonandai is also notable because it is one of the few buildings where traditional handicraft was successfully combined with manufactured customization, both organized to create an artificial rural landscape. A large sphere on the site is finished in silver and white aluminum to resemble a globe, and punched metal sheets on the site are cut into teardrops, clouds and other fanciful shapes. The roof-like pyramids used in the complex are also fabricated as varied but coordinated sets. These manufactured components successfully blend with the variations in crafted work, giving both a sense of unity and variety.

THE ARCHITECT AND INDUSTRY

In the twentieth century, manufacturing and construction are inevitably connected; this is because of the development of a system to produce cheap, standardized goods. Breaking down production processes into simple steps, achieved with the help of specialized machinery, slashed the costs of labor. For large batches, high equipment costs were also distributed, allowing for significant economies of scale. This manufacturing approach, called "Fordism" (after Henry Ford), was most popular in the United States. Fordism involved production characteristics that most Americans now consider inevitable in manufacturing; its basic ideas were also influential in architectural drawing production, housing construction and land development. Even today, Americans accept the following principles of Fordism as necessary in production:

- size or large quantities lead to greater economy;
- manufacturing must rely on specialized machinery – which can inhibit retooling and lead to production rigidity;
- managerial oversight of the assembly line is needed, because individual workers no longer grasp the larger complexities of the system;
- laborers do simple, repetitive activities, supervised by a small, privileged group of mostly white-collar workers;
- the skills learned by an individual worker are quickly acquired and easily become obsolete.

Fordism is most successful where the market is homogeneous and low cost is appreciated more than variety. In Europe and Japan, cultural values, educational opportunities, resources and technology all differed. Although Modernist intellectuals celebrated the potential benefits of universality, it was product differentiation, not standardization, that remained the norm. Systems of manufacturing in these communities, even where they seemed to imitate Fordism, were actually quite different as a result.

Beyond North America, approaches to manufacturing emerged that addressed the natural inefficiencies of Fordist models. Instead of inflexible machinery, the necessity of high inventories or the need for an extensive manager class to plan development, maintain systems and develop advertising to promote standardized output, the manufacturing systems in Europe and Asia took other paths. Most significantly, these markets remained small and there was less economic benefit to standardization. Still recovering from the devastation of World War II, these communities could not rely on the resources and capital necessary for frequent retooling or for stockpiling the material supplies needed to prevent unexpected production delays. Nor could they rely on a labor surplus, especially among people with technical educations. Instead, parallel assembly brought components together at the final stage, eliminating the need for large surpluses. Recently, economists began to recognize this approach, now commonly referred to as "post-fordism," as having advantages over Fordism, since it created opportunities for short production runs and experimentation.

Throughout the world, manufacturing is shifting from standardization and economies of scale to flexibility and economies of scope, using limited equipment to produce a range of products. Because these new systems evolved in very different production climates, there are important and notable differences between them.

"Post-fordist" systems of production, at least in Japan, are not new. Many academics date Japan's flexible production processes or their influences to the early seventeenth century.[2] During that period, Japan severely limited political and economic contact with the rest of the world, and the Japanese developed a different approach to industrial production. There was less concern for labor saving – in fact, governmental edicts of the time established programs intended to promote labor-intensive activities.

Japan then faced a very rapid industrialization in the mid-nineteenth century, essentially absorbing 400 years of Western technological development in only 150 years. Even today, some critics suggest that tariffs and other barriers to trade prevent economic factors from having full impact in Japan, propping up obsolete production facilities. According to this view, as barriers to trade fall, the older, inefficient production systems will disappear and many of today's opportunities for customization will be replaced by higher quality standardized goods.

A different explanation is that Japan has either sidestepped or developed beyond Fordist manufacturing approaches.[3] In this scenario, Japanese systems evolved from the work of Tai'ichi Ohno of Toyota, because of the need to maintain low inventories and longer use of highly adaptable equipment, while having longer-term commitments to individual workers. Responding to the failures of Fordism, newer production systems rely on general-purpose machinery run by skilled workers. In these systems, isolated segments of the assembly process allow the combination of segments used to be easily varied. Additionally, while some manufacturers or fabricators look little different from how they did thirty years ago, other small companies have access to advanced technologies, with the help of government and trade organizations. Thus, the Japanese system can respond quickly to new demands in the market because of the versatility built into production systems old and new.

Studies of Japanese manufacturing also have tended to focus on the importance of continuous improvement, especially through new high-tech and computerized processes. Most studies of Japanese construction will eventually refer to the use of robots, which range from programmable mechanisms that have greater strength or precision than humans, to equipment that has little or no innate intelligence. Robots are used for everything from concrete finishing and welding to sheet glass installation; on occasion, they are made especially for the particular needs of a project. However, these are a small part of the production landscape and much manufacturing is still relatively unsophisticated, relying on machines twenty years old (or more). Japanese manufacturers rely on flexible equipment to respond to changing needs. The production line is broken up into small steps, with older machines organized to allow for flexibility. With the small scale of many of these enterprises, a single machine or set of machines represents much of the investment in these businesses. Separate machinery is not only easier to retool; this adaptability becomes an opportunity for customization by the architect and design team. Thus, a tile, a railing, a corrugated panel or a window mullion can have a form that varies from others made on the same day. The process is potentially very simple: the manufacturer removes the customized piece from the production stream at key points, modifies it to fit the architect's specifications, and then returns it to the production stream; the processing and equipment does not require uniform shapes for conventional handling. In this way, the construction industry takes advantage of economies of scale for most production.

Some Japanese architects claim that standardized materials simply do not exist for many building components. Consumers and architectural clients accept the additional costs associated with specialization – which are relatively slight – because they see a benefit in a higher degree of particularity. Openness to such customization also allows Japanese suppliers to maintain a share of the market both at home and abroad without competing based on price. This encourages almost continuous product development as clients and architects bring new demands to producers – especially those architects I refer to as "lead users," who strive to anticipate future trends.

Japanese production occurs in a dual economy, defined by a few very large and many very small firms. In her book *The Technological Transformation of Japan: From the Seventeenth to the Twenty-first Century*, Tessa Morris-Suzuki demonstrates how the two levels of production systems in Japan work in tandem and supply different segments of the market. These two levels are the "center" (large-scale sophisticated production supported by governmental activities and major corporations) and the "periphery" (small, localized production).[4] These terms, although useful to someone who has observed Japan, are also misleading. The area she refers to as the periphery actually accounts for a sizable segment of production.

Over 50 per cent of Japan's factory workers labor in firms of less than a hundred workers.[5]

One of the modest and minor results of the greater number of small and medium-sized producers in the industry is that occasionally architects are commissioned to build something for these companies. Inevitably, the design team explores the possibilities of the materials and equipment these manufacturers supply. The best-known case of this is the small house at Kuwabara that Itsuko Hasegawa designed for a metals supplier. Her use of punched metal was published in journals throughout Asia and Europe, and quickly set off a craze for the material. Other examples are less well known beyond Japan's shores, but demonstrate that Hasegawa's design was not an isolated opportunity. Two that I have recently seen were a lovely glass box designed by the architect Makoto Takahashi, for Figula (a specialty glass supplier), and an office for a supplier of rubber hoses and tubing, where the partnership ADH (Yoko Kinoshita and Makoto Watanabe) cleverly exploited these tubes in handrails and an interesting set of screens and doors. A slightly earlier example is far better known: Ushida Findlay led the way in exploring the sinuous forms possible with computer-numeric controls, in their 1993 Truss•Wall•House, which was designed for the owner of a company that produced the internal structures for large-scale entertainment figures.

Small manufacturers share basic technology and may use customization as a way to segment the market. Even the flexibility established by size can be .the deciding reason for one producer being chosen over another. The silky concrete in Maki's Natori Performing Arts Center, for example, required white cement; to prevent any corruption by ordinary Portland cement, the plant was thoroughly cleaned and dedicated only to the Maki project. The small manufacturer of windows, metal screens or custom-made furniture responds to individual demands, often the result of close bonds, based on keiretsu ties, on-going relationships, or even old school friendships. In the current economy, this system continues to weaken. While keiretsu or neighborhood ties supported production earlier, the recession has reshaped the economy and reduced the power of these ties. Additionally, the cost differences between locally manufactured materials and components produced in standardized processes (especially goods produced overseas) continue to widen. One architect noted that although he has seen increased flexibility in production during the 1990s for many of the reasons I have explained, this was countered by tightened budgets. Therefore, he saw no net gains in flexibility for most architects, only industry leaders. It is likely that the slight but continuous erosion of the sectors served by small producers will continue and that the balance between customization and standardization will not noticeably shift.

IMPLICATIONS IN ARCHITECTURE

When standardized products remain unsatisfactory – which occurs often – architects in Japan customize. Because large corporations associate with small producers and use them as developing and testing grounds for new materials and products, small fabricators and the architects that work with them can even make use of the equipment or expertise found in larger companies. Architects working with larger companies are also passed on to small producers as their needs become better defined. In the Nagaoka Folly (also called Ten-Chi-Jin), Hajime Yatsuka had a very clear idea about the tile wall he hoped to develop; he wanted to achieve a gradation from deep red to a more purplish color. Initially, he also intended to use a relatively large size tile. In such cases, an architect will approach a large manufacturer, but may ultimately end up working with much smaller companies that are part of the keiretsu. The larger company fields out the less profitable, customized and craft production, while standardized tile shapes are made in a large, fully automated plant. In this case, two aspects of Yatsuka's design suggested the involvement of a smaller production facility: the size of the tiles and their color. As it became clear to the parent manufacturer that size was not as important as the color effects, Inax switched the plant where production would take place to one that could not work with larger materials but seemed most capable of achieving the desired color. This independent "craft tile" company supplied over 90 per cent of its product to Inax, which is Japan's largest tile producer. Two subsidiary plants made prototypes for the architect's review, at different stages in the development process. The one that was ultimately not used on this job did so at no cost to the project, or to Inax.

Staff in Fumihiko Maki's office have frequently mentioned to me that they will not customize if satisfactory materials are available. However, the opportunities to make adjustments may cause architects to be more exacting about their expectations. Maki's office, for example, sometimes uses a square tile with a shallow dome-shaped profile. The tile maker had six possible choices for white glazing, but in the course of developing the tiles, the staff rejected these colors in favor of a customized white glaze.

Diversification in the market is natural in the wealthy setting of a developed economy, as segments of the population demand greater individual satisfaction or accommodation of the needs of relatively small groups. Although for the most part manufactured products elsewhere are more often standardized, "manufactured customization" exists, too. However, with higher labor costs and less demand for customization, there is little motivation for customization among most architects or producers. "Lead users" exploit customization in several important ways. Most significantly, short production runs allow for niche marketing of technologies that better serve small, special needs populations. One excellent example of this kind of niche marketing is a toilet designed by Toto that tests urine for abnormalities such as high sugar content. Through daily monitoring, it may be possible for Japan's growing elderly population to remain at home and independent longer. Second, customization appeals to changing tastes. Some quirky architectural modifications are quickly apparent to the outside observer as signature elements: Arata Isozaki's "Marilyn curve" door pulls and chairs; the animal furniture found in work by Team Zoo; or the fractal geometries of Kisho Kurokawa's handrails. Third and less obvious (especially in the photographs which are the sole way many overseas architects know Japanese buildings), is the manner in which architects may reconsider relatively mundane problems, from the redesign of a drain pipe, a mullion or a wall tile, to the development of entirely new systems. Customization allows the architect to achieve a high degree of coordination between parts and to demand more refined detailing (e.g., using consistent spacing or modules) even when working with a number of independent manufacturers. This is the reason that Japanese architecture is widely perceived as polished and well detailed. Fourth, architects individually influence production, bringing new items to market by altering the form and composition of materials currently in use. The architect effectively moves to the beginning of the production process. With production flexibility, rapid delivery allows these new technologies to be tested in the market, without significant start-up costs. This "expeditionary" marketing permits manufacturers to respond quickly to evolving demands by the profession. In a well-known English language article, Fumihiko Maki has written about his team's development of a stainless steel roofing material for the gymnasium roof at Fujisawa. The material's rapid and widespread appropriation by other architects demonstrates how clearly Maki's interests reflected those of the profession.[6] Fifth, mass customization allows production to shift to the factory without compromising design decisions. Japanese architects find this not only reduces cost and accidents, but also enhances precision and quality control. The most obvious example of this is found in the use of CAD CAM equipment to cut heavy timber connections. In a tenth of the time a carpenter could produce these connections, a reasonable facsimile can be carved by a machine, based on shop drawings supplied directly by the architect. Finally, the speed of post-fordist systems allows for delivery that is more responsive. Decisions on major components such as elevators can be delayed to a point where coordination with other areas (such as interiors) is smoother. The

8.4
Fujisawa Gymnasium, by Fumihiko Maki. This area shows early use of the stainless steel roofing perfected elsewhere on the project.

timing also encourages designers to address construction at increasingly fine levels of detail. This shift from inventory storage to "just in time" deliveries indicates how the construction industry in Japan has already refashioned itself to mimic automobile manufacturing.

Customization is one of the reasons that manufacturers in Japan also produce numerous mock-ups for the construction industry, often at no cost and for relatively elementary components, through the use of flexibilities in production or in smaller shops geared to customization. I have visited dozens of fabricators and manufacturers, and almost without exception the facilities, no matter how modest, have included a set of smaller machines intended for building one-off and prototypical materials, with other areas set aside for testing.

Some of this is the result of public policies requiring unusual materials to be inspected at the fabricators before being shipped to the site, but much is also the result of common expectations in Japanese manufacturing circles. Some level of research and development is expected even at the smallest production facilities, and because research is rather loosely defined, client-driven innovations are easily rolled into the activities of these groups.

Mock-ups allow the manufacturer to fine-tune pieces for a specific project. Even where the architect or contractor has not required a mock-up, the manufacturer may sometimes decide it is wise to build one. These also allow architects and fabricators to begin to assess each other's capabilities and commitment to collaboration, sometimes identifying unex-

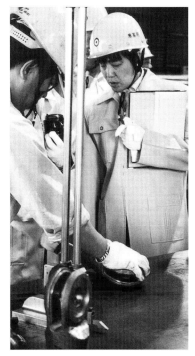

8.5
Yoko Kinoshita from ADH, inspecting structural connectors for a publicly funded project.

8.6
Makoto Watanabe, from the same firm, in a photograph documenting the inspection.

pected areas of disagreement. Even where architects choose a different manufacturer after investigating several, they learn how several manufacturers' strengths apply to their emerging interests and future work, because inspections often require multiple visits to the plant. During these visits, manufacturers will outline the ways that architects can modify specifications to reflect their needs, noting how staging or timing of different processes can affect the final results. As a JETRO publication geared toward promoting free trade noted, "For manufacturers of finishing (sic) materials and equipment, the provision of information to customers and designers is their most important sales activity."[7]

Small, widely read journals, among them *Kenchiku Chishiki* [Architecture Knowledge] and *Detail*, address alliances between architects and a wider range of constructors. *Detail* is very much in sympathy with the values architects bring to the table, but addresses how fabricators influence the work. A randomly selected issue, from October 1995, yields an article by the architect Hiroshi Naito, "Detailing Viewed from the Standpoint of Materials and Space-Form Relationship," with building sections illustrating an unusual concrete structure for the Sea Folk Museum. In other articles, attractive photographs and drawings illustrate inventive structures. Among these are: "Glass-box Observatory featuring Ultimate Transparency: Taniguchi and Associates" (on Taniguchi's Kasai Rinkai Visitors' Center, where the fire-resistant steel mullions play a structural role); "Heavy-weight Ceilings and Lightweight Floors for a Concert Hall: Arata Isozaki Atelier" (on Isozaki's competition-winning concert hall in Kyoto); and "Expressive Expansion Joint Design: Emilio Ambasz & Associates + Institute New Architecture" (regarding an undulating glass curtain wall in Hyogo Prefecture).[8] *Kenchiku Chishiki*, while more oriented to the trades, has popular appeal because of the careful selection of smaller-scale projects and its numerous accessible drawings. It sells over the counter in many bookstores, in spite of the technical emphasis of its subject matter. These publications as a whole also effectively demonstrate the importance of fabrication on architectural quality, and are one mechanism for explicitly integrating the concerns of different members of the building team.

LEAD USERS IN COLLABORATIVE DESIGN

On the positive side, the architect brings skills to the manufacturer that might otherwise not be represented in product development. These may include an interest in aesthetic and theoretic issues, but also extend to performance, maintenance, durability, construction costs, quality and many other areas that may not be readily apparent to others who work outside practice. However, some manufacturers do not appreciate collaboration and have told me that they feel compelled to compensate for architects' limited technical knowledge specific to their product. These complaints have for the most part come from North American producers accustomed to a system where interdependence is rare. Depending on the importance of the abilities and knowledge each party brings to collaboration, developing new or customized materials relies more heavily on one party or the other. In the case of components that have greater technical requirements, in fact, Japanese architects generally delegate design decisions to industry, while remaining involved enough to influence the outcome.

The approach is similar to the construction industry's "designated design development." Instead of giving the supplier detailed design documents, the client organization simply generates a general specification for the part and the supplier is asked to design and produce a component to meet these specifications. Jeffery Liker, studying the Japanese automotive industry, dubbed these collaborations "black box sourcing." As Liker outlined it, the practice "... has three characteristics; early involvement of suppliers, clear communication of the customer's [architect's] design requirements, and extensive design-related responsibility assumed by the suppliers."[9] Elsewhere he noted that, "Japanese automotive customers often initiate the design process by giving the supplier a general conceptual description of the part of the subsystem. This general description is followed by intense joint activity by the customer's and supplier's engineering staff."[10]

Takahiro Fujimoto found a similar situation, but discovered noteworthy variables. In 1993, he surveyed parts suppliers to see how they received orders. For completely new car models, car makers bid out 18 per cent of the parts based on detailed drawings; 49 per cent of the parts involved development competition among two or more suppliers, based on looser specifications supplied by the car maker; and 32 per cent involved selecting a particular supplier to then participate in the product's conception, planning and specifications.[11] This reflects what I observed in architectural practice, although the percentages of collaboratively designed components would be quite a bit different if counting *all* materials used in a building's construction. Nonetheless, whereas sometimes building materials were ordered by bidding from detailed drawings (a way Western architects would consider conventional) significant areas of the building – particularly finishes, critical subsystems and structural materials – were developed in partnership with one or more manufacturers.

As with Fujimoto, I found two types of partnerships. For a limited set of materials – those that were either essential to the overall success of the building design or represented previously untried technologies – cooperative design development would begin during the basic design phase of the building. For a broader palette of building components, manufacturer selection more commonly occurred after beginning design development and construction. In the latter case, contracts might also be offered to more than one supplier, for reasons I will discuss below.

With innovative materials or subsystems developed before bidding, it was generally the architects or the consultant team that sought out suitable manufacturers. Only a small subset of the companies capable of supporting flexibility will do so. However, some materials suppliers are widely known to be supportive of innovation. If an architect has a new idea involving materials produced by these companies, partnerships can be established quickly. Most designers can identify specific manufacturers and fabricators who they consider particularly open to customizations: Taiyo Tent, Kikukawa, Nihon Kentetsu, Technonamiken, and Nihon Chūzō are a few firms many architects suggested were open to experimentation. These producers were a small enough group that, on more than one occasion, while joining one architect in a plant inspection, I would see building components in production for another project I was following. In general, these firms were materials suppliers. As I mentioned earlier, some larger fabricators would split work off and delegate it to one or more smaller plants to accommodate customized production. This system allows the large manufacturers to accommodate customization within their corporate community.

Equipment or systems innovations are also found, but in these situations manufacturers were more likely to initiate work on a new internally derived technology that justified short-term alliances, rather than waiting for architects' overtures. Asahi Glass, for example, bought the Japanese patent rights to Peter Rice's innovative glass support system, and then invited leading architects to modify the "DPG" (Dot Point Glass) system (sometimes referred to as "spyder connectors" in English). They were aggressive about taking on responsibility for the structural support rather than pushing that off on to steel fabricators developing related parts of the system, when, for development of a one-off customization, they might have been happy to let other fabricators take the responsibility. In developing a range of customizations with leading architects, a number of solutions emerged. Asahi eventually brought some of these solutions to market and uses others as a basis for further development and customization.

When architects and manufacturers begin

working together during basic design, it is before bidding opens on a project, so there is no assurance that the manufacturer will ultimately obtain the contract. Not surprisingly, most architects tell me that when they have an idea for an innovative approach, they will contact many manufacturers about working together, and are frequently turned away. Architects sometimes joked about how manufacturers would "run away" when confronted with innovatory schemes. Professionals used a variety of approaches to find cooperative manufacturers. Introductions came from other architects, other manufacturers, materials brokers, engineers, old classmates and even family friends. Most commonly, the introductions are the result of other corporate ties, e.g., a small fabricator in an industrial district will work in cooperation with many other area shops and can introduce an architect to other fabricators. Cold calls are common enough for designers to feel comfortable doing the same overseas, however. On his first project in the United States, the structural engineer Kunio Watanabe apparently drove around and dropped in on area precasters to determine their capabilities before setting his parameters for basic design. Shigeru Ban has also mentioned using cold calls to find paper tube manufacturers willing to work with him and to locate donations for his work on behalf of those made homeless by the Kobe earthquake in 1995. There seemed to be no consistent pattern in identifying fabricators, except that contractors were never used to find these more cooperative manufacturers, for the simple reason that, prior to bidding, no contractor was as yet committed to the project. In fact, more than once I have known contractors to be in opposition to using the manufacturer proposed by an architect. This is usually an opportunity for the contractor to put added pressure on the manufacturer to accept lower prices in negotiations. The architect has a continuing voice in these decisions because while the contractors propose suppliers, the architects must approve these choices. More often than not, architects feel that the contractor selects companies based on price and corporate relationships. Consequently, architects tend to scrutinize these suppliers closely and are more likely to agree to split up important work, holding some back for the original fabricator, rather than to transfer those key areas of production to a manufacturer suggested by the contractor.

A private client may agree to indicate a preference for a collaborating manufacturer in pre-bid meetings, but public clients cannot pre-select fabricators, suppliers or manufacturers. It may seem odd that manufacturers offer support at this stage, when there is no guarantee of a contract or compensation, and a great deal of service is needed. Manufacturers expect that offering advice gives them an edge when a supplier is selected, both because they have greater technical information and considerable lead time for development, and also because the architect will want to continue the partnership during construction. Further, manufacturers work with the architect to develop specifications and these will include, if not favor, the advising corporation. This is especially true since specifications for innovative systems often outline production capacity, not product characteristics. Clearly, there are no guarantees between that architect and manufacturer. Understandably, therefore, many producers consider these collaborations expensive nuisances. Yet, some use the process as a form of product research that can lead to new markets and advance the manufacturer's repu-

8.7 & 8.8
Hajime Yatsuka's Nagaoka "Earth Man and Sky" Folly, exterior and interior with ceramic wall designed to draw heat from prevailing winds.

tation. Service or even building components may be offered for no cost, although most manufacturers will offer this higher level of care only on materials that are more expensive or assemblies, thus encouraging architects to make a higher financial investment.

Manufacturers will also offer new production support on the assumption that a leading architect can most effectively promote a new material – as was the case in a heat-absorbing ceramic wall for the government-funded Nagaoka Folly by Hajime Yatsuka. This wall, based on the same principles as the ceramic cores in automobile radiators, was used to draw heat off breezes as they entered a space, allowing cooling without enclosure. The idea for the product first came out of a meeting of cooperative organizations (firms in a *keiretsu*), where another corporation had introduced its new lightweight ceramic cores, designed to increase the efficiency of automobile radiators. Since the design was novel and untried, Inax treated the project as a form of *in situ* testing. Similarly, the aluminum industry approached Toyo Ito about developing an all-aluminum structure for a house completed in Tokyo in late 1999, and ultimately, the trade organizations subsidized the cost of materials. This seems to have engaged Ito's interest in the structural possibilities of aluminum. It was followed in the Summer of 2000 by an exhibit of Ito's proposals for future work with aluminum framing and supporting aluminum skins, at the GA Gallery in Tokyo.

One industry insider told me that most manufacturers make an effort to identify architects who are market leaders. Along with large architectural offices, these influential firms will be given continuous information on new trends and a high level of support for experimentation. This is one reason that the level of collaboration I have witnessed varies widely. Whereas young architects find limited support from manufacturers, lead architects find industry highly responsive.

However, this kind of exploratory design development, occurring while still in basic design, is usually limited to only a few areas of the building. Much component customization begins in design development, when construction is already underway. These later adjustments are less inventive than those noted above, but account for the refined character of Japan's best architecture. When customization occurs later in the design process, contractors and architects often employ an interesting tactic to assure that each manufacturer remains competitive. Two (or more) manufacturers receive contracts for the work, with the understanding that if either proves unsatisfactory, the team can drop them from the project with little difficulty. Both contractors and architects frequently employed this approach and the advantages of one fabricator sometimes became provocation in dealings with competitors. For example, one company might be able to make long sheets of steel, but not thin ones, whereas another can work with thinner steel — a situation I noted on a project by Riken Yamamoto. The architect and contractor note a competitor plant's strengths in negotiations, suggesting that, if the manufacturer could not meet similar standards, more of the work could be shifted to a rival. The design team communicates this message to both producers, in the hopes of getting thinner and longer steel sheet. In cases where multiple manufacturers are involved, the architects may also begin by proposing a challenging idea to the contender most capable of its production, then indicate to other producers that the lead firm has begun working on the problem, thus bringing them on board as well. As the noted economist, T. J. Pempel noted, in these situations, "Ultimately, power was concentrated ... Contractors typically divided orders among several subcontractors to gain multiple alternative sources ... They could shift contracts among subcontractors as rewards or punishments for past loyalties, current pricing problems, quality performances, or personal whim."[12]

Manufacturers respond to such pressures by bringing production staff into discussions at a very early stage. Initial on-site consultations generally involve both a sales representative and someone from production. If the architect's demands seem simple or the discussion does not require production advice, further consultation might only involve the sales staff. On projects where initial consultations require extensive involvement on the part of production staff, having them involved allows the manufacturer to concurrently design the component and its fabrication. Sales staff simultaneously advise the architects on how fabrication and material changes affect target costs, allowing these to be balanced in decision-making. Even so, such collaborations are expensive, and at least partially account for the fact that the prices of 87 per cent of all construction products are higher in Japan than in North America or other markets.[13] Still, most construction materials in Japan continue to be domestically produced, though the ratio of imported to domestic materials is falling. Customization allows Japanese manufacturers to maintain market share in spite of the economic benefits of using imported goods. In the case of Renzo Piano's Kansai Airport and Rafael Viñoly's Tokyo Forum, for example, the Japanese government hoped that by using Western architects, there would be more imported goods incorporated into the buildings. And in the basic design stages, initial bids reflected this — but as the projects progressed, just-in-time production and the opportunities for customization led to more and more materials being drawn from domestic sources. Even where there was an intent to promote the use of imports, customization offered a reasonable incentive to use more expensive domestic materials. Moreover, efforts to increase imports are in fact rare; various barriers to trade have maintained an oligopic marketplace.

BEING FLEXIBLE WITHIN CLEAR BOUNDARIES

In the collaborations I observed between architects and industry, the sides would first come to a verbal agreement about goals, without any contractual commitment and perhaps with no involvement by the contractor. This stage was exploratory. Questions might include the concept's feasibility, whether the manufacturer could produce the proposed component, what materials or shapes would be most appropriate for fabrication, etc. Even on buildings with generous budgets and the participation of leading architects, the team would drop some of the ideas discussed later. The reasons for deciding not to pursue proposals varied. On Hillside West, for example, Fumihiko Maki decided that an aluminum floor was too costly and the design team wanted to use the moneys elsewhere. On Toyo Ito's Sendai Mediatheque, a contractor decided that a sophisticated process involving lifting steel floor panels into place was unwarranted. In many cases, abandoning a proposal did not affect the overall quality of interactions between other constructors and the architects because these other parties had not invested effort in that particular area. There were occasions when other constructors had contributed to a collaboration, but only at a minor level. I can imagine that where a greater level of involvement was necessary — adjusting involvement following lengthy preparatory discussions or reducing the remaining work to be done — unilaterally abandoning a proposal has the potential to affect teamwork.

Jeffery Liker has developed the concept of "time windows" for decisions within collaboration and I have found this useful in understanding when designers propose innovations.[14] Although suppliers continuously fine-tune their production technologies, Liker noted that there are specific periods when suppliers introduce new technologies to purchasers — at the initial stages of the collaboration. This corresponds with what I witnessed. Contractors or manufacturers would alert architects to a target date for concluding decision-making, based on the construction schedule. Architectural staff similarly indicated to the contractor when they were working out detailing or material selection for specific areas of a building, and invited the constructors' input. In this way, members of the design team initiate the opening of a "time window." In most cases, the producers accepted proposed modifications to a material or subsystem only through the period shortly after review of a final prototype. When the design team required more than one mock-up, there was a tendency for major modifications to occur during development of the earliest mock-ups. Developing these is an iterative process; performance problems in the mock-up are not a serious problem, although failure to address them quickly is. I did see situations where later work in the field led someone to suggest additional modifications. Generally, the team quickly rejected even the question of alterations. However, because manufacturers continue to work out process technologies during fabrication, these sometimes resulted in changes to building components, and the design team aware of this on-going refinement might offer their own suggestions. In these cases, variations in the product run might be visible.

I discuss Japan's contractual flexibilities at greater length later. Briefly, however, in other nations, contractual written and drawn materials are privileged, while verbal communications are often referred to as "not worth the paper they are printed on." (The implication being that since they are not printed and verifiable, they have no value.) In Japan, challenging ideas are often investigated even before establishing a contractual commitment. Partners work verbally, perhaps using preliminary drawings or models. The Japanese consider these communications trustworthy; if a contractor says something is possible or estimates that it will cost a certain amount, this is treated as reliable information. In this way, architects can test various strategies related to cost, aesthetics, maintenance or other issues, without investing in a particular approach. Similarly, contractors or manufacturers can ascertain how committed the architect is to an idea and which factors initially proposed are flexible, determining appropriate resources and participants.

Liker also researched how teams function effectively; he refers to them "being flexible within clear boundaries."[15] For architects who have a clear formal agenda (thinner, more transparent, etc.) or easily articulated goals, it is relatively simple for builders to determine how these intentions affect a particular architectural component. The constructor can offer suitable guidance on available materials or forms that conform to the design team's intentions. Goals do not have to be communicated explicitly. In fact, when one of the functions of negotiation is to determine boundaries, the relatively fixed nature of drawings may not be the best mechanism. One salesperson representing a large furniture manufacturer told me he sees Japanese architects as being of two types: some "use paper," while others meet to communicate their needs. He described the use of written and drawn material as easier, but made the point that his company could then more quickly decide to refuse to put in a bid. In contrast, with verbally negotiated work, the prices were generally higher, but there was an opportunity to remove production barriers and avoid excessive expense.

Recently, offshore production is becoming a snag, hindering verbal negotiations. On major components, where architects feel collaboration is crucial, they do dig in their heels and refuse to approve overseas production plants. Sometimes, however, overseas outsourcing is not apparent. Some designers have found that Japanese plants offshore only some activities, such as shop drawing production. This becomes evident when designers make changes to the drawings and problems arise – architects may discover too late that discussing the proposal is not an option. For designers who depend on negotiation and advice over written material, the move to offshore production offers a genuine challenge.

Verbal communication, as noted above, usually occurs in conjunction with the use of models and sketches. On particularly complex or important components, architects, contractors or even government regulations also require mock-ups or prototypes, which offer an opportunity to check expectations against the more flexible instruments employed in discussions. Thus, the prototype offers a way to unearth misconceptions, a natural part of any construction experience. When Riken Yamamoto intended to use precisely formed precast concrete columns for the buildings on the Saitama University campus, for example, chamfered corners, evident on the two-story tall, two-bay mock-up, became a significant point of disagreement. The architect assumed that details drawn with squared corners would be understood as requiring higher care in production. The precaster, Fudo Kenken, had assumed the lack of chamfers in sketches was a simplification and that easy-to-fabricate corners were perfectly acceptable. The mock-up was built in May 1997, but the architects and fabricators had begun negotiations almost two years earlier, and document production, from January 1997, had not revealed the problem. After prolonged negotiations, the plant became committed to the required precision, to the degree that they arranged for the exposed face of each of the cast columns to be hand sanded as part of its processing. When two or more manufacturers supply materials, mock-ups also confirm that suppliers are producing comparable materials and confirm particulars such as finish and detailing.

GENUINE DRAWBACKS OF COLLABORATIVE METHODS

The Japanese approach to product development . . . requires an extraordinary effort on the part of all project members; eighty-hour weeks are not uncommon.[16]

Post-fordist systems have their drawbacks as well as benefits. Fordism was able to achieve the lowest possible price through standardization. Post-fordist systems reduced the costs of specialization, but they have not eradicated price differences between standardized and customized components. Furthermore, customization requires greater time commitments from designers, both for managing production processes and for absorbing information related to production opportunities. The manufacturer, too, faces greater investments of time. This is not only because of the greater level of service; both labor and management must maintain skills through continuous training.

Collaborations are potentially time-consuming and redundant. For Toyo Ito's Sendai Mediatheque, about thirty people – representing the architects, structural and mechanical engineers, contractors and various subcontractors – would sit down to a meeting which routinely took eight hours week after week. Some would travel from Tokyo or from fabricators specifically for this meeting, whereas others were based at the site. Those who were not directly concerned with the work at hand might occasionally wander off to take a call, but most remained in the meeting regardless of whether they were directly involved in the discussion – in part because there was an expectation that their input *might* be needed. The involvement of large numbers of staff is directly related to the fact that each problem is not tightly bounded, and most critics consider it inherent in the process of collaboration.

Paul Herbig, another researcher on Japanese management practices, observed that, "The Japanese innovation generation process has an unusually high cost associated with it in terms of the generation of problems and solutions, [a] high degree of social interaction . . . human exhaustion and overwork . . . mental exhaustion, and burnout."[17] The hours of effort I saw architectural staff put into a project struck me as nothing short of Herculean, and certainly entailed great personal sacrifice.

In the United States, liability problems, union opposition and regulatory context have undermined support for innovation. Another problem is sustainability; rapid product cycles lead to rapid obsolescence. Innovation may lead to quicker obsolescence for components considered lasting in buildings today, including elevators, HVAC systems, appliances and lighting. However, the opportunity to explore new materials with lower embodied energy costs and the reduced obsolescence of the production line may serve as a balance.

Although construction has never been said to have a high productivity, this sort of collaboration certainly works against contemporary efforts geared towards increasing efficiency. Moreover, although some observers still claim that the Japanese corporation continues to rate customer satisfaction as more important than profitability, the current economy has certainly rendered this attitude a luxury.[18] Furthermore, as Liker notes, ". . . it is increasingly recognized in Japan that a customer's focus can lead to unreasonable demands and sacrifice on the part of employees . . ."[19] For many manufacturers and contractors, where prestige is less directly tied to innovation, the high costs of collaboration, which recently have begun to include increased liability in Japan as well, are simply not justified today. Architects hold a different attitude about customization, reflecting the different goals of the profession.

WORKING WITH CUSTOMIZATION

Although most internationally recognized architects and designers in Japan take advantage of customization in their work, a few simple examples may suffice to demonstrate the benefits of manufacturing flexibility to architects. Fumihiko Maki, in a church built in Tokyo in 1995, brought together a wide range of components altered to fit his aesthetic goals, only a few of which I will discuss. The Tokyo Church of Christ is a simple building that achieves its elegance from the care Maki and his staff took in selecting components. The large trombe wall on the west facade, for example, combines products by Figula Glass and Nippon Kentetsu, both smaller, flexible manufacturers who see their work as supplementing the standardized products of larger suppliers.

Maki achieved a soft, even light through a west-facing double-skin curtain wall that

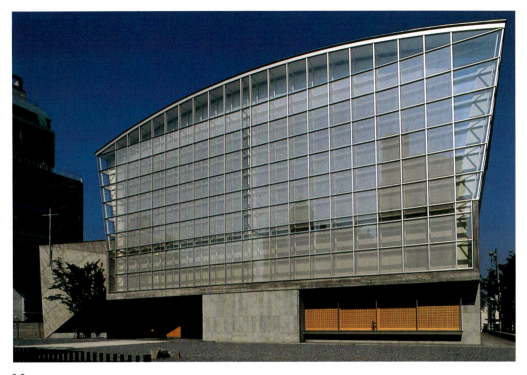

8.9
Fumihiko Maki's Church of Christ, exterior view.

stands at the front of the sanctuary. This required a combined approach. The outer wall has a fine, fritted finish. During design development, Maki's office asked several glass companies about the feasibility of the delicate patterns they were considering. The larger firms tended to say that a solution was too difficult for them to achieve and refused to supply samples, but the smaller and more aggressive Figula was able to supply samples and acceptable prices for all but one proposal. The work was achieved through the use of a computer-directed system to cut patterns on a vinyl protective sheet, machinery that offered a high degree of flexibility at minimum expense. In one case, though, Figula produced a sample, but no estimate – even this scrappy manufacturer had reached its limit. Maki's staff also learned the limits of their approach.

In addition to the fritted glass for the outer layer, a second, interior curtain wall combined the insertion of glass fiber tissue between the two panes and the assembly was completed by an etched finish on the inner glass surface.

Nippon Kentetsu and Maki's office worked together to develop the curtain wall itself, designed to respond to structural requirements, assist air handling and also dampen noise between the two sides of the wall – a busy street on one side and the sanctuary on the other. Air handling is based on a trombe system, drawing air through the space between the two curtain walls and either exhausting the warmed air at the top of the wall (which creates a positive air flow) or returning the warmed air for filtering before it is introduced into the interior, depending on the season. The

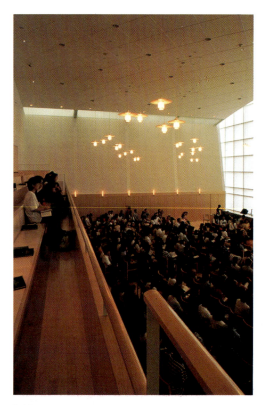

8.10
Interior of sanctuary, showing special finish and customized light fixtures.

gated aluminum panel with an asymmetrical profile was used to give the building greater luminosity. The staff developed this profile for an earlier project by Maki's office, Hillside Terrace, Phase VI. In the sanctuary, Maki's office worked with Daimaru Interiors to develop a ridged panel made of a porous sound-deadening material, conventionally produced as a denticulated trim. Normally, extruded and then cut into boards, Maki's office simply used the material in its extruded uncut form.

Maki's office also designed Wrightian pendant lighting fixtures and wall sconces, working with the manufacturer; the models of these fixtures, still under development, are shown in Plate 8.11. The development of these lighting fixtures is also notable because the manufacturer, who had worked with Maki on earlier projects, was becoming less enthusiastic about the fabrication of customized products. This was not a technical issue, but a legal one; until recently, any manufacturer in Japan had, by American standards, relatively modest legal responsibility for a product. However, influenced by trends in the United States, Japan has also begun to establish product liability laws. To date, small manufacturers are largely exempt from these new standards, but the trend is clearly moving in the direction of increasing liability. The legal context has hampered innovation in the States and, as I note elsewhere, has the potential to have the same effect in Japan, as much because of fears of the potential impact of legal changes as the reality. However, the economy has made it difficult for manufacturers to remain choosy, and it is possible that for many, the level of customized production will not change significantly – only their sense of risk, and the manner in which they are willing to customize.

structure is a vertical steel Vierendeel truss which is part of the curtain wall, thus becoming virtually invisible.[20] Nippon Kentetsu supplied both aluminum mullions at the second floor sanctuary and steel mullions at the ground floor entry area. The mullions below are steel to assure a thin profile while maintaining a high degree of impact resistance. Not surprisingly, Maki's office has described this wall as being the subject of "intense investigation at all scales."[21]

Maki's office also worked with manufacturers to modify materials used as panels in both the interior and exterior. In a discrete area on the rear of the building, for instance, a corru-

8.11
In the site office, models of the light fixtures at different sizes were mounted so that they could be considered over time.

ANCIENT EQUIPMENT

This collaboration between architects and manufacturers or fabricators is not limited to Japan's best-known architects. That even an inexperienced designer can, under Japan's system, develop provocative and well-detailed building by working closely with crafters and manufacturers may be best illustrated by the work of Dr. Terunobu Fujimori, an architectural historian. Fujimori is a popular architectural spokesperson and prolific scholar. He has authored dozens of books, writes regularly for newspapers and architectural journals, has interviewed major architects for a variety of books and private publications, and is himself interviewed frequently on Japan's public television station, NHK. Influenced by his mentor, Teijiro Muramatsu (known for his work on late nineteenth and early twentieth-century architectural production), Fujimori quickly became aware that if the opportunities of small-scale manufacturing were not integrated into contemporary design, they may be lost – he also seemed to feel that his own popularity meant he might be able to highlight the benefits of older equipment and craft in modern solutions. Thus, the architectural historian incorporates craft and production from small manufacturing facilities in his remarkable designs. It is not only his importance as an academic in Japan, but also the theoretic construct he has devised for his work that has attracted notice.

In his first building, the Jinchokan Shiryokan, Fujimori sought to confine himself only to finishes that reflected handicraft, including slate and other stone materials, a straw-embedded mortar coat which was also applied by hand, wrought iron door pulls and locks, and hand-made glass. (He was not entirely successful; fire-related materials such as extinguishers and exit signs are located by local officials in Japan – clearly unsympathetic to the project's intent – and much of the electrical equipment is manufactured rather than handcrafted.) In one notable example, he utilized boards split in a manner that apparently predates the saw, but wrapped them around the building as a skin in a way that was distinctly Corbusian. Using this material was a far from simple task; the first challenge Fujimori faced was finding someone still capable of splitting the equivalent of fifty *tsubo* (about 165 square meters or 1,775 square feet) of board in this fashion, since it is a disappearing art. Ultimately, through personal introductions, Fujimori was able to convince Chuu'ichi Yazawa to participate in the project. In the essay for *Shinkenchiku*, Fujimori describes Yazawa's day (due to his advanced age) as being "... in the morning, on an intravenous drip, and in the afternoon, splitting wood in a way he had not been called on to do for half a century."[22] But the use of traditional materials was not intended to be retrogressive; in the internal structure Fujimori utilized steel reinforced concrete, metal decking, and expanded metal. There was a clear decision to link the advantages of hand-finished and manufactured materials, exploiting the advantages of each.

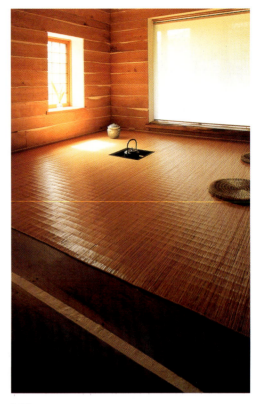

8.12
Terunobu Fujimori's Tanpopo House, interior showing plank walls.

More recently, Fujimori has shifted away from purely handmade materials and has begun to incorporate production from small manufacturing facilities, in recognition of the challenges this sector also faces. An example that demonstrates the way in which Fujimori has been able to customize production is his use of a local sawmill, Kakudai Seizai, to cut finishes for the Tanpopo House. He has known the family that owns the mill since he was a child, and they have been involved in several of his projects.

In the early part of the twentieth century, most sawmills in Japan were local mills, often close to forests. (In part this was because Japan's more rugged landscape made shipping logs downstream far less feasible than was true, for example, in the North American Middle West.) Large mills that operated in urban areas tended to cut primarily imported woods, and the small mills – that is, under nine employees – accounted for somewhere around 90 per cent of all sawmills in the country.[23] The importance of the local sawmill actually grew as access to power and small machinery made these facilities more competitive. Government surveys suggest that small mills increased in number by 70 per cent between 1919 and 1930, while large mills only increased 30 per cent in the same period.[24] Even today, there are 18,566 lumberyards and mills in Japan, of which roughly two-thirds – 12,147 – are staffed by fewer than ten people.[25] Small lumber yards can be seen in virtually any urban neighborhood, even the most expensive.

Even by these standards, Kakudai Seizai is a very small mill, run by a middle-aged married couple and the husband's father. This mill is very much in keeping with the scale and capitalization of the small producer or manufacturer. Machinery is only a large bed for the log, driven along a track, and a single, stationary bandsaw. The Kakudais achieve heavy lifting by using a truck-mounted articulated arm, the truck rented for the occasion. The logs for this project were large and a hard wood, so they also rented special saw blades. Fujimori directed the milling himself, using simple notes on a letter-size sheet of paper to review his needs and necessary thicknesses. With the participation of the Kakudais and two students from the University of Tokyo, the first of two logs was removed from the truck bed and Fujimori directed the setting of the log in the conveyor bed. When it was in place, he marked the narrow end of the log with chalk (primarily as a confirming device; this was not referred to during milling) and told the younger Kakudai how the wood was to be cut. Fujimori explained later that he did not feel it necessary to discuss his decisions with Kakudai because of his own long experience at the sawmill.

The larger logs were intended for wall finishes, built-in cabinetry and furniture, and were milled to a variety of shapes and thicknesses; because of the way the Japanese mill lumber, they retained a ragged bark edge which was exploited in the finished furniture. A smaller tree was used for window and door frames and was cut and trimmed to more standardized dimensions. Fujimori worked with Yoshio Uchida, also an architect and a professor at Toyo College, for practical support and advice on detailing and construction. Uchida also arranged for these materials to be delivered to the site.

In later discussions, the contractor on site told me that they preferred to arrange for materials themselves as they could control when they were delivered. (Japanese construction sites, being quite small, allow little room for storage.) Also, there is some labor saving to standardized wood sizes, although this is more than offset by the beauty of less uniform materials. However, since most contractors do tend to work with a variety of suppliers, there was not a significant resistance to the architect making other arrangements. Indeed, it relieved the contractor of any responsibility for material failure. Fujimori has taken that responsibility here and elsewhere in part because he designs for himself and close friends, giving him greater confidence in his freedom to contrive solutions.

Small producers are able to accommodate unusual requests because they have the

8.13
Fujimori marking wood for cutting at sawmill.

opportunity to rent the necessary equipment and materials, such as harder saw blades. The manner in which Japanese architects are able to exploit flexibilities in the production system thus differs in several key ways from American experiences, and offers architects a different set of opportunities. However, without the support of designers like Fujimori, these opportunities will disappear, and with them a level of control and experimentation.

many architects recognize that they have the potential to have a higher level of client support for component design and unusual technologies in a situation where the client has begun with a very public commitment to a difficult strategy.

POLITICAL SUPPORT

During the 1990s, public works accounted for between 40 and 70 per cent of total construction investment each year, a sizable proportion of revenues.[2] Consequently, in the catalog to an exhibition of Japan's public works, John Zukowsky declared public funding as, "what is at the core of Japan's design arts – the government, as patron and endorser."[3] One of Japan's major contractors, Takenaka Komuten, has traditionally been indifferent toward public works. Thus, the company, widely admired for its exceptional design and construction services, has been particularly affected in the current economy, with orders down almost 35 per cent. Of the other leading contractors, two reported 20 per cent drops in orders, but Takenaka literally stood alone.[4]

Overall, a greater proportion of Japan's GDP is spent on all construction (public and private, civil works and buildings) than in other industrialized nations, at a level totaling almost 15 per cent in 1998.[5] (Construction spending in 1972 reached a remarkable peak of 24 per cent of GDP, but the GDP was roughly one-fifth of what it is today.) Because construction plays such a large role in the economy, political support for public works is steady. This is particularly evident when comparing Japan's spending on public works with that of other governments. In 1996, Japan's municipal, prefectural and national governments spent 6.2 per cent of the country's total GDP on public works (not only buildings, but also infrastructure). In the same year, the US spent only 1.7 per cent of GDP on public works.[6] Expenditures have also been creeping up; in the three-year period from 1986–9, Japan spent a total of 29.9 trillion yen ($218 billion) on public works at both the local and national level. In the following three years, this rose to 41.2 trillion yen ($304 billion), and by 1993–6, 49.7 trillion yen ($477 billion) was spent on public works.[7] The dollar numbers are misleading, as they are affected by exchange rate fluctuations; the period from 1993–6 increased 67 per cent over expenditures in the 1986–9 period. In today's recession, the public works portion of construction spending has risen to 47.4 per cent of all construction spending.[8] These figures include infrastructure, and so this funding is often of more benefit to contractors than to architects. Nevertheless, architects also profit.

In most countries, construction (including public works) performs naturally, as "derived demand," rising and falling with broad economic trends. The amount of construction rises and falls in response to economic trends and other changes affected by the economy, such as population shifts. In Japan, government policies treat construction as a strategic industry, and smooth the profits and unemployment load of boom–bust cycles. These government policies have odd consequences: in the early 1990s, while Japan was in recession, the construction sector actually grew. Recent estimates suggest that the decade saw an increase of one million construction jobs, and about 50,000 licensed contractors.[9] As one politician explained, "Other countries use public money on unemployment benefits – we pay construction workers."[10] Through regulation, governmental support for the construction industry also extends into the private sector. In one extreme example, Prime Minister Noboru Takeshita proposed that developers be given minimum building heights, rather than maximums.[11] Public clients may also require that a certain amount of the total construction costs of a project favor local materials or small, local contractors, subcontractors and manufacturers. Small professional offices might be kept afloat with research contracts of no immediate consequence. The support preserves inefficient organizations, but protects local economies. It is accepted because the sector is perceived as one of the chief engines driving Japan's economy.

Japanese politicians use public works spending to revive and stabilize the economy, influenced by Keynesian theories developed in the 1930s, suggesting that planned approaches to the economy can solve unemployment and smooth dips. Most economists agree that this use of public works funding has been breathtakingly costly during the 1990s, especially when including debt-servicing obligations. Worse, these investments have little lasting economic benefit (unlike previous periods when government subsidies did revive the economy) although they may have made the difference between Japan being in a depression or a recession. Nonetheless, these policies are controversial because of their cost. Popular support for using public works to overcome economic fragility began to slip in 1997. In response, the government initiated a 15 per cent reduction in public works spending over the next two fiscal years. However, the result was a significant rise in bankruptcies among small contractors, followed by a return to higher public works spending.

GOVERNMENT SUPPORT

Governments calculate an internal, preliminary estimate for work and use this to set a minimum bid threshold – projects bid below this undisclosed amount are automatically rejected, to prevent contractors from making proposals that would lead to substandard work. This process encourages contractors to bid higher, allowing high prices to remain the norm even when labor costs are dropping. Furthermore, since projects are bid on a lump sum basis, the costs of individual parts or materials are not separately highlighted. Consequently, some decisions on public projects reflect different priorities than I, as a North American architect, would have expected. In one modest but memorable case, the project architect for Jun Aoki's "Snow Village Future Foundation" research laboratory ("*Yuki no Machi Mirai Kan*"), decided to promote a sense of public ownership in the building by individually casting 1,000 small steel snowmen, needed for slip resistance, into the concrete floors. Wax forms of the snowmen were individually boxed and distributed to villagers, who were asked to carve a pattern on the form and return it. The actual pieces were then created through a lost wax process. When I asked the project architect how much these efforts at individual customization cost, she was at a loss. I tried again: how much had the small boxes, the distribution effort, and the use of the lost wax process cost over simply using one permanent form to make 1,000 identical snowmen – still a potentially acceptable level of customization? The answer, simply, was that no one – neither the architect nor the public officials – had felt the need to investigate this question. The total cost for the snowmen came to less than 500,000 yen (about $5,000) and this seemed an acceptable amount for the expected goodwill, so their decision required no further analysis. I should note, however, that this attitude is not universal. Public officials, even on this project, have been generally vigilant about costs, especially where there is local pressure to reduce corruption or wasteful spending.

There is good reason for concern on both sides. The lucrative opportunities in public works safeguard the construction sector; many estimates suggest that the profit on a publicly supported project in Japan is 10–16 per cent.[12] Even more impressive (although difficult to confirm), Chalmers Johnson argues that profits from collusion amount to between 16 and 33 per cent of industry revenues.[13] This is a significant sum. Annual net profit among the six largest contractors in 1990 was between 25 and 50 billion yen each, or roughly $173 to $345 million at the time. This declined to net profits of between 13 and 35 billion yen for 1994 – approximately $127 to $342 million, the dollar differences tempered somewhat since the dollar had also fallen sharply against the yen.[14] Even in the mid-1990s, contractors were still reporting 10 per cent profits, double the conventional expectations for contractors in the United States. Japanese organizations, however, use less than straightforward accounting procedures and these numbers may be inflated by losses downplayed elsewhere.

However, high profits also ensure a broader flexibility. Accompanied by relatively consistent demand, this structure allows contractors to afford losses on a single project. When the need arises, they may decide that the continuing relationship with an architect or – more likely – with a public client is more important than profit on the project. The reasons that contractors may take higher risks on public works and will sacrifice profits for quality are further explained in the following section.

Construction costs on a per square meter basis also show a disparity, one that cannot be accounted for on the basis of the quality of construction alone. According to an annual report from JETRO (the Japan External Trade Organization), the Ministry of Construction figures for 1997 show that on buildings for the private sector, costs are about 195,000 yen per square meter ($155 per square foot). For comparable publicly funded buildings, the costs shoot up to 299,000 yen per square meter ($238 per square foot).[15]

The budgets set for public works are often galvanizing. In surveying the published costs of buildings from the late 1990s, I found community centers tended to range between $220 and $300 per square foot in construction costs, third sector projects with luxury shopping and hotels ranged from $259 to $655 per square foot, and museums – none particularly notable by international standards – ranged from $202 to $703 per square foot. Not all projects were as generously funded, however. Schools, for example, tended to be only $133 to $314 per square foot, with most under $250 per square foot. Although such a budget would be generous in North America or Europe, this is not very high for Japan, in light of the higher overall costs for construction. Lower budgets for schools may perhaps reflect the fact that teachers have been considered mostly leftists and thus at odds with Japan's leading political organizations, which are conservative.

Beyond generous budgets are other means to protect the construction industry. Most public works contracts require that the public agency acting as client pay the contractor 30 per cent (or more) of scheduled costs shortly after signing a contract. Under normal circumstances and in Japan's private sector, payments do not exceed the value of completed work, because the differences between the utility of an unfinished building and its remaining costs become too great. The generous dispersal of public works funds instead offsets the drain on resources that commonly affects contractors because of payment withholding. Government agencies at all levels believe the process of awarding public works contracts – and the potential threat of withholding future work if a contractor performs poorly – is a sufficient deterrent against poor construction.

PRESSURE TO PERFORM

Governments use a satisfaction rating that strongly influences access to future work. These rankings are compiled and used by the national government, prefectures and most large cities to establish a short list of professionals and constructors able to design or build public works. The governmental agencies that make up these lists cannot hire other firms. Inclusion in this set is established based on the amount of government-funded work done by the office in the previous year, performance results (including a specific item related to accomplishing the original project goals) and an assessment of completed projects. The July 2000 arrest of the former Construction Minister Ei'ichi Nakao on suspicion of accepting a 30 million yen bribe (about $270,000) to add Wakachiku Construction to Tokyo's designated bidder list has raised questions as to whether other factors might also be involved in making up these lists. Even in this case, however, the bureaucracy insisted that no such changes had been made, in spite of the bribery.

In the city of Tokyo, only 200 architectural firms were ranked and could be considered for public work funded by the city, which has a population of over 12 million. In 2000, this list included offices headed by Tadao Ando, Toyo Ito, Kisho Kurokawa, Fumihiko Maki, Kenzo Tange and Yoshio Taniguchi. However, Arata Isozaki, to give one example of a respected architect with significant public experience, was not on the list. This could be the result of the city's rankings system or a decision by the firm not to register for review. Someone from the firm's management must do the registration each year, during a very limited period of time. Therefore, architects from small ateliers cannot register throughout the country; they will try to select locations to register based on rumor, on-going work and perhaps proximity. Few offices, however, can afford the luxury of forgoing public works in Japan's largest city – especially when their offices are located there.

The use of a ranking system, at both the national level and by major municipalities, is one of the reasons that Japanese contractors place a high value on craft. The total quality of the construction is an important factor in these rankings, whereas cost overruns are not, in part because inflation and other reasons for cost variance are outside contractors' control. In addition to linking future survival to past performance and assuring good work without enacting financial penalties, the system also protects a small group of established contractors and professionals. Not surprisingly, it is frequently identified as a barrier to free trade, since professionals from outside Japan are unable to include their overseas experience in assessments. The impact is also felt at home, however. It is difficult for young Japanese to get public works contracts; without previous experience, the architects have no buildings to assess for future work. Governments have responded to these criticisms with set-aside programs for architects, allowing foreign professionals and young designers to establish public works experience. The Tokyo Forum and Kansai Airport competitions allowed limited access to Japan's construction market for foreign firms (and Renzo Piano continues to build in Japan), and programs such as Kumamoto ArtPolis opened smaller public works projects to young professionals. Such programs, however, maintain the system of control over access to the lucrative public works market, and they have been much less conspicuous as the recession has dragged on.

Today, local governments seem to be attempting to curtail the volume of work contracted out, by doing much of the supervision on public works. Public officials do design inconsequential buildings, and thus consider their skills to overlap with those of professional consultants. Architects have responded in a variety of ways: Tadao Ando, for example, has been quite open to the use of public employees for day-to-day supervision, whereas other architects have been more inclined to resist. The reasons for concern may be at least partially explained by the example of Saitama University, which follows.

THE ROLE OF PUBLIC COMMISSIONS

For many of Japan's best architects, institutional projects are the core of their work. In one remarkable example, in a twenty year period, close to 80 per cent of Yoshio Taniguchi's output has been public works – even more notable when one remembers that Taniguchi's buildings are exceptionally refined.[16] It is perhaps not surprising that Taniguchi once worked in Kenzo Tange's office, where public works projects also dominated. Yoshio Taniguchi's earliest museums, public commissions, resulted from his close friendships with leading artists. Regional authorities asked both Gen'ichiro Inokuma and Kai'i Higashiyama to donate their works to the community, and tax laws made it advisable for them to do so. Both negotiated for dedicated facilities for these collections, and insisted that Yoshio Taniguchi be the architect. The importance of government funding pervades the industry. A review of recent "yearbooks" published by *Japan Architect* illustrates government support of design quality in Japan. These publications represent the best work of each year; Fumihiko Maki, Tadao Ando, Toyo Ito and other leading architects appear regularly. Although few descriptions include information on financing, in 1999 eleven of the twenty-seven published buildings were clearly public: libraries, culture centers, museums and social service facilities. Six were private, including one Sunday school

9.1 & 9.2
Yoshio Taniguchi's Gallery of Horyuji Treasures in Tokyo, exterior and interior views. Completed in 1999, this is the most recent in a long string of highly refined public works Taniguchi has designed.

building, two office buildings, a retail complex, an atelier and a distillery. Financing for four of the projects I did not count as public works is unclear. All could qualify for third sector support (public–private partnerships, with public incentive funds): an "art village" resort complex, two small houses Tadao Ando has reworked to accommodate art installations in Naoshima, and a small museum by Kazuyo Sejima. Six private residences rounded out the list. Excluding them, nearly half of the projects considered exceptional in 1999 were public works, and possibly as many as fifteen out of twenty-one.

In the 1998 yearbook, nineteen projects are clearly public buildings and twenty-five are private – twelve of these are private residences, leaving only thirteen others. Two projects are ambiguous, either privately funded or built with third sector support. Again, excluding private residences, nineteen to twenty-one of thirty-two projects were public buildings. The 1998 yearbook also gives construction size: public buildings range from 746 square meters (8,030 square feet) to 30,572 square meters (329,080 square feet) – but only one project falls below 1,000 square meters (slightly more than 10,000 square feet). Private projects, excluding the private residences, range from 83 square meters (893 square feet) to 20,098 square meters (216,335 square feet), but five of the twelve projects are under 1,000 square meters. This suggests that where good design occurs in larger buildings, public works are even more frequent.

Although no yearbook is published in the United States, the annual American Institute of Architects awards offer a useful comparison, as these also attempt to recognize good design by a nation's architects. In both 1998 and 1999, one-third of the projects receiving these awards were public works or received the equivalent of third sector public funds, as in the case of the Intelligent Workplace at Carnegie Mellon. According to a press release, this proportion also follows the typical ratio of government-funded projects in AIA members' offices.[17]

As the yearbooks reveal, there is also a broader range of project types that receive public support in Japan. In addition to institutions such as museums, convention and conference facilities, schools and town halls, the yearbooks include many health services and day care facilities for the elderly, reflecting the rapid aging of Japan's population; a hostel allowing residents of one of Tokyo's wards – especially schoolchildren – to spend time in the country; and a teahouse, part of the Hanshin Earthquake Recovery Project. Recently, there has also been some enthusiasm for "media centers" coupling new technologies and the arts. Culture centers are also surprisingly common, in spite of the fact that my experience suggests most are underutilized. A 1997 survey counted 1,257 public culture centers, for a national population of only 126.5 million. To some degree, this is the result of a lack of coordination between different levels of government. For example, in 1997, three public halls opened in Tokyo: a new national theater, in the works for over twenty years, costing 75 billion yen ($620 million); Tokyo Forum by Rafael Viñoly, with four halls totaling almost 8,000 seats, cost 165 billion yen ($1.36 billion); and a more modest hall built by Sumida Ward, requiring about 20 billion yen ($165 million) in construction costs and another 9 billion yen for land acquisition. Immediately adjacent to the national theater, the private "Opera City," housing an opera hall, shops and offices, opened shortly thereafter. At times, the construction of these facilities seems driven by competitive pride between communities: the lavish "Act City" musical complex for Hamamatsu's 555,000 people was quickly followed by the "Granship Shizuoka," designed by Arata Isozaki for a neighboring community of 471,000 – the two theaters only minutes apart on the bullet train's line. Isozaki was also simultaneously responsible for a smaller experimental theater facility in the hills above Shizuoka.

During Japan's Bubble, government projects were particularly ambitious; aspirations for public works linger. The latter half of the 1980s saw stimulating architectural design featured in expositions in Tsukuba (1985), Nara and Yokohama (1989) and Osaka (1990). Celebrated architects served up memorable structures. The dazzling work by young, untried designers drew international attention. Osaka in particular was known for the small "follies" by visionaries such as Daniel Libeskind, Zaha Hadid, and others linked to the Architectural Association of London. Young Japanese architects, including Hajime Yatsuka and Itsuko Hasegawa, also made an impact with their designs. Plans for a 1996 "Urban Frontier" exposition in Tokyo, coordinated by Toyo Ito, would have included structures by the next generation of young designers – but rising public concerns about the costs of these festivals led to its cancellation. Still, Japan's politicians remain enthusiastic about expositions, and another is anticipated for Aichi Prefecture in 2005, with costs expected to reach 180 billion yen (approximately $1.7 billion). Interestingly, the International Bureau of Expositions has raised questions about the intentions of this fair, suggesting that it "appears to be a pretext for development."[18] In response, Kisho Kurokawa, who often allies himself with major public projects, proposed an alternative plan for the exposition.[19]

More amazing – especially considering the length of Japan's recession – has been continuing support for plans to move the capital from Tokyo. Experts assume the projected costs of at least 14 trillion yen (approximately $130 billion) are inaccurate, since these do not include the costs of roads, rail or airports. Nor do estimates include the costs of housing – yet during the 1990s, 30 per cent of housing in Japan was publicly financed; in the post-war period, over 40 per cent was. Although politicians postponed the new capital proposal several times during the 1990s, site selection and programming proceed, and the groundbreaking is optimistically projected for the first half of the decade ahead. Precedents for these ambitious plans include those by Kenzo Tange and Kisho Kurokawa for Tokyo Bay (both unbuilt, and perhaps never meant to be built, but widely published), and the Osaka Prefectural government's stated intentions to raise the bed of their own bay by 15 feet, with the use of landfill – thus adding 4,600 hectares for construction.

On the local level, many governments use public works to reshape dismal communities, frequently with national support. This led one visitor to acclaim:

> When one visits Japan one marvels not so much at the corporate headquarters or the spectacular high rises, but at the wealth of small government-funded buildings and like constructions throughout the country, from concert halls and health-care facilities to police stations and museums of all kinds.[20]

Arata Isozaki and Hajime Yatsuka have carried over tactics acquired in managing exposition design to the local coordination of public works projects in Kumamoto, where architects have designed a wide range of publicly financed facilities throughout the prefecture, including a livestock breeding research center, public toilets, a dam control facility, bridges and even the ventilation opening for a highway tunnel. Yatsuka notes, "The principal significance of [Kumamoto] ArtPolis resides in the fact that, except for temporary buildings for world fairs, it is the first time that so many avant-garde architects have designed major public projects."[21] This is because "Isozaki, rather than members of the prefectural government, underwrote the quality of design."[22] Smaller schemes inspired by Kumamoto, coordinating public works in the city of Shiroishi, in Yokohama, in Nara and in Toyama Prefecture, have had limited effect, nonetheless resulting in several memorable structures.

A bolder undertaking can be seen in Saitama Prefecture, near Tokyo. Publicly financed construction totaling 1.8 million square meters (19.4 trillion square feet) and costing $1.35 trillion will shift Omiya from a bedroom community to a government center. The scheme involves offices for ten Ministries and national agencies, including a twenty-eight-story building for Japan's Ministry of Posts and Telecommunications, offices for the Ministry of Construction, and a major transfer point for the bullet train. This effort makes use of national funds, but local public works support is also high. In response to Tokyo's sprawl and the resultant explosion of Saitama's population, prefectural public works projects number in the thousands each year, with local city and village governments also supplying a demand for construction.

In the case of Saitama, national support and local needs agree. This is not always the case. The Ministry of Construction develops and advances plans from Tokyo; centralized decision-making can be indifferent to local concerns, proposing new building as a reflection of territorial equity or political influence. As the government stepped up its construction spending, the number and scale of public works grew. Many facilities proposed today did not naturally emerge through local initiatives, but were established to create opportunities for construction and to diffuse funds into local economies. Increasingly, the face of public works is that of seldom-traveled highways, costly toll bridges spanning waterways once plied by inexpensive ferries, and dams designed for 150-year floods. Because of this, an unusual level of public opposition has emerged: one magazine rather hysterically described "recent mass protests against unwanted dams, airports, roads, and bridges that have suddenly broken out all over the country."[23] Although this is an exaggeration, voters are pressuring the government to reduce demand for public works, and this is affecting architects. Remote rail lines include plans for train stations, unpopular land reclamation plans include warehouses, and those little-traveled highways include toilets and rest stops, which are sometimes designed by ambitious young architects. The protests may also be the beginning of a deeper danger for architects, since the looser expectations for these buildings have offered designers an appreciated opportunity to experiment programmatically and stylistically.

Still, for the moment, architects are not yet perceived as benefiting from public works support by creating a public burden – unlike the construction industry. But with the costs of upkeep and the modest visitors' numbers for many of the baubles being built today, it is possible that the profession is undermining future public support. As one protestor noted, "we have come to realize that public works are not for the public."[24] Architects are not blamed; anger is directed toward politicians and construction companies tied to unpopular civil works. However, architects will be affected if recent efforts toward effective cost–benefit reviews are successful; the mechanism is now in place for members of the public to demand greater utility in new projects. To date, though, in spite of newly required cost–benefit (re-) analyses, only thirty-five projects of 8,000 reviewed have been affected. It is possible that communities will grow more savvy in the use of cost–benefit reviews to stop superfluous facilities, in which case architects will likely see fewer of the most open-ended projects.

Movements toward transparency have also led to the decisions about competitions being held in public forums. Today there is very little effort on the part of most architects to educate the public; designers are instead content to operate within the most powerful sectors of Japanese society. New ways of selecting professionals may offer a useful forum for architects to increase public awareness, but it may also shift decisions toward more conservative choices.

CRONYISM AND "DESCENDING FROM HEAVEN"

Corruption is widely considered endemic in the construction industry, although architects do not seem in any way directly involved. However, three forms of corruption dominate, and each has some potential effect on architectural practice. Corruption can be broken into *dango*, collusion related to bid rigging and pre-determination; *amakudari*, construction companies hiring retired politicians and bureaucrats; and bribery.

The impact of collusion is the most obvious, accounting at least in part for the inconceivable building costs I cited earlier in this chapter. Newspapers representing the public interest have complained about *dango* at least since the Meiji era, with no obvious effect. In one government audit in the early 1990s, *dango* was discovered in 90 per cent of public works projects audited.[25] Professionals are surprisingly comfortable with its existence, if not all of its effects; Matsushita goes so far as to suggest, "... collusion is in fact routine, and many people think it is legal."[26] The Japanese publishing and professional communities are also for the most part sanguine about collusion. Yasuyuki Hippoh's report on construction practices notes simply, "... this practice is too traditional and prevalent for contractors to abandon it ..."[27] Hideo Tanaka's 1995 essay on bid-rigging in Saitama Prefecture goes further, suggesting why bid-rigging remains viable: "... the authorities decided not to prosecute ... for several reasons, among them: there were no precedents for prosecution of bid-rigging ..." Further, he states that governmental oversight was hampered because a "... case involved sixty-six companies and would have exceeded the JTFC's [Japan Fair Trade Commission's] investigative powers ..."[28] In fact, it is not entirely clear that collusion is illegal, as there are no directly applicable provisions of the penal code. Instead, arrests are often for other, related, violations. Public bodies thus sustain collusion, whether deliberately or unwittingly.

The need for pre-bid estimates also may sustain *dango*. Agencies unprepared to handle cost estimations internally contract out to local firms. The decision about which contractor to consult may have more to do with personal friendships than with expertise. In this way, a privileged builder enjoys lead time for bid preparation, greater intimacy with the agency's goals, and inside knowledge about the minimum threshold for bids. Other contractors have less incentive to bid and generally appreciate knowing if there is an advantaged bidder.

Periodically, however, the government does step in to reduce collusion. Both the government and professionals may hold conflicting positions on the practice. Architects have been known to argue that they appreciate collusion, because manufacturers and subcontractors can rely on pre-determination in contracts. Thus, consultants find manufacturers supportive in the early stages of design, making costly samples or mock-ups and testing materials before a contract is in place. The manufacturer is not assured the job, but a case can be made among peers that earlier involvement and invested costs are reasons for a specific manufacturer to be given a contract. Based on this, some professionals claim collusion is ethical, at least for the constructors. Contractors certainly appreciate that the system not only reduces the costs of preparing unsuccessful bids, but the less competitive environment also maintains higher costs. This makes the system less fair to clients and the public. Professionals aware that *dango* increases costs in specific sectors will attempt to shy away where its influence can draw too much capital from projects with limited funds. However, because costs seem capricious and unpredictably affected by *dango*, architects have less incentive to address these costs. Japanese architects sometimes seem to miss the fact that the high costs of construction have created a split market and that the independent professionals thus design a far smaller portion of the built landscape.

Japan does not have a monopoly on collusion. According to Ronald Goldstock and others, in New York, "Inspectors generally . . . believe that there is significant fraud on *every* major public construction project."[29] Corruption is estimated to raise the overall costs of construction in that city by at least 40 per cent, which is comparable to the 50 per cent increase that JETRO reports on charges for public works in Japan. There are several reasons that collusion is found in the construction industry. The same authors note that construction projects are almost impossible to closely audit; cash payments to day laborers and small suppliers are common, and the vast number of suppliers on construction projects makes it easier to establish illusory corporate entities. Since there is no gross standardization, and unforeseen problems frequently require an immediate response, this also creates a looser approach to financial management in construction. In addition, Goldstock's team lists other factors that encourage corruption. These include the fact that large amounts of money are involved and illegal payments can be passed on to consumers.[30] Japan's public works projects cost tens or even hundreds of billions of yen (hundreds of millions or even billions of dollars), so they certainly require large amounts of money. There have been some nascent efforts at establishing accountability, but tax systems today support accounting practices that allow cash payments. These payments are also supported by public citizens, who may benefit by receiving untaxed *mendōryō* (literally, "the costs of bother") payments from adjacent construction sites. As with many other aspects of Japan's construction industry, the problems are not unique, even if the combination that defines Japan's context for practice is.

One example of ethically questionable practice that is difficult to find in most developed countries is the widespread practice of *amakudari*. The word literally means "descent from heaven," and implies that retired officials hired by private concerns bring with them special powers, like gods coming to earth. The practice is not new, nor is it confined to the construction industry. T. J. Pempel noted that in the 1960s, the Ministry of Finance, the Ministry of International Trade and Industry, and the Ministry of Transportation all had higher numbers of retired officials in private employ than the Ministry of Construction. However, a 1996 survey by Teikoku Databank showed that of 2,995 management positions in the top one hundred construction companies, retired public servants filled an estimated 517 jobs – one out of every six.[31] In recent research on the practice, former bureaucrats served as various versions of managing directors at Shimizu and the medium-sized Tokyu and Toda Construction companies (*senmu*); Fujita, Maeda, Hazama and a road-building affiliate of Obayashi (*jōmu*); and at Kajima and Kumagai (*torishimariyaku*).[32] (*Torishimariyaku* is a general term for directors, and *jōmu and senmu* are high-ranking directors.) Through their contacts, former officials influence government agencies' decisions, promoting the continuation of generous budgets for public works.

Bribery and generous political donations from the industry simply bolster these relationships and seem as integral to construction practices as *dango* and *amakudari*. One author notes that, "Of the hundred or so bribery scandals each year in Japan, over half involve construction companies."[33] Professionals have very little direct involvement in bribery and the effect on design and construction quality has been minimal. Thus, architects remain unconcerned. For the moment, however, design professionals benefit from the friendly ties between large construction companies and government. The danger is that as bribery becomes increasingly unpalatable to the Japanese public, architects will find their reputations tarnished – with little opportunity for recourse, since they are not directly involved. For the most part bribes are a way to *obtain* work, not as a way to get shoddy work accepted. In fact, there is very, very little evidence of shoddy work. Perhaps this is the reason that bribery is punished lightly. Contractors may find that exposure leads to relatively short three- or six-month periods when they are unable to bid on public works. Many will not even face these penalties, as the statute of limitations for any prosecution is relatively short (three years).

Even today, architects often discover that efforts to address corruption can affect design practices.

RIKEN YAMAMOTO AND SAITAMA UNIVERSITY

The Saitama University campus, originally designed and constructed as Saitama Nursing College, is a beautiful complex that projects an unruffled serenity. Ironically, its construction was one of the most antagonistic processes I have witnessed in Japan. Architects and contractors spoke to each other in a strained, overly-formal Japanese and frequently raised their voices and stalked out of meetings – behavior quite rare on most sites, especially those involving major contractors.

The strained relationships on site were at least in part caused by concerns the client, Saitama Prefecture, brought to the project. In the early 1990s, pressure from the US government to open the construction market to foreign firms drew attention to corruption in the construction industry. Saitama Prefecture, a booming district adjacent to Tokyo, figured in several scandals, perhaps for no other reason than its relatively high rate of construction activity. The largest of these scandals was the exposure of the "Saitama Saturday Club," a group of contractors that met regularly to determine winning bidders on public works and arrange joint venture partnerships. As a result, the prefectural government made efforts to develop a more fair system of contract awards and oversight, but – at least on this site – the new system had a rough beginning.

Anti-corruption efforts included awarding construction contracts in a complex manner, resulting in five separate construction contracts for the site, each conferred on a different joint venture contractor. Sixteen different general contractors, including three major ones (Obayashi, Shimizu and Tokyu), participated in these five joint venture organizations. The unwieldy numbers at Saitama University – twenty-nine staff in the architect's office alone and weekly meetings of thirty to thirty-five people from the consultants, contractors and major subcontractors – prevented a sense of teamwork from developing on site. The architects reported that even early discussions about relatively small decisions such as formatting drawings were prolonged and fruitless.

9.3
Saitama University designed by Riken Yamamoto, exterior showing bridge.

The decision to use so many contractors may seem peculiar, but it was not uncommon during the recession and was also used in the 1970s to sustain the construction industry. In 1998, I also saw three contractors linked as a joint venture on the relatively tiny 611 square meter (6,577 square foot) "Snow Village Future Foundation" by Jun Aoki. As public works projects moved toward more competitive bidding, there was a concern that these approaches would exclude the smaller, local contractors, who naturally have less impressive qualifications than Japan's major contractors. Because local governments are also concerned with area employment and with maintaining local enterprises, joint venture arrangements, linking larger contractors to local firms, were a popular arrangement. So although the system is economically inefficient, its targeted social benefits parallel minority set-asides in the US construction industry.

Joint venture arrangements are not inherently problematic, but the large number of participants set the stage for problems at Saitama University. This was exacerbated because Riken Yamamoto, the architect, was committed to creating a unified character that contributes to the sense of calm on site, but requires extensive coordination. Yamamoto also had limited experience on large, public projects and saw this as an important point in his career. Other architects, faced with breaking the site up between contractors, have been more likely to establish a mixed vocabulary of materials and manage each block with a distinct team, thus allowing the team and the specific joint venture contractors to establish a rapport internally, and creating looser ties between the groups. At Saitama, Yamamoto's desire to have close coordination between the different contractors often meant that subcontractors and fabricators were also required to coordinate detailing and materials selections. Where the architect was able to insist on a single fabricator, as in the thousands of precisely made precast columns produced by Fudo Kenken, the project is most successful. But the constructors also produced customized and coordinated curtain walls as much as 325 meters (1,066 feet) long, with minimal variation in detailing – not, however, without a great deal of painful negotiation.

In addition to coordination problems, oversight by the client was stepped up: the prefecture had five public officials with construction experience on site, there were unsuccessful efforts to establish heightened control through ISO 9000 series approaches, and even the architect had a full-time accountant on site, although she was concerned with internal costs, not estimating. Putting these efforts in place caused considerable delays, and the architects found themselves having to respond to a construction period of only nineteen months, from July 1997 through to January 1999, for a 102,265 square meter (1,100,780 square foot) site with a building area of 54,080 square meters (582,120 square feet).

The oversight by Saitama public officials eventually interfered with design development. It was my sense that their strongest mandate was related not to design impact or even construction quality control, but rather to cost containment. Saitama Prefecture had a great deal of publicly funded work under construction at the time, and the combination of voter concerns over construction scandals and the possibility of simultaneous cost overruns on several extremely large projects amply justified such concerns. These officials were knowledgeable on construction matters and often impressed me with their awareness of fabrication issues during their participation in visits to fabricators and on-site materials inspections. However, they were not sympathetic to architectural concerns, such as the higher standards for detailing that Yamamoto's staff brought to the project. This may in part be because local officials do occasionally design projects internally, but these tend to be built from relatively crude production documents, with little design development.

Eleven months into construction, officials overseeing the project had become so nervous about the potential for ambiguous cost fluctuations resulting from design development that they attempted to place a moratorium on changes and insisted that the architects use

9.4, 9.5 & 9.6
Care was shown in even the smallest details. Here, the pattern of holes on screens were extensively drawn and observed in models before production of the final materials. Shown is an exterior view of the punched metal finish, looking from the interior, and one of the firm's on-site staff with a mock-up of the same material.

earlier drawings rather than further detail the work. When design development and detailing were necessary, the Saitama officials attempted to determine whether this resulted from performance or aesthetic concerns, with a willingness to eschew aesthetic interest. For the most part, the project was not affected by this moratorium, because by this time major areas such as the envelope were already worked out. However, the architects were still resolving the space frames that cap each building. The soaring canopy roofs linking several of these buildings were particularly affected and do not show the refinement seen in the skin and interiors, for example.

Nevertheless, what most architects would consider design development did continue, and at a high level of refinement. A list of the elements considered for approval in July 1998 included sixty-three items; these ranged from landscaping items like signage and plantings to detailing connections at the envelope, roof copings and window fittings. Most, however, were for interior finishes and cabinetry. These approvals very often involved a significant level of design decision-making, and illustrate how integral refinement is to construction supervision.

An on-site furniture inspection of proposed library shelving in September 1998 offers a good example of how some areas were being developed. The number of participants in the inspection varied throughout the afternoon, but included as many as eight staff from the architect's office, three people representing the furniture designer, a "broker" who was overseeing the alliance between these two consultants, four people from the fabricators, three of the contractor's staff, three Saitama Prefecture employees, and one person from the electrical subcontractor. People moved the shelves closer to a stair, checked the bulb heat, and tried to scratch and mark the finish with fingerprints – activities consistent with an inspection. In addition, the bracing design was rejected for reworking and welding quality was cited as a potential problem. The participants also made choices between two types of bookend connections and square or rounded corners on the bookends, shelves made up of parallel bars or panels and with or without a back, splayed or straight legs on the shelving units, and different resolutions for the base of the cabinets – all activities that can better be considered design decision-making.

How could a moratorium on design development be in place while this level of refinement was openly under consideration by a large group, including several public officials? The furniture inspection involved a customization that was already underway and the details under consideration were routine production variants. Detailing had shifted from the hands of the design consultants to the fabricators. On the other hand, further development of the roof canopies would have required negotiation by the consultants and the contractors involved, so it was not possible to pursue. Thus, even while officials fought the architects' efforts at refinement and constructors bridled at coordination efforts, the overall care and craft the constructors brought to the work remained high. As I have already noted, public reviews and future contracts – both those between the contractors and the prefecture, and those between the subcontractors and contractors – depend on performance and assure quality in production.

1. N. Pollock, "Designing for the Japanese Public" in J. Zukowsky, ed., *Japan 2000: Architecture and Design for the Japanese Public*, Munich and New York, Prestel, 1998, p. 31.
2. The 70 per cent figure is from J. Lewis, "Review of Recent Works on Construction and Public Works" *Social Science Japan*, no. 10, August 1997, p. 33 and the 44 per cent figure from NIST [National Institute of Standards and Technology], *Innovation in the Japanese Construction Industry: A 1995 Appraisal*, Washington, DC, US Government Printing Office, 1996, p. 116. The comparable figure for the United States is 28 per cent.
3. J. Zukowsky, "Introduction" *Japan 2000: Architecture and Design for the Japanese Public*, Munich and New York, Prestel, 1998, p. 17.
4. "Kenchiku Juchū de Obayashi ga Kentō, Takenaka ha Kusen [Construction Orders Show Obayashi's Good Fight and Takenaka's Hard Fight]," *Nikkei A-kitekuchua* [Nikkei Architecture] no. 655, 13 December 1999, p. 5.
5. *Kensetsu Hakushō, Heisei Juichi Nen* [Construction White Paper, 1999], Tokyo, Ōkurashō Insatsu Kyoku [Ministry of Finance Printing Office], 1999 p. 494.
6. JETRO [the Japan External Trade Organization], *The Survey on Actual Condition Regarding Access to Japan*, Tokyo, JETRO, October 1998, p. A1-1. Annual figures for Japan only are published in the *Kensetsu Hakushō* [Construction White Paper]. In 1998, public works accounted for 6.8 per cent of GDP.
7. K. Kase, "Economic Aspects of Public Works Projects in Japan," *Social Science Japan*, no. 17, December 1999, p. 19.
8. *Kensetsu Hakushō, Heisei Juichi Nen* [Construction White Paper, 1999], p. 495–6.
9. *Kensetsu Hakushō, Heisei Juichi Nen* [Construction White Paper, 1999], p. 504.
10. G. Tett, "Endless pump-priming bloats Japan's construction sector," *Financial Times*, 12 November 1999.
11. K. Fujita and R. C. Hill, *Japanese Cities in the World Economy*, Philadelphia, Temple University Press, 1993, p. 101.
12. J. Lewis, "Review of Recent Works on Construction and Public Works," p. 33.
13. C. Johnson, *Japan: Who Governs? The Rise of the Developmental State*, New York, WW Norton, 1995, p. 77. Johnson is referring to the work of John McMillan in "Dango: Japan's Price-Fixing Conspiracies" in *Economics and Politics* 3:1, November 1991, p. 201–18.
14. *Japan Company Handbook 1*, Tokyo: Tokyo Keizai, 1994. Taisei, p. 53; Obayashi, p. 54; Shimizu, p. 55; Kajima, p. 63; Kumagai Gumi, p. 95. Figures are not available for Takenaka Komuten. These figures cluster even more tightly if one does not follow the convention of including Kumagai, whose profits were 13 billion yen in 1994. The figures for the other four firms were between 29 and 33 billion yen.
15. JETRO, "The Survey on Actual Condition Regarding Access to Japan," p. A2–4.
16. N. Pollock, "Designing for the Japanese Public," p. 46.
17. http://www.e-architect.com/pia/membero/pa/aug_99/awards.asp
18. Y. Shimizu, "Vote Deals a Blow to Public Works," *Nikkei Weekly*, 31 January 2000, p. 5.
19. "Kaijō Atochi Riyō Megutte Iron Zokushutu [Objections are raised about using vacant lands]" *Nikkei A-kitekuchua* [*Nikkei Architecture*], no. 655, 13 December 1999.
20. Zukowsky, *Japan 2000*, p. 17.
21. H. Yatsuka, "Introduction to ArtPolis" *AD Architectural Design, Japanese Architecture III*, no. 107, 1994, p. 35.
22. Quoted in Pollock, "Designing for the Japanese Public," p. 35.
23. "The Perils of Pork and Gravy" *Economist*, vol. 351, no. 8123, 12 June 1999, p. 38.
24. Ibid.
25. M. Tilton, *Restrained Trade: Cartels in Japan's Basic Materials Industries*, Ithaca, Cornell University Press, 1996, p. 112. The original source was *Nihon Keizai Shinbun*, 4 November 1993 with an English language report in the *Weekly Japan Digest*, 8 November 1993.
26. F. Matsushita, *Design and Construction Practice in Japan: A Practical Guide*, Tokyo, Kaibunsha Ltd., 1994, p. 53.
27. Y. Hippoh, *The Construction Industry in Japan: A Survey*, Asian Productivity Organization, n.d. (c. 1983), p. 234.
28. H. Tanaka, "The Role of Law in Japanese Society: Comparisons with the West," in K. Fujikura, ed., *Japanese Law and Legal Theory*, Aldershot, Singapore, and Sydney, Dartmouth Publishing Co. Ltd., 1996, p. 100.
29. R. Goldstock, *Corruption and Racketeering in the New York City Construction Industry: The Final Report of the New York State Organized Crime Task Force*, New York and London, New York University Press, 1990, p. 129. Emphasis mine.
30. Ibid., p. 62.
31. Teikoku Databank "*Amakudari Jittai Chōsa*." Published in English as "Amakudari in Construction Companies," 13 December 1996.
32. *Nihon no Jinmyaku to Kigyō Keiretsu* [Japan's Company Alliances and Lines of Personal Contacts], Tokyo: Tōyō Keizai Shinjô Sha, 1994, p. 18.
33. B. Woodall, *Japan Under Construction: Corruption, Politics and Public Works*, Berkeley and Los Angeles, University of California Press, 1996, p. 39.

Legal issues

In my descriptions of collaborative teams, I have already indicated that liability and contractual responsibilities differ in Japan. In the sections that follow, I outline some of the key ways that two areas of the legal system assure flexibility.

CONTRACTS

Any North American architect observing Japanese design development cannot help but wonder at the ability of Japanese architects to negotiate the quality and execution of design after a project has been bid and contracts negotiated. I have seen the site survey done at the onset of construction, for example, after the project has been bid. Suppliers and the quality of building components found in later stages of construction (windows, doors, etc.) are determined shortly before installation. The tolerances for the structure are established by existing standards, but designers successfully press fabricators to work at tolerances only one-third of those allowed. Contracts often remain unsigned until well after the engineer's calculations and such have been completed – and one author notes a case where a contractor had demolished an existing building and begun advertising units for sale in a new building prior to contracts being signed on the project.[1]

The basic assumptions found in legal systems in the United States and Japan are diametrically different, with the practices of most other developed nations standing somewhere between the two. Although elsewhere it has seemed most appropriate to present Japan's context without explicitly drawing comparisons, expectations in Japan regarding the influence of US practices lead me to believe that it is best to more explicitly compare and contrast the two systems. In the US, contracts are considered to tightly define the relationship and responsibilities of each party, without regard for the fairness or appropriateness of the agreement. Therefore, US courts will strictly enforce a contract. But, as the legal scholar Hiroshi Oda noted, Japanese courts have decided that contracts should be reviewed, "taking into account the doctrine of good faith and fair dealing ..."[2] More significantly, as another leading scholar noted, "in case after case ... the courts continued to refuse to enforce contracts according to their explicit terms."[3] Consequently, in Japan, contracts are generally perceived as being inexact, adaptable instruments.

Thus, the foundation of the Japanese contractual relationship encourages contracts that are vaguely executed. Japanese legal scholars are unequivocal on this point: Ei'ichi Hoshino notes that, "the general notion of the binding power of contracts is weak in Japan" and that, "... the precise drafting of a contract itself is not very desirable. One can say, in a word, that in Japan little interest is paid to what are called contracts."[4] And Oda claims that "the binding force of contract is not as strict as in Europe and the United States."[5]

Furthermore, the Japanese doctrine is that, as Oda states, "contracts concluded where one party is in a strong bargaining position and which contain excessively disadvantageous clauses as regards the other can be null and void ..."[6] In the United States, by contrast, the courts will enforce a morally tainted contract (the common example is trading one's inheritance for a bowl of soup) on the assumption that both parties felt it a worthwhile bargain at the time of execution.[7]

Contracting parties in Japan do not pay much attention to the content of contracts, and may even work with no more than an oral agreement. In 1979, the Ministry of Construction found that over one-quarter of all construction contracts were no more than a simple written order and its acknowledged acceptance. About 80 per cent of general contractors surveyed normally completed a contract with owners, with an additional 12 per cent using only a written order and/or its acceptance, and slightly more than 5 per cent undertaking work on the basis of an oral contract.[8] Subcontractors or architects also enter into projects with little more than a verbal agreement, further eroding those claims to tailoring their legal rights which Westerners consider necessary. Practices between subcontractors and the general contractor were even looser, with only 39 per cent utilizing contracts, and 9 per cent relying only on an oral agreement, although the Construction Business Act does require a written contract.[9] On the same page, the author drily notes, "... this is a normative rule and cannot invalidate the legal effect of an oral agreement."[10] (The reasons that a contractor is more likely to require a contract when working with a client, and less concerned about binding legal documents with subcontractors, is a point I will further address below.) Manufacturers, too, as I have noted elsewhere, offer testing, prototype development and other services for free and without contracts. Almost universally, the construction industry will ignore the specificity of clauses, although the use of precisely drafted contracts is increasingly being promoted by contractors. For the moment, however, it remains true that while many cultures value contractual minutiae, in Japan the contract simply serves as a departure point for on-going negotiations.

One reason that it may be beneficial to draft contracts without extensive clauses (which Western academics have referred to as "incomplete contracts") is that it is often quite costly to develop an agreement that covers all possible occurrences – and even then, as many architects are aware, the interpretation of these clauses on each side may differ, leading to problems. Bob Greenstreet, in a discussion of lawsuits against architects, goes so far as to note that, "Many of the cases ... often result not from design failure ... but from a breakdown in the contractual relationship, due to misunderstandings, miscommunications, or a general lack of comprehension."[11] It is conventional in many countries for architects, prior to commencing construction, to produce extremely detailed construction documents as part of the contract, but in spite of this, not all aspects of the building can be adequately addressed in such documents. In addition, changes in material prices and availability or less than ideal conditions on site may require that tightly written construction documents must still be modified by change orders. Greenstreet notes that, "... the change order process is a fertile area for the inception and growth of disputes."[12] Therefore, one legal text on construction practices in North America notes grimly that, "Construction is a dispute-prone industry, and claims are a fact of life. Even successful projects have claims. Claims are a natural outgrowth of a complex and highly competitive process during which the unexpected often happens."[13]

Instead of a detailed agreement, Japanese contracts simply call for unforeseen events to be addressed in a cooperative spirit. The idea is that the use of contracts not only encourages mutual trust in the relationship, but allows for adaptability in unforeseen circumstances. In a lengthy essay on contracts, Takeyoshi Kawashima notes that this approach has even been preferred by the contractors advising the national government. He wrote,

> On one occasion I suggested that the contents of the standard provisions of the construction work contract of the Ministry of Construction be made as complete, inclusive, and definite as possible. This was because I thought that it was, above all, necessary to narrow the margin for deciding disputes between the contracting agency and the contractor through negotiation ... There was opposition to my proposal from the business world [e.g., contractors] ... If the obligations under the contract were made definite and fixed, it was said, an uneasiness was felt that such contracts would "lack flexibility".[14]

Because of this tendency toward versatility, agreements are frequently drawn up without the involvement of legal counsel. Yoshinobu Ashihara has even been quoted as saying he will not accept projects when the client uses a lawyer in negotiations.[15] And Tadao Ando summarized the Japanese attitude in noting, "If in Japan you came to a meeting and said 'this is my lawyer,' the person you were meeting would get upset. But in America, you have the feeling that people say 'that's right. I don't trust you.'"[16] Regarding this approach, Fumihiko Maki said, "In Japan, we are still able to change design in construction without too much litigation ... We have taken advantage of this. The final product is a collaboration."[17]

CONTRACTS IN JAPAN'S LEGAL AND SOCIAL COMMUNITY

Two scholars who have studied legal practices in the United States and Japan, Minoru Nakazato and J. Mark Ramseyer, refer to the US approach to contracts as a negotiated "private legal regime" and many scholars consider the US approach to be overly "legalistic." Most further suggest that the Japanese legal context allows for simpler contracts because there is little occasion for privately negotiated variations. Thus, not only is there less need for highly specific documents, there is little opportunity to utilize them. Generally speaking, the Japanese courts will not only consider a specific contract, but also look to industry norms and to practices that already existed between contracting parties. The Japanese courts have noted that custom has greater weight than the language found in contractual agreements – the precise opposite of what one would find in US courts. For example, the Tokyo District Court has dismissed detailed boilerplate in a lease as no more than "a model" and "not intended by the parties to have any effect."[18] This attitude is also found outside the courts. In a 1971 and 1976 set of surveys by the *Nippon Bunka Kaigi* [Japan Culture Forum] the questions included "What would you do if a contract became unsuited to the actual situation a few years after it was made?" Slightly more than 31 per cent of respondents agreed to the answer, "However unsuitable, a contract is a contract and I would abide by it," but over 60 per cent of all respondents selected the answer, "I would discuss with the other party whether the contract could be ignored."[19] Notably, renegotiating the contract and writing a new one was not even offered as an option in the survey.

One point that many scholars writing on Japan's legal system tend to regard as central to the flexibility of contracts is the impact of "changed circumstances." In both the United States and Japan, it is possible for one to be excused from carrying out contractual obligations if there have been unforeseen changes that make complying impossible – US scholars, for example, tend to discuss the impact a war has on shipping supplies. And in fact it was circumstances surrounding World War II that led the Japanese Supreme Court to decide that a contract is no longer binding if the context under which it was written has changed. Broadly speaking, the definition of changed circumstances is similar in the United States and Japan. In the United States, a contract may become moot when its purpose has been destroyed, e.g., when an architect has been hired for particular expertise, but passes away before being able to complete a project. Additionally, changed circumstances may make it physically or commercially impossible to complete a contract, for example when an earthquake makes a building site unsound. These points are usually outlined in three conditions under which a US contract becomes untenable: first, the change in circumstances must not have been foreseen; second, the party attempting to nullify the contract must not have directly or indirectly accepted the risk associated with the change; third, the party seeking to nullify the contract must not have been responsible for the changed conditions. However, one notable difference between the two systems is the potential scope under which these changes are considered.

Thus, in Japan, the conditions that can lead to a contract becoming invalid are broader, and by coincidence more closely relate to the practice of architecture. In fact, the issue of changed circumstances takes up a considerable amount of space in the relatively short standard contracts used by most architects and contractors. Standard contract forms permit the parties to demand renegotiation if one year has passed and if "... the contract price has become inappropriate due to changed wages or commodity prices ..." or because of "... drastic changes in the economic conditions ..."[20] The contract does note, however, that contractors are to be liable for the initial 15/1000 (1.5 per cent) of costs impacted by such unforeseen economic shifts.

Although contractors have attempted to limit the cost of fluctuations during the 1990s (because they create economic uncertainty), an earlier survey demonstrates the use of this clause. In the early 1970s, the combination of a shift from the gold standard in the United States and rising oil prices created a sharp drop in Japan's economy. At that time, the Tokyo Chamber of Commerce and Industry surveyed its 300 member firms regarding exploitation of the "changed circumstances" clause in construction projects. Two-thirds of all firms attempted to exploit this clause, and one-half did so successfully, with larger firms generally more fortunate.[21] Thus, normal practices are such that architects and contractors treat contract documents, which are often ambiguous in any case, as pliable – especially as they relate to price and deadlines. Bluntly stated, no contractually agreed upon costs can really be treated as binding, because of the nature of construction.

CONTRACTS IN JAPAN'S ARCHITECTURAL COMMUNITY

One leading Japanese legal scholar claims that "even if detailed provisions are inserted into contracts, they do not have very much significance; and consequently, the parties do not read them carefully or regard them seriously."[22] And Fumio Matsushita, legal counsel for one of Tokyo's largest design offices, noted:

> A contract is not finally binding upon the parties, no matter how exactingly bargained and drafted. If one party experiences difficulty in performing, he can and usually does propose a change to the contract and the other party is expected to give certain consideration.[23]

He continued, "In Japan ... negotiations do not precede, but follow the conclusion of a contract and continue without end."[24]

As one example of how this is evidenced in architectural practice, legal deadlines are more flexible. Firm deadlines, particularly the imposition of to-the-minute bid deadlines on government projects, are a source of amazement and amusement to Japanese architects and contractors who have had experience in the United States. In general, many contractual deadlines are targets, and under circumstances, such as for payments or completion of work, complying within a few days is considered acceptable. As Kawashima noted in his essay, "The Legal Consciousness of Contract in Japan," "... even something such as the due date of a debt is not thought of as something strictly defined but as fixed 'give or take a few days.'"[25] Kawashima additionally notes that construction contracts tend to offer a great deal of leeway through built-in extensions, and that as long as the other party is not inconvenienced, these extensions should not incur penalties.[26] Furthermore, because the precise scope of work in each phase is more loosely defined, architects and contractors can frequently shift incomplete work to the next stage of production when necessary, although final completion dates are still important because of their potential impact on satisfaction ratings.

In one extreme example, a project was officially completed in December, but apparently remained without an operable air handling system until June – in spite of the fact that the building had been specifically designed and constructed to study the mechanical systems, which included some relatively unusual features. Office staff moved in in February, with space heaters to offer some comfort. I visited the project on the day the air handling systems were first put into operation, and found that the client representative and mechanical contractors were on cordial, even friendly, terms. The client representative confessed that there had been some rough days initially, but noted cheerfully that he hoped these were behind them. The mechanical contractors were more chagrined over their delays, but worked in a professional and unflappable manner.

In general, the relaxed attitude toward fine points in agreements leads to some willingness to crib on small points. One author suggested that between 1969 and 1978 as much as 8.4 per cent of all projects included violations to the Building Standards Law.[27] I do not see evidence that such attitudes extend to anything that might be life-threatening – in fact, the performance of recent buildings in the 1995 Kobe-area Hanshin Earthquake would suggest the opposite, in that major damage as a result of negligence by contractors was singularly insignificant. Nonetheless, Japanese architects will try to fudge small points, opening up balustrades along stairs or creating ambiguous rooms that are presented to the authorities as not intended for occupancy. This is easier to accomplish because for the most part there are no building inspections. Rather, contractors report progress to the authorities using photographs taken at each stage of construction.

While the current shift to performance specifications will have a significant impact, today uniform standards generally establish specifics such as tolerances, not project-specific contracts.[28] In the case of construction tolerances, I found the agreed upon norms already more precise than would be expected in North America – but I also observed architects successfully putting pressure on fabricators to work within still tighter tolerances for particularly important parts of the building, without any contractual rights to do so. Contrast this with Western practices, where instead of a measure of a reasonable maximum variation, tolerances are often treated as the acceptable slack by builders. Since in Japan the emphasis is on the relationship between parties, rather than a legalistic assertion, the fabricators tend to either work harder to meet the architects' stated higher standards, or to ignore them in such a way as to indicate a reluctance to continue the working relationship. In the latter case, as I note elsewhere, other firms generally exist within the building team and are able to take on production, and this is the more likely response than the dubious attempt to pressure a reluctant fabricator to work at a higher standard.

Furthermore, if parties in Japan do not specify the quality of a material and it is not covered by accepted standards, the courts have generally mandated intermediate quality. As a result, much of the detail of North American

Legal issues 153

specifications is not initially necessary in Japanese documents, and the documents that exist for the most part resemble outline specifications. Japanese architects may write performance specifications, but these are generally related only to the production of unique or previously untried building components. Rather than relying on the architects' specifications to establish quality, I have noted the use of extremely specific agreements produced during the construction phase. These are usually drawn up by the contractor, with modifications suggested by design professionals before document approvals. As one example of such an agreement, on one site I was shown a binder several inches thick, related to unfinished concrete finishes on the project. Topics covered included the state of the formwork to be used, its thickness, form ties and separators, the composition of the concrete, supplier location and the distance from the plant to the site. In reviewing the document, the architect noted a desire to assure that the nail heads in adjacent panels of the formwork would be aligned, a level of detail probably beyond the scope of most North American specifications.

Although an open-ended legal context allows for the professional to react quickly – detailing and measuring for existing construction, or taking into account changes in the cost and supply when selecting materials – the environment is not one that is entirely positive. First and foremost, loose contracts mean that each project requires a new relationship to be established between the architect and contractor, and the actions possible on one site might, in spite of the architects' best efforts, be unavailable on the next. Even where the same contractor is involved, much depends on the inclinations of the individuals representing both sides on site. As I note elsewhere, the ability to successfully negotiate such relationships is not one that comes easily. Although the best projects exemplify the innovations possible under a flexible legal structure, Japanese architects also recognize the benefit of a tightly defined contract. As one example, I have observed many projects where the budget is redefined during construction, generally reducing the funds available. Such shifts mean that architects in Japan must constantly renegotiate areas that many architects consider fixed.

POLITICAL ECONOMISTS' JUSTIFICATION FOR "INCOMPLETE CONTRACTS"

The flexible attitude to contracts tends to be linked to a strong inclination toward mutual trust. In that regard, Japan's relatively closed community has made such contracts more likely, although there are certainly other environments where similar agreements are possible. Legal scholars suggest that a society's willingness to enforce contracts tightly or not is in part a result of expectations regarding the longevity of business relationships. As Cooter and Ulen note, "Sharp dealing is far more likely when the contractual partners never expect to see each other again than when they have an interest in continuing trade."[29] In game theory, this is referred to as the "End Game Problem." In short-term relationships, the benefit of cooperation is not perceived as being significant, but in ongoing relationships the reverse is true.[30]

In a discussion of similar attitudes toward contracts found in rural communities in the United States, the legal scholars Nakazato and Ramseyer argued,

Whether in Japan or the United States, how much firms A and B use and rely on legally enforceable contracts will depend on several often closely related factors:

- the extent to which A and B are tied to a small, closely knit community
- the speed and accuracy with which information travels among the firms with which A and B deal
- the number of other firms with which A and B do business
- the degree to which A and B have invested time and resources in their reputations for integrity
- the extent to which A and B can use assets, guarantees or controlling stock interests to secure their performance
- the degree to which, wholly aside from these factors A and B can credibly convince each other that they can rationally expect to continue to do business with each other in the future.[31]

Or, as Howard Davis noted more simply, "The more explicit contract is necessary in order to enforce centralized control over the building's construction, in a situation in which shared cultural understandings and informal social sanctions are not strong enough to guide construction."[32] Clearly, some of the points that Nakazato and Ramseyer outline are closely related. In a small, closely knit community, it is much easier to rely on quick, accurate information, especially on issues more likely to be communicated informally. Similarly, a limited number of firms and the small size of the community begin to collapse when one is considering specific groupings, such as the construction sector. Finally, if this group is closed, either because of language or other barriers, then firms will of necessity find that they work together repeatedly.

Going through this list is sobering, because all of these factors have to some degree changed in the recessionary 1990s. Elsewhere in this book I have pointed out that the number of contractors has risen, and small, local contractors, although perhaps affiliated loosely with the "Big Five," are the ones that most worry architects. There are fewer guarantees of performance, and long-term reputation is less likely to be a concern to these contractors. With greater numbers of builders, it can be very difficult for architects to get accurate information about their strengths and weaknesses. Contractors have room for similar concerns, because of the rising number of registered architectural offices. Without reliable information, an individual architect's tendency to make changes or drag his or her feet are less likely to be known. Additionally, the increasing number of professional offices and licensed contractors reduces the likelihood of parties working together again in the future. Increasingly, architects prefer the largest contractors, and contractors and clients tend to favor the more established architectural offices. There is less trust and less willingness to work together in local settings.

The long recession of the 1990s has also weakened the extent to which both parties can use assets, guarantees or controlling stock interests to secure their performance. Assets have been reduced to such a degree that several major contractors would already have been declared bankrupt in many countries – and it is possible that one of Japan's major contractors may yet be declared bankrupt before this book reaches print. Further, cross-holding shares of stock, a practice that has held together contractors, suppliers and architectural firms (most

Japanese corporations, whether small professional firms offering architectural services or larger manufacturers, are *kabushiki kaisha* or joint-stock corporations) is also declining and the banks are far too weak to offer support. It has become harder for the construction industry to bear the expense associated with uncertainty in design and construction practices. This precarious situation means that the use of precisely drafted contracts is also being promoted by contractors as a way of protecting limited resources.

However, even with these changes, most of Nakazato's and Ramseyer's criteria are far more descriptive of the context for architecture and construction practice in Japan than they are, for example, in the United States. Scholars discussing the fabric of Japan's business communities noted that, "The literature on business transactions and contracting in Japan suggest a predominant emphasis on repeated deals based on relationships established over time and avoidance of spot transactions with strangers."[33] I discussed oligopoly at greater length earlier, but it is also worth repeating here that the limited number of major contractors, developers and architects working on larger and more significant projects in Japan make ongoing relationships the norm for a part of the construction sector. Whereas a small firm may have to worry about a local contractor's performance, because of their reputation and the nature of their work, leading architects are likely to find themselves working only with the "Big Five" or with joint ventures that include these larger companies. Japan's smaller size and a common language also contribute to a sense of working in a bounded community – which may explain why some European countries also have a loose attitude toward contracts. However, even on this point, Japan's linguistic and regulatory barriers are certainly most effective. As long as Japan's construction community remains restricted, the authority of long-term relationships over specific contracts will probably continue, albeit in a weaker state than has been found recently.

The pressure on Japan to accept free trade may change the landscape of construction in ways both beneficial and problematic to architectural practice. Over the past ten years, the US, goaded by Senator Frank Murkowski, has attempted to force open Japan's lucrative construction industry to international trade. Understandably, the differences between Japanese attitudes and Western attitudes toward contracts and agreements is one of the major factors that has contributed to the continued failure of US–Japan trade agreements. Many times, the agreements have been perceived by the US as fixed, while the Japanese expect them to be as adaptable as other contracts. Thus, to date these efforts have been balky and only partially effective, but there has been impact. In its economically weakened state, Japan has been forced to concede to the US on a number of important issues; as the Japan External Trade Organization acknowledged in a survey on access within the construction market published in 1998, "Japan has made a particular effort to open its markets through deregulation and other measures . . ."[34]

If US efforts become successful in opening the construction industry, this will impact on currently flexible attitudes regarding contracts in Japan's construction and design community, since it changes the context for contracts. Japan's construction would no longer be controlled by a small, closely knit community, information would no longer be as reliable, and – with a much larger number of firms involved – individual corporations would no longer believe that repeat business was likely. There has been a history of minor US successes, interspersed with periods when the US efforts stall or fail. As a result, the potential for trade efforts to affect the industry can be raised only as a question.

Thus, while adaptability in contractual relations remains possible today, many fear this flexibility is waning. In society as a whole, and especially within the ailing construction industry, a more legalistic perspective is developing. Although to date I have seen only minor changes in what is possible on site, there is a greater rhetorical shift; contractors and owners seem more likely to initially resist modifications to original contract documents. Since the loose practices of the past have meant that most projects are bid on documents and specifications that lack specific and particular information, shifts in practices may result in design and detail development, once enriched by the flexibilities of contracts, being severely curtailed. Because this change is one in basic practices, many fear what the future may hold.

A recent article in the *Nikkei Weekly*, for example, stated simply, "... the policy of contractual goodwill is coming to an end. The ambiguity of practices seen until now and the breadth of responsibility and liability [held by architects and contractors] is an issue moving towards its conclusion in a impassioned way."[35]

It is my sense that the openness to change still found in construction practices will be eroded in the years to come, but that much of what I describe will remain possible in the best work, if only because of the investments major contractors have made in their reputations for technological sophistication and their commitment to buildings that are well detailed and constructed. There is, however, one area where real changes are already emerging in the legal community, and similar shifts have severely impacted on practice in the United States – that is in the area of liability. In the next section, I argue that there, too, fear regarding the potential impact of these shifts is probably greater than the actual impact will turn out to be, but this is nonetheless a significant constraint.

TORT: COVERING THE COSTS OF LIABILITY AND NEGLIGENCE

Architects are primarily affected by two particular areas of the law: contract law and tort. ("Tort" is defined as a wrongful act that is addressed under civil – not criminal – codes, with the potential for damages to be financially compensated rather than through the application of criminal penalties.) In both these areas, Japan's legal context differs notably from the more restrictive United States. In this section, I will look first at how tort has changed in the United States during the post-war period, essentially shifting toward a more exacting definition of the acceptable quality of professional services. From there, I will discuss the Japanese system and its impact in detail. One of the reasons for looking closely at these two systems is that many fear Japan's legal system is growing more like that of the United States. Although there are shifts in Japan, these are unlikely to result in a climate as onerous as that found in the United States.

Until the 1960s, the US tort standard was based on whether an architect had been negligent. Today, many believe that the US system has evolved towards a standard of "strict liability." Negligence, roughly speaking, assigns fault based on a lack of proper care or a level of performance not up to industry standards, but strict liability is based on the expectations others (such as users and owners) hold of remaining injury-free or trouble-free. An alternative view is that liability has simply expanded as the courts have shifted costs from first to third parties, e.g., insurers. Regardless of which position one takes, it is almost universally agreed that liability has expanded. This shift can be dated to around 1965, when, in response to slightly earlier court decisions that began the move to strict liability, the American Law Institute attempted to clarify the situation, and outlined the new standards of liability in its Second Restatement of Torts.[36]

The result has been significant, leading some legal scholars to conclude that,

> Tort law is in turmoil in the United States. The scope of harms for which plaintiffs have been allowed to bring actions and the size of judgements they have received have been growing very rapidly. In fact, the growth has been so fast and expansive that there is a wide-spread belief among some thoughtful commentators that the tort system has broken down and needs to be extensively reformed.[37]

Architects working in the United States are well aware of the impact of these changes, and one author even uses the provocative phrase "extinction by legal liability" when noting that, in 1985, 43 per cent of insured US architects reported a claim against them.[38] Many tort claims are for relatively minor problems, and less than 10 per cent of all disputes in the US go to trial but, as I will discuss below, damages awarded in court may be affected by jurisdiction, the type of trial, and other factors, thus leading to a sense of uncertainty and crisis.

Today, architects in Japan fear that a similar transformation in the legal standard of care is occurring, in imitation of US practices. Scholars note that there has been a "change in [Japanese] law consciousness," shifting from mediation to resolution in the courts during the post-war period.[39] Professionals' liability is such that the architect or contractor is not responsible for defects in those areas where they were not solidly negligent. However, as Japanese liability cases have begun to shift to the courts, authorities sometimes conflate negligence and expectations of defect-free construction, although the latter are closer in spirit to strict liability.[40]

In some ways the shift from negligence toward strict liability seems a natural direction for Japan, since normal business practices make it difficult to assign fault; strict liability is more concerned with the expectations of the owner or user than in assigning negligence to the architect's actions. This also fits more compatibly in light of the difficulty of pin-pointing responsibility with multi-organization design teams, where approvals often include non-hierarchical listings with as many as twenty seals, the Japanese equivalent of signatures. However, I believe liability costs are unlikely to become as onerous as those in the United States and that Japanese fears on this point are misplaced. Notably, although liability cases are being tested in the courts, at the time of writing I know of none that has been decided for the plaintiff based on strict liability.

The major problems associated with tort breakdown in the United States are related to areas of the legal system not found in Japan.

Further, I believe that there are legal and cultural restraints that discourage confrontation and litigation, although this is a controversial point among legal scholars. It is possible that these restraints will erode over time, but Japan's legal system cannot change quickly, regardless of the reasons for its current low level of litigation.

Even though architects in Japan may be held to a higher standard of care than they have in the past, there are several key reasons to believe that tort cannot reach the level of crisis seen in the United States.

THE JUDICIAL SYSTEM

There are two legal traditions, civil and common law. Japan and many European countries are civil law countries, whereas the United States is a common law country. Some argue that these two systems are growing more alike, but the difference between them is important. Under a common law structure, there are a variety of sources for laws, loosely ordered. The legislature, the constitution, the judiciary or other institutions may make laws, and those laws may conflict. Notably, under common law, many of the laws affecting architects originate with judges. Additionally, in the United States, lay people may make legal decisions, through participation on juries.

Under civil law, the source of law is more restricted; in Japan, all laws are made at the national level by the Diet (equivalent to the US Congress). Judges do not make laws in civil law nations; Japan also has no jury system. The most significant result of this difference is that legal outcomes are more predictable in Japan than in the United States. There is one set of laws guiding judges, and judges are not able to step outside of that law, even when larger, "universalist" issues of justice exist.

This predictability is particularly important in establishing the costs of negligence or liability. The two cultures emphasize differing attitudes toward judicial fairness. In Japan, the belief is that like cases should have like outcomes, whereas in the United States, the belief is often that litigants' particulars, especially related to issues such as material wealth, emotional distress, or other individual circumstances, should influence awards. Koichiro Fujikura, in comparing the two systems, cites the Lawrence Friedman book *Total Justice*, in which Friedman suggests that justice in the United States includes "a general expectation of recompense – the idea that people who have suffered some form of personal economic harm should be made whole ..." and a concept of "Plural equality" which Fujikura notes takes into account individual differences.[41]

So, for example, in the United States, an award related to a wrongful death will be based on factors such as the anticipated wages of the person in question (a practice that is also more expensive and time consuming, and may in part account for per capita representation differences in the two legal communities). In Japan, pain and suffering awards are standardized. One set of legal scholars noted that, "For breadwinners, the courts award about 24 million yen. For dependants or unmarried persons, they generally award 17–21 million yen."[42] The precise amount has increased as the relative value of the yen has declined, but the existence of guidelines has not. Similar formulae are also compiled for various levels of damage and injury. Although non-binding, the ideals of the judiciary, its relative power, and even the manner in which oversight is managed encourage consistency, and contribute to creating a high level of predictability for damages awards.

Thus, legal scholars agree, in most cases litigants do not perceive any need to go as far as the courts in Japan, settling instead through mediation. As Nakazato and Ramseyer noted, "Whether parties to a quarrel can settle will depend in part on how nearly their risk-adjusted estimates of the litigated verdict converge ... The more nearly the parties' estimates of the outcome of litigation converge, the greater the odds are they can settle."[43] Another leading scholar on Japanese law, John Owen Haley, notes, "Lawyers can and do routinely predict how judges will interpret and apply legal rules in most lawsuits [in Japan]."[44]

Even more significantly, Japanese courts limit awards. As Nakazato and Ramseyer note, "... courts do not award unforeseen extraordinary damages. Neither do they award nominal or punitive damages."[45] The expectation to date has been that reckless or egregious conduct should be addressed in criminal courts, not through the mechanism of monetary awards. I should note here, however, that this is one of the areas where the Japanese legal climate is shifting. Although there are no cases that relate directly to architecture and construction, there have been several successful civil suits associated with particularly reprehensible crimes, such as the murder of a child or the rape of a student by her teacher. In these cases, the courts have accepted the cases as civil rather than criminal and they have resulted in sizable awards that do seem intended to be punitive. In the United States, it is often punitive damages by juries that are the most unpredictable and costly in liability cases. One law professor was recently quoted as saying of punitive awards, "It's an enormous, incredible windfall to whoever gets it ... It turns the court system into a lottery."[46] US juries may, in sympathy to a litigant, award huge sums that bear no relation to the material harm caused to a plaintiff, and the possible amounts, however unlikely, are effectively so large as to make them almost impossible to plan for. However, such awards rarely stand up to appeal and, as Carl Sapers pointed out in an earlier review of this chapter, "Most US disputes are arbitrated ... This puts in serious doubt the relevance of juries." Nonetheless, higher awards affect the system as a whole, as extreme awards create unrealistic expectations in the minds of plaintiffs.

Thus, the general lack of such awards in Japan increases the predictability of settlements. As Nakazato and Ramseyer also note, "Plausible reasons why Japanese disputants might be able more readily to agree on the litigated verdict are easy to find. First, Japanese courts do not use juries ... unlike juries, judges take pride in uniformity across place and time ..."[47] With even greater cynicism, they later note, "... claiming levels [for liability] are high in the United States because juries sympathize with accident victims and are easy to fool ..."[48] Because there are no punitive awards in Japan, not only is the amount awarded to rectify or address damages more predictable, but it is smaller and offers less incentive to litigate. This is also the reason that US insurance policies explicitly exclude coverage of punitive damages.

Furthermore, in Japan, restitution may not be paid at all; instead, other means are more common in resolving construction-related problems. In a 1998 survey, 309 architects were asked whether compensation had been paid in architect-designed residential projects where a construction problem emerged.[49] Nine per cent said compensation had been paid, while 86 per cent said there had been no compensation. (Five per cent did not answer.) Instead, architects and contractors may simply work together to find a resolution, as in the case of the Kumamoto Dome, substituting labor for compensation. Further, contractors serve as an effective check to insure building performance. Although architects are responsible for design, contractors hold primary responsibility for construction and may even be liable for many design decisions. This probably has less to do with the source of a concept than it does with a simple economic fact: contractors in Japan, especially those on the larger projects that are most likely to concern the courts, have greater financial resources and long-term stability than architects.

Because of their liability, the contractors and other members of the construction team will attempt to work with the architect to assure that difficult details or new materials are thoroughly considered. Where they do not have confidence in approaches proposed by the architect, other members of the design team will challenge the architect to accept liability for any performance failures. This shared liability, and the oversight that is a part of it, gives architects tremendous confidence in their capacity to propose untried or challenging approaches in their designs, especially at the preliminary stages of design. In addition, the design team incorporates complementary skills and checks that insure the application of reasonable care. By contrast, many architects in North America act in a more conservative fashion, in order to compensate for possible gaps.

Shared liability extends beyond the design and construction team. With any award for damages, there are various groups who may actually cover the cost of the harm. Again, these expectations differ in Japan and the United States. Simply put, tort costs can be covered by a victim, the injurer or some third party, such as the government or an insurer. Commonly in the United States today, there is an expectation that damage awards are paid by an insurer or the injurer, and – most importantly – the relationship between the plaintiff and these groups is short-lived. In Japan, however, many of the independent architectural offices report that 70 per cent or more of their projects are derived from long-term relationships. Long-term obligations also differ. Architects and contractors, based on warranty expectations, will make at least one follow-up visit a year after completion, to check on building performance. If other projects for the same client are undertaken or even simply anticipated, there may be frequent contact over a longer period. In this way, problems are often recognized when they are still small and most can be corrected more easily.

Japan also retains a third-party "safety net" in the form of national health systems and other governmental programs. Thus, plaintiffs have access to third-party compensations for potential health problems. In this way, governmental programs ameliorate the need for immediate compensation against any dormant damages. This may also reduce the necessity to decide awards based on the defendant's greater ability to pay, a trend that emerged in the United States in the 1980s as a result of court decisions regarding the long-term health effects of DES (Thalidomide).

In lieu of governmental support, and because the possibility exists that awards will be extraordinary – with no predictability – US architects are more likely to rely on insurers for third party compensation. Robert Cooter and Thomas Ulen summarize the relationship between coverage and potential liability.[50] Initially, if potential liability remains low, it may not be cost-effective to pay annually for insurance coverage. The assumption is that risk can be kept low, and thus any damages award would be less than the long-term cost of insurance. However, as the potential for awards becomes higher, the possibility emerges that the immediate costs related to an award might bankrupt a firm, and insurance becomes commonplace – as long as the relative annual costs of insurance are not onerous. However, as occurred in the 1980s when the price for insurance rose rapidly, high annual costs may lead firms to risk possible bankruptcy through a damage award, rather than take on the certain economic loss imposed by the cost of insurance. Architects in the United States, where possible damage awards are higher, tend to fall in a range where insurance is either perceived as necessary, or crushing.

In Japan today, when liability awards remain low, it should not be surprising that the majority of Japanese architects do not carry liability insurance – even some of Japan's largest architectural firms do not have insurance.[51] The fact that Japanese design professionals may not feel insurance is necessary simply reflects their opinion that any potential judgments against them are low enough to be an acceptable risk. However, although still quite rare, reliance on insurance seems to be growing.

DISCOURAGING LITIGATION

In addition to the fact that the potential rewards for litigation are significantly lower in Japan than they are in the United States (one author recommended removing a zero[52]), most scholars agree that Japan's legal system actively discourages litigation. There is, however, some controversy over which mechanisms actually suppress litigation levels, and even whether the tendency to litigate is rising or falling. The arguments concerning a Japanese reluctance to sue tend to focus on either the function and infrastructure of the legal system, or, alternately, a societal aversion to conflict. The latter, although developed by a leading Japanese academic, is viewed with some suspicion in North American academic circles because it supports potentially stereotypical assumptions about Japanese culture.

Most scholars, however, do agree that there is simply less opportunity to litigate because the Japanese legal system remains limited in scope. There are fewer lawyers and judges per capita in Japan than in most industrialized nations, cases take longer to decide and litigation is more expensive. Hiroshi Oda, in an overview of the Japanese system, gives the population per attorney for several developed countries, based on a 1987 survey. There was one lawyer for each 358 people in the United States, West Germany had one for each 1,291 people, and France had one for each 3,468. But Japan's lawyers numbered only one for each 9,199 people.[53] Judges are similarly scarce. An updated version of John Owen Haley's essay "The Myth of the Reluctant Litigant" includes population figures for lawyers and judges. According to these numbers, there is one judge for every 43,924 people in Japan, a total of only 2,823 judges in 1990.[54] Because the number of lawyers and judges are determined by the passing rates for examinations and thus entry into a two-year training program required of all career judges, most argue that the limited number of judges and lawyers is condoned and even desired by the Japanese government.

Therefore, each judge carries a heavy caseload and will address an average of 1,100 cases or more per year (civil and criminal), considering many simultaneously.[55] Furthermore, whereas juries in other countries make it necessary to have a trial proceed quickly, Japan's judges are under no such pressure. Consequently, trials are lengthy. Haley notes that an initial trial in Japan may take two years, with appeals stretching cases out for an average of five years.[56] Even trials of ten years, he argues, are not uncommon, and many critics have noted how frequently litigants die before the completion of all appeals.

Filing a case is also expensive. In the United States, the filing costs for a million-dollar lawsuit are only about $120, while in Japan, according to Yamanouchi and Cohen, the same filing would be about $5,000.[57] Obviously, the lower awards in litigation, combined with the high costs of actually going to court, encourage many potential litigants to settle instead. Not surprisingly, when surveyed, over half of all Japanese respondents agreed with the statement "Litigation is expensive and time-consuming, and even when you win, you will usually lose money."[58] The cost of litigation can suppress the inclination of plaintiffs to turn to the courts, even if the range of liabilities expands.

Several other theories on why litigation rates are significantly lower than in other industrialized nations point to work developed by the University of Tokyo law professor Takeyoshi Kawashima, who claimed that litigation and the pleasure of trumping an opponent directly opposed a social tendency toward consensus. In addition, he argued that "... modern law radically diverges from the social norms by which Japanese structure their relations. Where modern law imposes universalistic principles, Japanese follow what are fundamentally popularistic ... norms."[59] Although these theories are controversial, in my experience it is true that Japanese architects and contractors seem reluctant to litigate. A general reluctance of the population is also backed up by surveys, such as that of the *Nippon Bunka Kaigi* [Japan Culture Forum] taken in 1973 and 1982. To the question, "Would you consider suing if your rights were violated?" the majority of respondents replied, "No, unless the matter were extremely grave."[60] In my previous discussion on contracts, I suggested some reasons for this reluctance, related to the community size and repeat interactions.

Whichever justification one is inclined to accept, the result today is the same: "Japanese litigation rates are consistently lower than all comparable industrial states."[61] The relaxed tort conditions, which both architect and contractor have enjoyed in Japan, are significant reason that architects and contractors share responsibility and decision-making on site. A shift in perceptions regarding tort is one that does deserve concern. Nonetheless, as I have outlined, the impact of tort in Japan should remain relatively benign.

SENDAI MEDIATHEQUE IN CRISIS

In December of 1998, the contractors on Sendai Mediatheque, a remarkable building designed by Toyo Ito and the structural engineer Mutsuro Sasaki, discovered a major problem: three of the structural "tubes" at the first floor were assembled out of position. Parts of one tube were misaligned by almost 30 centimeters (about a foot). I had witnessed the extraordinary care both architects and engineers had taken up to this point, insisting on tolerances of no more than a millimeter on steel pipes seven meters long, when legal tolerances were at least three times greater. I recognized that the contractors and fabricators had gone to pains themselves to assure this precision. Now, all that work was moot and the design team faced a challenge: could the structure be put right? Members of the design team repeatedly described the situation as extremely tense, since the responsibility for this problem was so widely shared: the design of the structure, the first of its kind, certainly contributed; there were questions about decisions related to assembly and welding; questions were even raised about the quality of information supplied by the fabricators.

When the parts of the first lattice-like tube had been welded together, the assembly was constantly surveyed to assure that all parts remained in position. The structure had not moved, and based on greater confidence in the temporary connectors, a decision was made to weld the next three tubes without simultaneous surveying. When these assemblies were completed and a follow-up survey done, the problem was discovered. For six weeks, new structural work on the site was at a standstill, an expense borne by the contractors. Ultimately, a solution emerged from round-the-clock meetings between the architects, engineers, fabricators and contractors. From the first, it was important to everyone on site to understand the roots of the problem, since there was a great deal more work to be done on the structure above. However, after identifying the various potential causes of the trouble, the team worked together to determine a set of solutions, not to assign blame: what could be done to make sure the structure remained in place during welding, and how could the misaligned areas be fixed?

As a group, the design and construction team thoroughly explored their options. This required an ongoing level of mutual trust and commitment to the project that would not be typical if such a situation occurred in many countries. Finally, everyone on site came to a decision. Recognizing the need to move forward, they agreed to a novel approach that heated the steel and moved it back into position. The designers understood that the result would not be perfect (a slight bend to the heated pipes is still evident) and that this compromised the character of the building. It was all the more disappointing for the location of these tubes. Not only were these the first to go in, but they were in the large entrance lobby, and would be the first parts of this building's remarkable structure that visitors would see. Most people will not notice the fact that the tubes are no longer completely circular in plan where the repairs took place, but the architects' staff seemed unable to miss it each time they passed.

Yet the project did move forward, and a year later, as the final parts of the structure were put in place seven floors above, the building was completed nearly on time – in

10.1
Two-story tube sections at 1st floor. Tube in the foreground was the first to be assembled on site.

10.2
Tubes showing a variety of approaches to fire resistance, based on use.

10.3
Tube finished with a ceramic "fire-proofing" called "Taika-Arock."

10.4
Sendai Mediatheque, nearing completion.

spite of the fact that the structure took six months longer than the contractors had expected, both because of the problem with the tubes and problems that emerged in welding the steel floor plates together. I found it notable that from the beginning, the source of the problem was openly discussed among members of the team and even with me, an outsider. By May, a brief discussion of the problem made its way into one of the published *GA Japan* reports on the work at the site.[62] The speed with which construction resumed is also notable. There was no need for an outside arbitrator, nor did the parties attempt to preserve the structure in its unfortunate state while assigning blame and expense. The design and construction team not only agreed to the problem's resolution, but afterwards made numerous decisions together about the use of other new materials and assemblies for the project. Ito, for example, eschewed his original plans for a sophisticated fiber optic system to bring daylight into the tubes, settling instead on a relatively modest set of adjustable mirrors. Moreover, in the closing days of construction, architects and contractors remarked on the importance of teamwork in the project. This is perhaps the best illustration of how Japanese architects benefit from the expectations of cooperation at the heart of Japan's legal system.

1 F. Matsushita, *Design and Construction Practice in Japan: A Practical Guide*, Tokyo, Kaibunsha Ltd., 1994, p. 44.
2 H. Oda, *Japanese Law*, London, Dublin, and Edinburgh, Butterworths, 1992, p. 199.
3 J. O. Haley, *The Spirit of Japanese Law*, Athens and London, University of Georgia Press, 1998, p. 141.
4 E. Hoshino, "The Contemporary Contract [*Gendai no okeru keiyaku*]" translated by J. O. Haley. In K. Fujikura, ed., *Japanese Law and Legal Theory*, Aldershot, Singapore, and Sydney, Dartmouth Publishing Co. Ltd., 1996, pp. 82 and 84.
5 Oda, *Japanese Law*, p. 197.
6 Ibid., p. 147.
7 R. Cooter and T. Ulen, *Law and Economics*, New York, HarperCollins Publishers, 1988, p. 214.
8 Y. Hippoh, *The Construction Industry in Japan: A Survey*, Asian Productivity Organization, n.d. (c. 1983), p. 242.
9 Matsushita, *Design and Construction Practice in Japan*, p. 33
10 Ibid.
11 R. Greenstreet, "Laws and Order," in A. Pressman, *Profession Practice 101: A Compendium of Business and Management Strategies in Architecture*, New York, John Wiley, 1997, p. 204.
12 R. Greenstreet and D. Chappell, *Legal and Contractual Procedures for Architects, Fourth Edition*, Butterworth and Oxford, Architectural Press Legal Series, 1994, p. 216.
13 N. J. Sweeney, et al., *Smith, Currie and Hancock's Common Sense Construction Law*, New York, John Wiley and Sons, 1997, p. 206.
14 T. Kawashima, "The Legal Consciousness of Contract in Japan," in K. Fujikura, ed., *Japanese Law and Legal Theory*, Aldershot, Singapore, and Sydney, Dartmouth Publishing Co. Ltd., 1996, p. 34. This article was originally published as a chapter in the book *Nihonjin no Hou Ishiki* [Legal Consciousness in the Japanese Mind], although it has frequently been republished in the shorter form.
15 W. Coxe and M. Hayden, "UIA Project Work Group: Trends in Private Practice. Report from Japan," unpublished report dated 20 March 1993, p. 14.
16 Kawamura, "*Digitaru to no Tatakai no Zenyō: Fo-towa-su Gendai Bijutsukan* [Digital and the Fight for the Whole Picture: Fort Worth Modern Art Museum]," *Nikkei A-kitekuchua* [Nikkei Architecture], no. 623, 5 October 1998, p. 112. Translation mine.
17 Coxe and Hayden, "Report from Japan," I address litigation issues further in the next section.
18 Haley, *The Spirit of Japanese Law*, p. 145.
19 S. Miyazawa, "Taking Kawashima Seriously: A Review of Japanese Research on Japanese Legal Consciousness and Disputing Behavior," in Fujikura, *Japanese Law and Legal Theory*, p. 385.
20 Matsushita, *Design and Construction Practice in Japan*, p. 134.
21 Ibid., p. 135
22 Kawashima, "The Legal Consciousness of Contract in Japan," p. 36.

23 Matsushita, *Design and Construction Practice in Japan*, p. 57.
24 Ibid., p. 59.
25 Kawashima, "The Legal Consciousness of Contract in Japan," p. 35.
26 Ibid., pp. 28–9.
27 T. Igarashi, "*Kenchiku Fujuyu no Jidai* [The Era of Constrained Building Construction]" *Nikkei A-kitekuchua* [Nikkei Architecture], 1981, p. 129, noted in Matsushita, *Design and Construction Practice in Japan*, p. 72, no. 1. Matsushita's citation is incomplete, giving only the year.
28 On the changes to contracts, see, for example, "*Kanri ha dare ga yaru: Henbō wo semarareru 'kanrisha' no shigoto to sekinin* [Who will do construction supervision? The supervisor's work and responsibilities shaped by transformation]". *Nikkei A-kitekuchua* [Nikkei Architecture]*,* 14 June 1999, no. 642, pp. 32–53.
29 Cooter and Ulen, *Law and Economics*, p. 244.
30 Ibid., p. 245.
31 J. M. Ramseyer and M. Nakazato, *Japanese Law: An Economic Approach*, Chicago: University of Chicago Press, 1999*,* pp. 65–6.
32 H. Davis, *The Culture of Building*, Cambridge, Cambridge University Press, 1999, p. 181.
33 Haley, *The Spirit of Japanese Law*, p. 208.
34 JETRO [the Japan External Trade Organization], *The Survey on Actual Condition Regarding Access to Japan*, Tokyo, JETRO, October 1998, introductory page (unpaginated).
35 "*Kanri ha Dare ga Yaru* [Who will do construction supervision?]," p. 32.
36 Cooter and Ulen, *Law and Economics*, pp. 422 and 433. See also V. Schwartz "Making Product Liability Work for You," in J. R. Hunziker and T. O. Jones, eds., *Product Liability and Innovation: Managing Risk in an Uncertain Environment*, Washington, DC, National Academy of Engineering, National Academy Press, 1994, p. 30.
37 Cooter and Ulen, *Law and Economics*, p. 326.
38 Greenstreet, "Laws and Order," p. 204.
39 H. Tanaka, "The Role of Law in Japanese Society: Comparisons with the West," in K. Fujikura, ed., *Japanese Law and Legal Theory*, Aldershot, Singapore, and Sydney, Dartmouth Publishing Co. Ltd., 1996.
40 See Omori, *Nikkei A-kitekuchua* [Nikkei Architecture], no. 638, 19 April 1999, pp. 39–40.
41 K. Fujikura, "Introduction: Legal Culture in a Non-Legalistic Tradition," in Fujikura, ed., *Japanese Law and Legal Theory*, pp. xxi–xxii.
42 Ramseyer and Nakazato, *Japanese Law*, p. 89.
43 Ibid., pp. 92–3.
44 Haley, *The Spirit of Japanese Law*, p. xviii.
45 Ramseyer and Nakazato, *Japanese Law*, p. 89.
46 A. Pollack, "$4.9 Billion Jury Verdict In G.M. Fuel Tank Case," *New York Times*, 10 July 1999, p. A7, national edition.
47 This is a crucial issue in Ramseyer and Nakazato, *Japanese Law*, see pp. 93–4.
48 Ibid., p. 106.
49 "*Kekkan: Kaitousha Sannin no Futari ni Kekkan Amamori ha 'Kenchikuka no Akashi* [Defects: Two of Every Three Architects are Blameless in Water Leakage Defects]," *Nikkei A-kitekuchua* [Nikkei Architecture], no. 625, 2 November 1998, p. 78.
50 Cooter and Ulen, *Law and Economics*, pp. 448–9.
51 Coxe and Hayden, "Report from Japan." The UIA report found 20 per cent of firms carried insurance. Matsushita notes that 30 per cent of AIJ (Architectural Institute of Japan) members carry insurance, but this coverage is offset when the combined memberships of the AIJ, JIA (Japan Institute of Architects), and JFAOA (Japan Federation of Architect Office Associations) are considered. In that case, coverage drops to roughly 5 per cent of all design firms. See p. 227f.
52 Matsushita, *Design and Construction Practice in Japan*.
53 Oda, *Japanese Law*, Appendix 2.
54 J. O. Haley, "The Myth of the Reluctant Litigant," in Y. Yanagida, *et al.*, eds., *Law and Investment in Japan: Cases and Materials*, Cambridge, Massachusetts, and London, Harvard University Press, 1994, p. 475.
55 Haley, *The Spirit of Japanese Law*, p. 97. This is down from a caseload of 1,708 that Haley noted in 1974. See "The Myth of the Reluctant Litigant," p. 473.
56 J. O. Haley, "The Myth of the Reluctant Litigant," in K. L. Port, ed., *Comparative Law: Law and the Legal Process in Japan*, Durham, NC, Carolina Academic Press, 1996, p. 118. This is an updated version of the original cited in Yanagida.
57 Yamanouchi and Cohen, "Understanding Incidence of Litigation in Japan," p. 107. I am using an exchange rate of 100 yen to the dollar for these numbers.
58 Miyazawa, "Taking Kawashima Seriously," p. 385.
59 As paraphrased in Ramseyer and Nakazato, *Japanese Law*, p. 91.
60 Miyazawa, "Taking Kawashima Seriously," p. 385.
61 Haley, *The Spirit of Japanese Law*, p. 33.

62 "*Sendai Mediateku Genba Reporuto 2: Chūbu to Hanikamu* [Sendai Mediatheque Construction Site Report 2: Tubes and Honeycomb]," *GA Japan*, vol. 38, May–June 1999. The discussion of this problem is on pp. 155 and 156. This interview occurred on 29 March, less than two months after the problem had been resolved. The architects and engineers graciously review several probable reasons for the tubes to have shifted during construction, and note that one of the potential reasons for the problem was that the precise locations where siting was done at the fabricators were not marked for on-site verification. The architects and engineers explicitly remarked that they were equally responsible, since they had not recognized the potential for a problem without marks, either.

Conclusion

Japanese architecture may be fashionable, even faddish, but enthusiasm has not necessarily been matched by understanding. At best, interpretation is superficial or stereotyped. At worst, it is patently incorrect.[1]

(William Coaldrake)

Initially, and perhaps not surprising considering that I stumbled on Japan during the heady days of the Bubble, I was drawn to the beauty and provocative compositional character of the buildings I saw around me. Over time, however, I became interested in the process that generated these buildings. This came about not because of my own inclinations, but because of the issues that people around me emphasized in our discussions. For architects in Japan, architecture is not simply a noble art within the context of – or completely unallied with – the building industry. Instead, architecture, for even the most elite of Japan's leading architects, is a part of building. Practice in Japan derives its greatest excitement from the new opportunities that exist in the construction industry. Repeatedly, people told me how they took swift advantage of changes in what was possible. Structural engineers, celebrating the new analyses possible with computers, took up bolder, more complex systems and often goaded architects into their use. Fabricators, using the same technologies, were willing to explore the practical limits of robotic welding and computer numerically controlled production and drew architects into seeing the potential in manufactured customization. Sales people dropped by architects' offices to speak of an unusual product their companies were trying out. Contractors, aware of shifting economic demand, drew on new types of industries to subcontract production – and architects recognized new possibilities in their work. This willingness to engage change pervaded many discussions I had with architects, and it is one I hope I have communicated here. Often, exploratory investigations came to nothing: the material was not ready for production, there was not enough money in the budget, or someone decided that an idea was more exciting than reality, and unworthy of further effort. Yet an openness to trying something new lingered, even when individual efforts were aborted.

To some degree, I found special conditions that allow for greater flexibility in architectural practice in Japan. Political support emerged as much more significant than I had at first expected. In addition, the way that competitions push innovation is important. Finally, public works rankings of constructors and consultants effectively assure that both commit to quality in construction.

The legal flexibilities in Japan are also noteworthy. Japanese architects, working in an elastic legal context, find that "incomplete contracts" accommodate the team working out the details of construction cooperatively. Because of contractual differences, costs remain negotiable further into the construction process (and occasionally after construction completion), allowing all members of the team to feel that their potential risk, when taking on uncertain work, is lower. Limited judicial opportunities for relief also assure that all members of the construction team find negotiation a more desirable route for resolving disputes. In addition, because contractors hold liability, both constructors and professionals have a vested interest in design issues, promoting collaboration. Large contractors have reinforced their role in design decision-making by bringing professional consultants in-house. Although there are disadvantages to the profession in this arrangement, a point I return to below, it creates a group of individuals who connect the interests of designers and constructors.

It is also significant that Japan's shift from a feudal society to a modern one was rapid and incomplete. Some valuable opportunities found today in the building industry are rooted in history. Most importantly, the continuing presence of craft has allowed architects to draw on a broader palette of materials and maintains an awareness of the value and process of customization. This has probably been one of the reasons that Japanese architects were able to quickly embrace the possibilities of manufactured customization as machinery changed.

These, however, only establish a context. As my discussion of the models of practice in Japan suggests, what architects do within this context can vary considerably. Some architects practice very much as they do in my own country; some have frighteningly limited interest in the practicalities of construction. Other architects, though, have an admirable involvement with the details and execution of their works. They not only command – or, on occasion, deliberately reject – remarkable levels of refinement, but also engage in the development and investigatory trials of new materials and new systems. It was work by these architects that first inspired me to study Japan's buildings more closely. They offer a model in which architects, contractors and manufacturers share knowledge and expertise and expect learning to be a part of practice.

The advantage of collaboration with constructors is clear. With rapid technological change and the increasing complexity of buildings today, no one field can demonstrate sufficient understanding of all the issues facing the building team. The generalist tendency in the profession serves a very real purpose in drawing together the opposing values of other members of the team, especially when an architect also has established credibility on topics driving the project, such as aesthetics, programming, or social goals such as sustainability. Architects, however, cannot truly be generalists without a deep understanding of construction. Collaboration must, of necessity, occur before and during construction. Professional consultants benefit from being able to observe the realities of construction on a daily basis, and constructors benefit from contributing to the decisions about execution. Notably, it is not possible to engage in shared decision-making until other members of the production team are on board.

Tomorrow's architecture will result from the efforts of lead architects who engage today's emerging opportunities. I borrowed the term "lead users" from an economist, but it is important to recognize the potential of a specific subgroup of elite architects to lead through their experiments. It is not enough to draw provocative imagery. The true ability to blaze a trail comes from implementation, and this comes from working with industry. Japan illustrates the benefits and challenges of a different approach, rooted in teamwork and daily interactions not only with abstract media, but also with the machinery and processes of construction and fabrication. The architects I spoke with showed surprising confidence, because they drew not only on their own expertise, but on the work of many others.

There were times when I was tempted to become a missionary for the systems I found in Japan, but I was also painfully aware of the long hours and expense that went into architectural practice. The field is demanding anywhere, but nowhere more so than in Japan. On the other hand, almost every time I find some promising young architect trying to incorporate construction and fabrication into Western architectural education or practice, I learn how experiences in Japan shaped their outlook. Clearly, in spite of the difficulties, the satisfactions of allied practice have persuaded many of us that it is worthy of greater study and offers a praiseworthy alternative to the way young interns in more litigious societies learn, through the routine and repetitive production of abstract representations. It is worth noting that, historically speaking, until relatively recently architects considered it natural and normal to be involved in the day-to-day activities of the construction site. Many argue that the complexities of contemporary buildings preclude this kind of intimacy – and yet architects still routinely work from the site in Japan, *especially* on the most complex buildings where deeper understanding and quicker responses are necessary.

INCREASINGLY INNOVATIVE

A focus on architecture as mere art will tend to marginalize the profession; a focus on architecture as mere fashion will tend to trivialize the profession; and, most dangerous, a focus on architecture as a luxury product that is either unavailable or unnecessary to the majority of people will ultimately destroy the profession.[2]

(Stephen Kliment)

Whereas architectural practice in a cooperative team can be both satisfying and critically successful, it is not without its dangers. The appeal of architecture – especially architecture as it emerges from less conservative practices – is tied to economic and political currents.

Whether in Europe or Japan, recessions bring reduced demand. In this book, I addressed the process of design decision-making in allied practice, but this process cannot occur without demand. I have tried to avoid treating the current recession as wholly representative of Japan's post-war experience. Legal norms, government demand and even Japan's position as the world's second largest economy will preserve many of the features of practice known today. Yet, there is ample room for concern and the flailing economy has forced changes on the construction industry.

Ironically, the Japanese government's efforts to prop up the construction industry requires architects and contractors with proven records of accomplishment to become even more committed to innovation. Although there are fewer remarkable buildings being built today and architectural styles are understated, the materials and processes of construction have been rethought in a way never possible in the busier, flashier 1980s. Japan has enhanced its ability to create the world's finest architecture, even during a prolonged and painful recession. The architects able to take advantage of this situation are almost all in their fifties, sixties, and even seventies; they struggle with reduced demand and a higher level of risk and oversight involved in the commissions they receive. For younger architects, there are simply few opportunities for work. Talented architects have given up practice and retreated to teaching, retired early or simply never entered the profession. These conditions might be true in any country contending with recession, but in Japan, cranes continue to dot urban skylines. It is simply that developers and contractors – rather than architects in private practice – are designing more and more buildings for the private sector.

Disturbingly, areas once considered securely under the control of the profession are seeing competition. Contractors are making inroads into designing public institutions; both developers and government offices are also doing more design in-house, in an effort to have greater control over costs and the effects of corruption. But it is questionable whether government participation in design has any positive impact on costs, judging by some resulting inefficient, ugly, but expensive buildings. Frequently, the quality of in-house design services is curbed, and these services are perceived as no more than an unwanted necessity. Although architects working for contractors and developers are capable of care and craft, it is in part because independent professionals have been able to act as goads and to establish standards for the building industry. A weakened profession cannot play this role for long.

In Japan, architects grew complacent; they enjoyed the support of politicians and contractors. Work came easily in better times. Architects were the darlings of the media and celebrated like rock stars in Japan only ten years ago. Today, the profession struggles. These two faces of practice are more related than many are willing to admit; the recession's threat is rooted in the fact that architects chose to foreground only one of the profession's strengths. When the economy was good, architects in private practice designed those aesthetically demanding projects that were less profitable to contractors. Especially now that the economy is poor, architects must be clearer about what, besides aesthetic benefit, the profession offers. It does not serve the profession well to be thought of only as artists, since art will always be expendable in downturns.

Oddly, the role architects play in the construction industry is one highly valued in many of Japan's industrial sectors. The Walkmans, tiny telephones and fuel-efficient automobiles exported by Japanese manufacturers have their roots in similar alliances with a central coordinator committed to a range of elusive concerns. The difference is that manufacturers profit from these innovations through export successes, and Japan's construction sector remains for the most part rooted at home. Construction has some support from politicians because it has a domestic economic purpose, but the differences between the benefit of a good building and a poorly designed one are so far perceived by many as marginal. That architects in Japan are struggling suggests that it is not sufficient to construct buildings well; the face of the profession must be reworked to articulate the benefits of its efforts.

The problem is that we as a profession have failed to recognize the benefits created by lead users and the differences in their approaches to practice. Professional distrust, for example, is reflected in a recent call for papers from a small academic journal: "What happens to the built environment when the exceptional case sets the standard for mainstream designers (with mainstream budgets)?"[3] As Howard Davis argued, "... for most of this century, the operative assumption has been that architecture must follow the means of production rather than lead it."[4] Such attitudes overlook the remarkable practitioners who have found a way to lead. Von Hippel's work suggests that rather than being suspicious of these lead users, we as a profession should recognize the impact they have on our future. He does not argue that they unerringly reflect the demands of the market – but instead, he suggests that by judiciously studying lead users, and considering how they identify trends in practice, we can more effectively work with the construction industry, both today and tomorrow.

LEARNING FROM JAPAN

I do not think that Japan has a monopoly on lead users producing fine architecture, but only that the circumstances for making fine buildings exist there today. Senior architects in Japan remember a time when they envied the fine craft of North American buildings, a point ratified in works by Kahn, Mies and other architects of the post-war period. Even today, buildings elsewhere demonstrate the advantages of allied practice, both those linked to better-known designers such as Calatrava, Gehry and Piano, and the fruits of smaller studios from New York to the Sonoran desert, from Helsinki to Madrid. Why, then, study Japan? In part, because the activities of lead architects are accepted within the construction industry and their activities are better integrated. In part, simply because it is a place well known and poorly understood.

Earlier I noted the difficulty many Japanese architects have had building abroad. How, then, can other architects hope to follow their example? I do not think it lies in imitation but in thoughtful study. By understanding the range of support for architects in Japan, it may be possible for each of us to find challenges relevant to our own situations.

For Japanese architects, the challenge is to discover what, indeed, is central to their successes. As demand has dropped in Japan, there have been fewer interesting projects at home for leading architects, and overseas projects have become more significant to their practices. Over the last ten years, Fumihiko Maki has had numerous opportunities to engage in practice internationally. He has worked with the subsidiaries of Japanese contractors, has relied heavily on mock-ups during construction, and his staff's efforts at collaboration even resulted in Alcoa naming a color "Maki gray." Even with these efforts, his North American work, at San Francisco's Yerba Buena, lacks the polish of those buildings he has undertaken in Japan. As this book goes to press, however, plans are underway for a new building by Maki to go up on the MIT campus. This one will be executed under conditions similar to those Maki's office has enjoyed in Japan; the building has received considerable support from the client, from North American fabricators and from the contractor. Although at least one of the fabricators is allied with a Japanese company, most of those involved in the project are not. In a way, Maki's experience suggests that it is not the context for practice that is most important, not the cultural background of the players – it is the team.

The direction Maki has traveled suggests the lessons outside observers can learn from Japan. What follows are some suggestions for students, academics and professionals.

Successful teams include people with disparate disciplinary values and differing expertise. In Japan, architects understand that they cannot achieve what they hope to without recognizing the strengths of others on the design team; architecture students everywhere can benefit from learning the same lessons. In academe, teaching students to understand the value of teams is often difficult. How do you grade achievement or create an organizational structure when all students are equal? In part, the problem results from the fact that students team up with other students – often other architecture students with similar educations and interests. Students should work with students from other departments, especially those, like engineering, that will yield future allies. This may also serve to break down the way our universities promote disciplinary isolation.

In addition, I try to locate some of my students' activities on site and in shops – in the natural territory of fabricators and contractors. For the most part, students have been excited about these opportunities, and they develop a deeper understanding of the relationships between architecture and building. To get students on site requires a well-defined problem, limiting the number of students who will interact with any one organization and accepting that contractors control the situation while students are on site. Even when the economy has boomed, builders generously take the time to help students appreciate the demands of construction in a way that is difficult to achieve in the classroom. Contractors and fabricators understand that an informed architecture student has greater potential to be an informed architect.

In the classroom, academics also need to be more willing to recognize the connections between process and product, and between basic design and construction. We expect students to make intelligent choices about which materials are suitable to attain different intellectual or aesthetic goals, but we do not illustrate these connections in our lectures. I am not afraid to tell my students that one of the reasons for selecting a material is aesthetic. I'll use a sexy building when reminding them what galvanized steel looks like. And, like many people who teach technology, I wish most of my colleagues teaching students would discuss how technology fits within architects' decision-making. This also requires a different approach when preparing course materials: it is not sufficient to use a single image of a building, with little recognition of the choices in materials or orientation. We need to help students recognize that a building designed for Japan will respond to the norms of fabrication and construction in Japan: that concrete structures are encouraged over steel frames, the crafts resulting in unfinished concrete are not uncommon, and that, for the most part, one can depend on flatter, larger sheets of glass. This requires that each of us discussing buildings do so from a deeper level of understanding. When students propose imitating a Japanese building, their interests offer an opportunity to teach, not naivete to be ignored or simply dismissed as impractical.

It is not easy for those of us who teach to stay current on the norms of practice – especially now, when they change so quickly. I suspect that this may be the reason for the old adage that "them that can't, teach." We as faculty need to stay in touch with the realities of the field and the realities of the industry. Professionals and builders can help us do so, not simply by speaking to us of their concerns, but by bringing us back into their offices and sites on a regular basis, both physically and rhetorically. Young engineers willing to take on a challenge have always been popular on the lecture circuit in architecture schools. We should also draw on the contractors and fabricators who go beyond simply executing standard details, and help architects realize ambitious choices. Their stories help students to understand that the idealized isolation of ateliers is an artificial and unrealistic one.

In lectures, we can recognize how architecture exists within the construction industry by drawing other members of the team into discussions. At the very least, we should all acknowledge the contributions of the engineers, fabricators and contractors who engage design in the space between the dreamy sketch and its fruition. Too many times in lectures, practitioners clothe their accomplishments in abstract language, without telling us how these accomplishments came about.

As a profession, we need to revive an awareness that architecture is a part of building, and develop a greater commitment to the production opportunities available to us. The largest projects already demand this, because customization can be a way to squeeze inches and dollars out of construction. For smaller projects, collaboration on site often appears an expensive luxury. However, the reality is that isolation from the field not only makes our designs more conservative and our profession less essential – it also prevents us from exploring the creative side of architecture that first excited us. Everyone in the building industry is frustrated by the schisms between contractor and architect, so clearly at odds with the increasing complexity of the buildings we produce. Japan offers a provocative solution to some of this dilemma. Although not every project will invite this involvement, an awareness of the crafters and industries in our communities can prepare practitioners for those projects that will benefit from allied practice and innovative solutions.

The profession of architecture, drawn by an illusory idea of the nature of professionalization, has drifted a long way from its roots in construction. To be truly effective, we must look to those places where alliances between design and execution remain – and learn from them.

1. W. Coaldrake, "Myths & Realities of Japanese Buildings," *Architecture*, September 1988, p. 113.
2. S. Kliment, "Remarks on the New Client and Market" in W. S. Saunders, ed., *Reflections on Architectural Practices in the Nineties*, New York, Princeton University Press, 1996, p. 32.
3. Call for papers, for *Threshold 18*.
4. H. Davis, *The Culture of Building*, Cambridge, Cambridge University Press, 1999, p. 243.

Index

Page numbers appearing in **bold** indicate figures

ability to pay compensation 161–2
academics 51, 174–5
acoustic testing 53
advice: contractors 77, 78; manufacturers 114
aesthetics: benefits 172; shared responsibility xv, 1, 78
air handling 121, 153; equipment 42
alliances 95 *see also keiretsu*
aluminum housing 115
amakudari 142
Ando, Tadao 2, 50, 150; design development model 35–6; post-graduate experience 30
Aoki, Jun 51, 52, 132
apprenticeship 6, 14, 20, 25–6, 30–1; modern 101
Araya, Masato 54
architects: attitudes related to collusion 141; competitions 129–30; conceptual model 34; crafts 100; customization 109, 120–2; job completion 62; manufacturing 105–8, 109, 111, 112
architectural documentation 66; *see also* drawings
architectural education 20, 21, 23, 27, 78
architectural practice, emergence of 19–21
artisans 6, 33, 47; *see also* craft
Asahi Glass 113
assembly lines 66
assignments: interns 27
automated plants 96
autonomy 28–9
avant-garde architecture 128–31
awards: limited 160

Ban, Shigeru 51–2
bank lending 91, 94–5
bankruptcy 95
bidding 132; alliances 91–2, 95; competitive 73; rigged 140–2; *see also dango*
black box sourcing 112
bribery 142
budgets 133–4
building manuals 14

CAD CAM systems 109
Campbell, John Creighton 29,
capital of Japan: new 138
careers: assistance 130
carpenters 8–9, 18, 102; apprenticeships 26; as architects 7–9, 18
carving 11
cement 107–8
ceramics: heat absorbing 115
change: flexible contracts 157; willingness to 169
changed circumstances: contracts 151–2
choices: models of practice 39
civil law 157–9
class structure 100–1
clients 8; conceptual model 34; as contributors 12–13, 74
Coaldrake, William 7–8, 169
cold calling 114
collaboration 119–20, 113, 170; architectural practices 28; builders and architects xvii, 21, 58

177

collusion 140–2
common law 159
communications 50, 59; liaison staff 77
communities: contracts 155
community buildings 138
compensation 159–60
competition 172; bidding 73; manufacturers 116; for work 75–6
competitions: architectural 27, 84, 88, 129–30
complaints: architects/contractors 79
computers: design 121; jacking systems 88; literacy 31
conceptual models 34–5; buildings 41–5; goals 49
Conder, Josiah xiii, 17, 20
conflict: North American practices 48; in Japan 79, 143
connoisseurship 6–7, 100–1
construction 173; bribery 142; collusion 140–2; conceptual model 34; GDP 131; industry 2; innovative 86; site model 36–8; supervision xvi, 33, 34, 62
construction site 28, 35–9, 44, 62, 77
consultants 36, 49, 54, 76, 85
consumers: crafts 7, 101
context of buildings 74–5
continuity 54–5
contractors: as building designers 33, 74–6; bank support 91, 94–5; collusion 141; company size 36, 72, 93; design decisions 49; employing architects 20–1, 74, 76; manufacturing 114; national 73; ratio of building construction to civil works 73; Saitama University 143; Shimizu Construction 17; *see also* Fujita, Kajima, Kumagai, Obayashi, Sekisui House, Shimizu, Taisei, Takenaka
contracts 148–57; AIA 48, 80; weak/incomplete 149–50
contributors: designs 4
Cook, Peter 91
coordination: Saitama University 144
corporate structures 33
corruption 140–2
cost-free changes 38
costs: alliances 95; construction site 63; damage repairs 89; design-build alliances 80; innovations 60, 61; Kumamoto Dome 85; litigation 163; manufacturing 108; of materials 95, 116; per square meter 133; public works xvi, 85, 131, 132–3; Saitama University 144
courts: detailed contracts 151
crafts xi–xii, 170; architects' support for 100–2, 123–6; contractors' support for, 101; decline of 13; historical 6–7; implications of keiretsu 98; in public works, 134; revival 14–16; schools 23;

Cram, Ralph Adams 14
cranes 86
cronyism 140–2; *see also nakama* 130
culture centers 137
curriculum: architectural 20
curtain walls 40, 57–58, 82–3, 120–1; Sendai Mediatheque 43–5
customization 4, 96, 100, 108, 116; costs 132–3; development 119–20; manufacturing 107, 109, 113; model 38–9

Dai'ichi Kōbō xviii, 84–9
damage: Kumamoto Dome 88–9
damages: legal 160
deadlines 152–3
debts: contractors 73, 94–5
decision-making: architectural practices 28–9; shared 79–80
dependency: subcontractors 94
design: advice on choices 78; architects 74; changes 63–4; characteristics 8–9; collaboration 112; computers 121; contractors 74; decisions 1, 4, 49, 104, 172; details 28, 38; manuals 18; on-site 33, 36–8; processes 3–5, 21, 84–5; shared decisions 82–3; Western-style 16–17
design development 115–16; model 35–6; Saitama University 146
design-build: alliances 79–80; packages 33
details: design 28, 38
directors: retired officials 142
disagreements 59
disciplines: university 23–4; architecture and engineering together xiii, 53
discussion: problems 166
diverging goals 48, 79
diversification 109
diversity: contractors 72–3
documentation xiv, 63–6
Domino system 41
drawbacks: collaboration 119–20
drawings xiv, 25, 28, 49, 63–6, 118, 150
Dyer, Henry 20

early modern Japan 6–7
ecological collapse 7
economics: contracts 152; government spending 132; stability 97–8
economizing 32
education: architectural 20, 21, 23, 24–5, 174–5; buildings 16; computer courses xiii, 31; construction 21
Eisenman, Peter 34
employment 93, 131–2; leaving 29–30
encouragement 27
Engel, Heinrich 8
engineering departments 24, 175
engineers 51–2, 54, 57, 77, 85, 114, 169; *see also*,

Araya, Masato; Matsui, Gengo; Sasaki, Mutsuro; Watanabe, Kunio; Kanebako, Yoshiharu
examinations 25
expectations: liability 158
experience 30–1, 77, 171
expertise 77–8
expositions 138

familial office relationships 29
feedback 54
female architects 81
Figula Glass 120
Findlay, Kathryn 49–50; *see also* Ushida Findlay
Finn, Dallas 18
fireproofing 42–3
First National Bank 17
fixings: curtain walls 82–3, **83**
flexibility: architectural practice 170; contracts 150; deadlines 152–3; legal 170; manufacturers 106–7, 117–19; production 4–5
floors: construction 41–2
Ford, Edward R. 100
Fordism 105
foreign issues: architects 19, 34–5; enclaves 16; influences 7, 9–10; international projects 174; study 20
foundations: Sendai Mediatheque 42
frameless curtain walls 43–5
Frampton, Kenneth 9
free trade 156
Fujimori, Terunobu 123–6, **126**, 129
Fujimoto, Takahiro 112–13
Fujisawa Gymnasium 110, **110**
Fujita 84–9
furniture: Saitama University 146

Gallery of Horyuji Treasures **136**
Gifu Multimedia Workshop 81, **82**
glass xiv, 57–58, 96, 97, 113, 120–2; fire-resistant 43; "honeycomb" 85–6; walls 43, 45
government: collusion 141; spending 129, 131, 132–4

harmony 55
Hasegawa, Itsuko 4, 102–4, 107, 129
Hayakawa, Kunihiko xvii, 36
high school education 24
horizontal alliances 91–2
housing: public 138

iemoto; *see* apprentice
imitation 27
imported materials 117
in-house architects 74
inappropriate behavior 30
Inax 108, 115

individual responsibility 28–30
industrial modifications 38
inexperienced architects: advice 77
influences 1
information 35–6
innovation 7, 78, 169, 171–3; alliances 98; competitions 130; customization model 39; development 120; lead users 40; liability 122; manufacturing 106, 113–14; Sendai Mediatheque 41; team efforts 84–9
inspections: building 152–3
insurance 162
international projects 174
invalidation: contracts 151–2
ISO 9000 series: Saitama University 144
isolation 175
Isozaki, Arata xvii, 4, 65, 69, 138–9; collaboration 52–3; conceptual model 34–5
Ito, Toyo xvii, 3, 4, 28, 81, 115, 119, 129, 164–6; networks 54; Sendai Mediatheque 41, 67

jacking systems 88
Jinchokan Shiryokan 124
job changes 29–30
joint ventures 130, 143–4
journals 29, 53, 111–12,
judges 159
judicial system 159–62
juries: competitions 130
just-in-time concept: delivery 66; design 38

Kajima Corporation 17, 92
Kakudai Seizai 125
Kanebako, Yoshiharu 84
Kano Tan'yū 11, 12
Katsura Imperial Villa **9**, 10–13, **11**
Kawashima, Takeyoshi 150
keiretsu 91–2, 95, 98, 108
kenchiku, meaning 23
Kinoshita, Yoko 107, **111**
kinship: apprenticeships 25–6
Kliment, Stephen 171
knowledge: exchange of 55–7
Kora Munehiro 11
Kumagai 91, 92
Kumamoto Dome 84–9, **85**, **86**, **87**, 139
Kurokawa, Kisho 1, 84, 138
Kusumi, Akira 102–4

labor-intensive work 106
laboring classes 6
laws: contractors 78
lawsuits: contractual misunderstandings 150
lead users 39–40, 107, 109, 112, 116, 171, 173
leaders: North American practices 47–8
Leatherbarrow, David 47
legal issues 148–66

liabilities: collaboration 120; contractors' 161; legal 48, 157–9; products 88–9, 122
liaison staff 76–7
licensing 75, 76; contractors' employees holding licensing 72–3
lift-up systems: Teflon roofs 86–8
lighting 122, **123**; Teflon roofs 85
Liker, Jeffery 112, 117–18
litigation: discouragement 162–3; levels 159
local alliances 79
long-term employment 29

machine tools 110
Maekawa, Kunio xiv, xv, xvi, 78
Maki, Fumihiko xi–xvii, 2, 3–4, 41, 51, 108, 109, 110, 174; Tokyo Church of Christ 120–2
management: Fordism 105; project 39–40
manuals: architectural 29
manufacturing 13; collaboration 51, 112–13, 146; collusion 141; craft-based 104; customization 39; design decisions 49; documentation 64–6; flexibility 5; multiple 116; new materials 40; responsibility 59–60; sawmills 124–5, working with contractors 149; *see also*, fordism, post-fordism
materials xii–xiii, 7; contracts 153; design decisions 35; innovations 45, 78, 85; keiretsu 92; oligopolies 96
Matsui, Gengo 51
mediation 160; Sendai Mediatheque 164
meetings 59, 61, **61**, 119
Meiji Restoration period 13–16, *yatoi* 19
mentoring 77
Ministry of Construction 139
misunderstandings: contracts 150
Mitsui Bank 17
Miyake Design Studio Gallery **52**
mock-ups xiv, 65–70, **65**, **67**, **68**, **69**, 110; modifications 118, 119; Sejima, Kazuyo 81
models 50, 63, 66–70; of practice 33
modernization: oligopolies 96
modifications: industrial 38
monumental architecture 12
morals: contracts 149
Morse, Edward 14
mullions 122
multiple manufacturers 116
Murano, Togo xiv–xv

Nagaoka Folly 108, 115, **115**
negligence 157–9
negotiations: contracts 149, 151; costs 61; preliminary 117; trade-outs 60
networks 54
niche marketing 109
Niigata Concert Hall 104
Nikken Sekkei 74

Nikko 10
Nippon Kentetsu 120
Nishizawa, Ryue 57–8
North America: collusion 141; common law 159; construction 54; contracts 151, 155; innovation 120; practices 47–8; public buildings 137; tort 157–8; trade agreements 156

Obayashi Corporation 17, 92
observational learning 25–6, 29
Oda, Hiroshi 149
offices: development 35–6; on-site 35–6, **37**, 62–3; relationships 29; Takenaka Komuten **75**; training 25–31
officials: private employment 142
offshore production 118
Oita Convention Center 4
oligopolies 93–8
on-site design 33, 36–8
on-site work by architects 62–70
Ota Rest House **56**, **57**

paper tubes 51–2, **52**
parallel assembly 105
participation: interns 26
partnerships: manufacturing 113
pass-rates 25
payments: compensation 161; public works 134
performance: by companies 134; collaborators 55
period of construction 63
personal development 27–8
personality 58
phases: design/construction 62
photochromic glass 45
Physic 2B building 34
Pilkington glass 43
plank walls 124, **124**
plaster **103**, 104
politics 16; public buildings 128–9, 131–2
post-fordism 105–6, 119
post-graduate experience 30–1
post-war architecture 129
potential liability 162
power: design 47
practical education 23
pre-bids: documentation 63–4; estimates 141
precision: contracts 149
predictions: litigation 160
prestige buildings 75
Pritzker Prize xix
problem solving 50–1, 53
processes: architectural 2, 3–5
production: architects 109; control of 47–8; processes 3–5; systems 107
professionalism 19
profits 133

project management 39–40
promotion 30
proportion 12
prosecutions: collusion 140–1
protests: public buildings 139–40
public buildings: access to 134; percentage of total construction 131; politics 128–9, 131–2, 142–3, 144; programs involving multiple projects 84, 89, 135, 138–9; protests 139–40; range of building types 137; redundancy 137; style 128–31; in yearbooks 135–7
publications 53, 135–7

quality: contractors 73; craftsmanship xii, 14–16; design 47; design-build packages 76; international projects 174; labor 93–4, **94**

ranking systems 134–5
recession xvi, xviii, 63, 73, 97–8, 172; contracts 155–6; public buildings 138; increase in number of architectural firms 32
recognition 53
registration: ranking system 134
relationships: architects/contractors xiv, 79; companies 54; contracts 148–9; corporate 91; long-term 6, 161; longevity 154, 156; office 29; Saitama University project 143; suppliers 92; work communities 77
research: applied 51
responsibility 55, 75; Kakudai Seizai 125–6; shared 78; tort 158
retired officials 142
risk-taking 53; subcontractors 94
"river": Shonandai Culture Center 102, **103**
roles: architects 5; contractors 18

safety: innovative construction 86
Saiseikan **18**
Saitama Prefecture: corruption 143; public buildings 139; Saitama University 142–6, **145**
Salat, Sere 38
Sasaki, Mutsuro 41, 54, 164–6
sawmills: manufacturers 124–5
scale of buildings 12
schedules: construction 88
Sejima, Kazuyo 57, 81–3, **82**, 130
Sendai Mediatheque 41–5, **42**, **43**, **44**, **67**, 164–6, **165**
sharing: liability 161; responsibility 78; sense of values, 24; work 108, 130
Shimizu Construction 16–17, 21, 88, 92; Shimizu, Kisuke, 16–17
Shōiken Pavilion **11**
Shonandai Culture Center 4, 102–4, **103**
shop drawings 64–6
Shugakuin Villa **8**

site offices 35–6, **37**, 62–3
size: legal system 162–3
skills: acquisition 27; crafters 101; expected 31
snow cooling 51, **52**
Snow Village Future Foundation **52**; bids 132
social conditions: litigation 163
sound handling 122
span ratios 41
specialization 19
specifications 154
sports domes 84–9; Kumamoto Dome, 88–9
staff: burnout 120; interchangability 76–7; manufacturers 116
stainless steel roofing 109, **110**
standardization 105; lack of 107, 108
steel construction 4, 14, 41–2, 45, 55, 57
stress 29
structural problems: Sendai Mediatheque 164–6
students 174–5
styles 3–5; choices 9–13; public buildings 128–31; Western 16
subcontracting 91, 93
subcontractors: customization model 39
sukiya 10
supervision: architects 80; local government 135; Saitama University 144–6
supports: floors 42; Teflon roofs 85
surface finishes 81, **82**
surveys: Sendai Mediatheque 164
Suzuki, Edward 34

tacit knowledge 50, 59
Taisei Corporation 17, 73
Takahashi, Makoto 107
Takahashi, Tei'ichi 65, 84–9, 129; *see also* Dai'ichi Kōbō
Takenaka Komuten: xii, 21, 73 alliances 92, 97; architects 20; design-build 74, 75, **75**; origins 13; public works 131
Tange, Kenzo xii, xiv–xv, 129
Taniguchi, Yoshio xii, 135, **136**
Tanpopo House 124, **124**
Tatsuno, Kingo xiii, 20
Team Disney building 53
Team Zoo 102
teams 2, 174; building 48, 50, 55, 58–60, 84; Japanese practices 48; organization of teams, 144
technology: education 5; innovations 16, 60
Teflon roofs 85
temporary staff 40
temporary supports 88
testing 53; dome stability 88; mock-ups 69
third-party compensation 161
tiles 4, 102, **103**, 108, 108–9
timber cutting 125
timescales: customization 119; production 117

time windows 117–18
Todaiji 14, **15**
Tokugawa era 6–7
Tokyo Church of Christ 120–2, **121**, **122**
Tokyo Metropolitan Gymnasium **2**, 4
tolerances 66; contracts 153
tort 157–9
Toshogu 10, **10**, 11–13, **12**
trade agreements 156
trade-outs 60–2
training: small practices 32
trust xiv, 55, 58, 62, 118, 154

Uchida, Yoshio 125
undergraduates 24–5
unfinished concrete 35, **94**
universities: collaboration 51; education 23–5, 174–5
Ushida Findlay 107

vaguely bounded job demarcation 28, 53, 55, 76–7
variation 69; design 10
verbal agreements 118, 149
vertical alliances 92

vertical movement 45
Virtical movement 45
Von Hippel 40, 50

wages 93
Watanabe, Jun 60
Watanabe, Kunio 114
Watanabe, Makoto 107, **111**
weathering 69
Webster, Anthony C. 36
Western issues: beliefs 1–2; influences 13, 14
work: hours 61, 63; importance of 77
writing systems 27, 31

Yamada, Shuji 102–4
Yamagata University **17**
Yamamoto, Riken 54, 119, 129, 130, 142–6
Yatsuka, Hajime 1, 108, 115, 130, 138–9
Yazawa, Chuu'ichi 124
yearbooks 135–7
Yoga Promenade: Tokyo 102
Yokohama Care Center **3**

zenecon 72–4; *see also* contractors